THE BAR IS OPEN

Photography by
Feo

Text and editing by
David Misialowski

ISBN 978-1-944854-12-6

www.poodpawprints.com
facebook.com/poodpawprints
youtube.com/@poodpawprints
instagram.com/poodpawprints

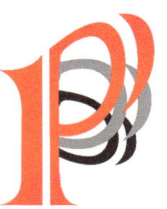

THE BAR IS OPEN, Published by Pood Paw Prints, 18819 71st ave NE, Kenmore WA 98028, United States. This book copyright 2023 FEO and Pood Paw Prints. All rights reserved. No portion of this product may be reproduced or transmitted, by any form or by any means, without the express written permission of FEO or Pood Paw Prints.

According to lore, the bar originally opened illegally in the 1920s as a "to-go" shop, filling buckets of beer for take-out, and became Chappy's in the 40s. In the 1960s, it took on the name Wilson's 10:30, for the starting time of the nightly craps games held in the basement, as evidenced by the craps table unearthed during renovations. Although it was named Spring Lounge in the 70s, it has been known throughout the neighborhood as the Shark Bar, due to the large stuffed sharks that are prominently displayed.

— *From the Spring Lounge Website*

The bar is known for being open 24/7/365, but in early 2020 it was completely shuttered, like most other establishments in the city, because of the Covid pandemic. It stayed closed for about three and a half months. Now, it's back, and better than ever.

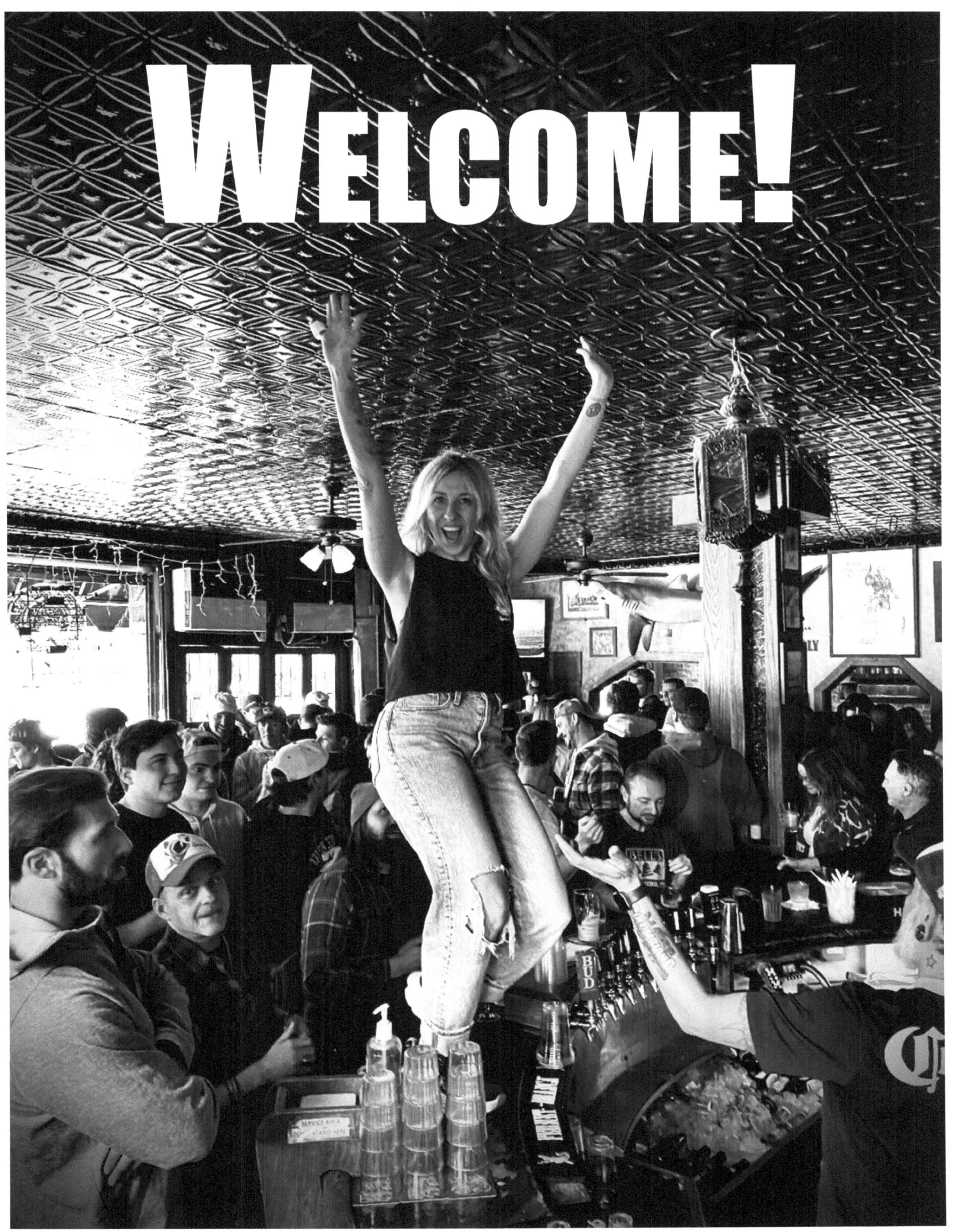

THE BAR IS OPEN

ENTER HERE

6 - Life Is Short
12 - The Bar Is Open
16 - Publicans
30 - Patrons
56 - Profiles
66 - Premises
86 - Sketchbook

SPRING LOUNGE

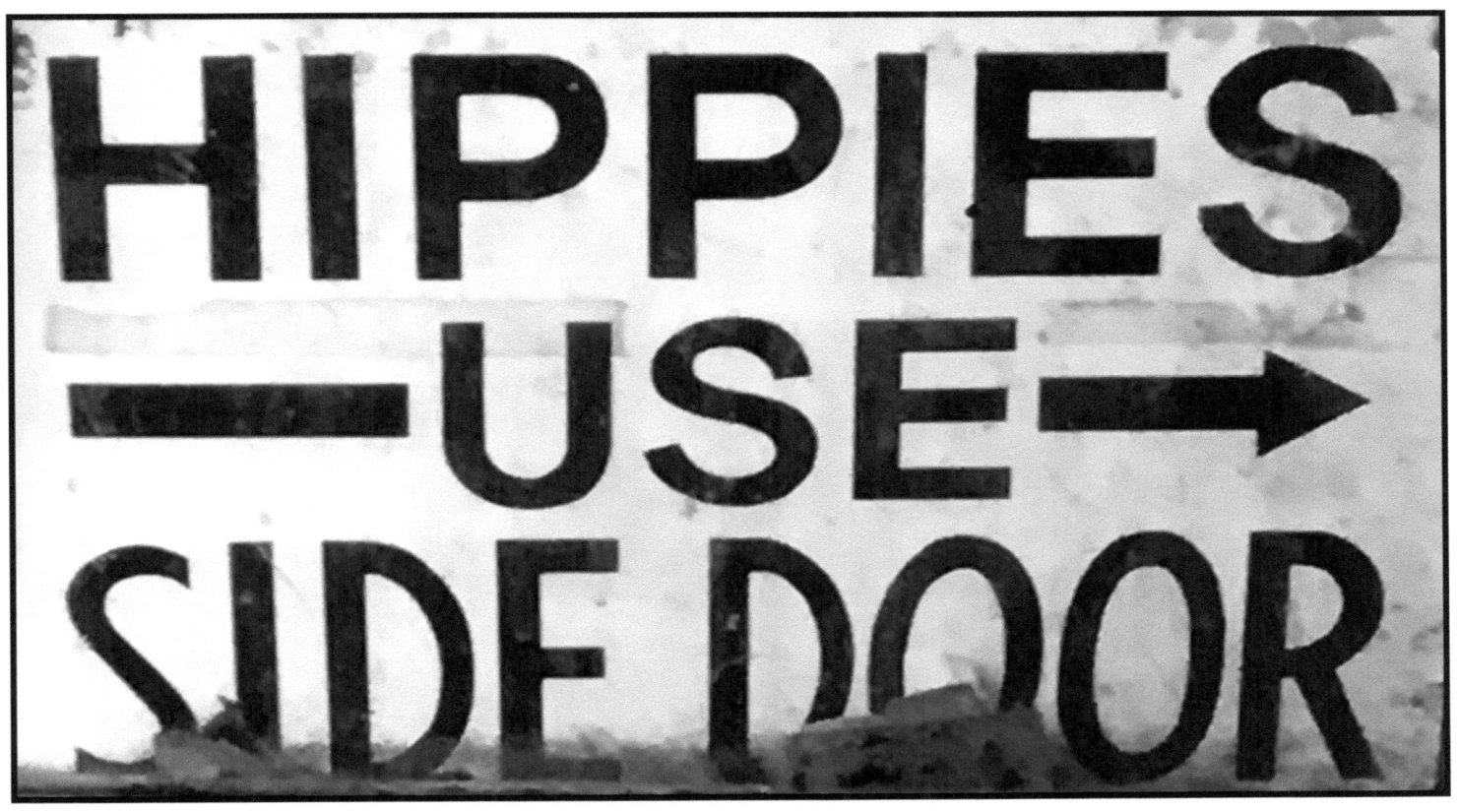

THE BAR IS OPEN

Life is short. Drink early.
That's the motto of the Spring Lounge. Of a crisp Autumn morning, doughty Gina, pushing 90, toddles out of her redbrick walkup apartment building on Spring Street, directly across from the bar, and trundles her shopping basket in front of her. In it, on a nest of blankets, sits Rosie, her ragamuffin white dog with black-button eyes.

Gina's of Italian descent, living in the vicinity of a nabe known as Little Italy, because more than a century ago it was a magnet for immigrants from the boot. Now it has shrunk to a few square blocks. The order of the day, in the cybernetic 21st century, is gentrification: out with the old, in with the new. Gina is old guard.

Once, a lifetime ago, Gina was voted the queen of the San Gennaro street fair. She was young and fair, just 17 years old. Her whole life was in front of her.

Now, pushing her cart with Rosie inside, Gina, old and bent, shuffles past a wall

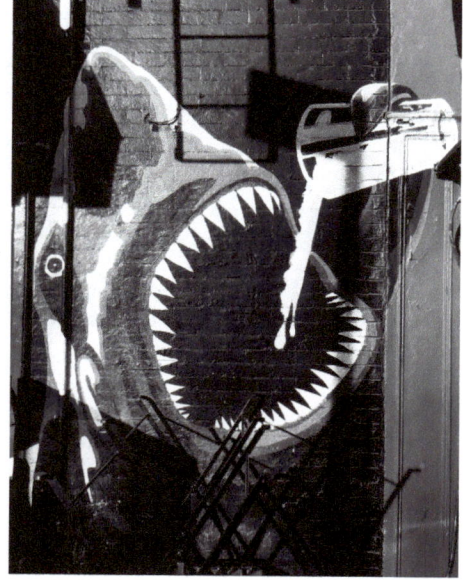

painting of a shark arching upward. One fin is curled around a pitcher of brew, which is tipped downward toward a gaping maw ringed with teeth. The ambrosia flows down into it.

Rosie hops out of her basket and onto the sidewalk. Then she gallops ahead on stubby little legs, now and then casting backward glances in search of Gina, who is still shuffling along and pushing her cart on her way to the corner bodega. Gina never puts her dog on a leash, preferring to let her run wild and free. Rosie is everything to her, all that she has left.

Continued on Page 8

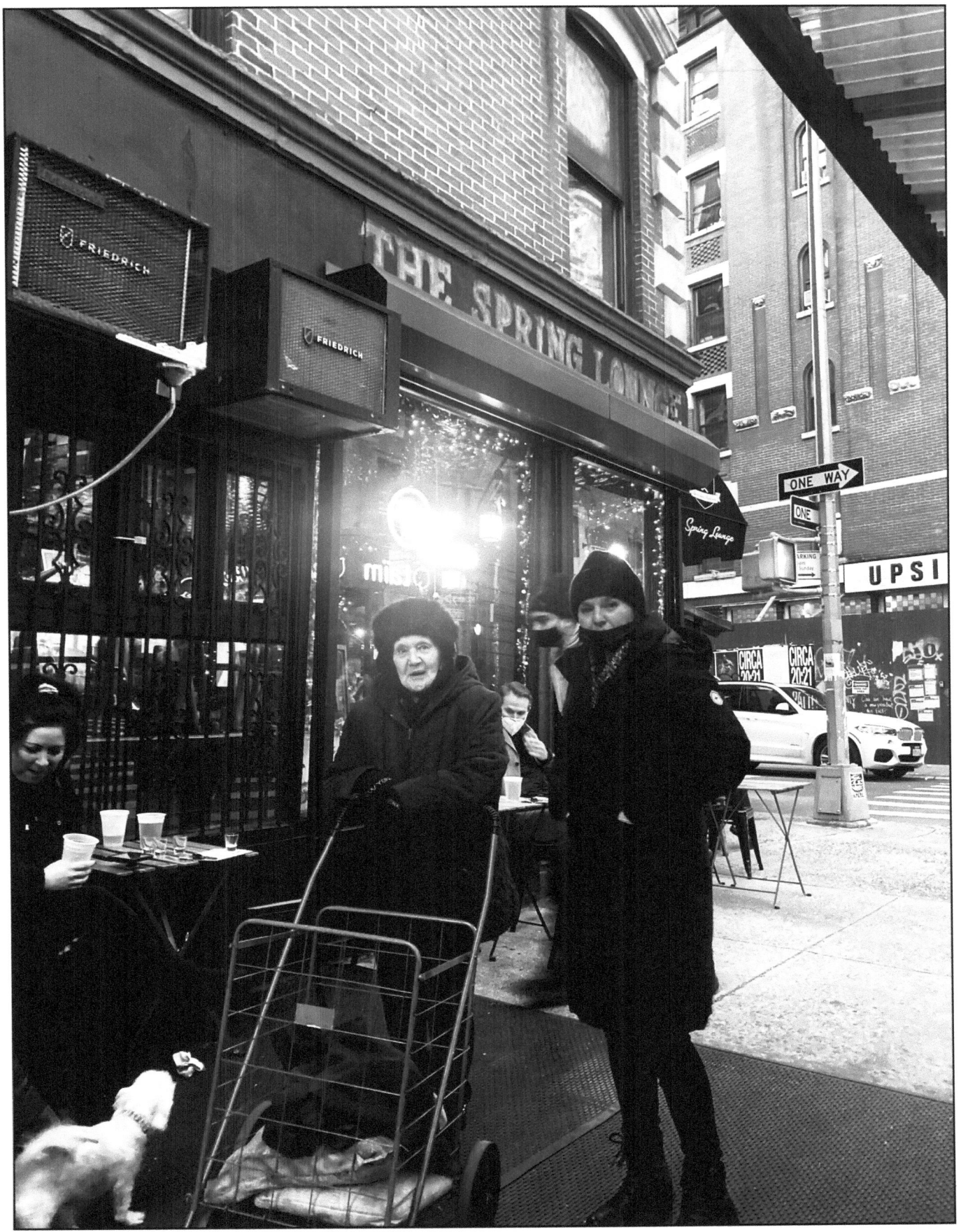

Little Rosie with her human, Gina, who is pushing a cart. At right is Michelle, a former Spring Lounge bartender.

The Bar Is Open

Or, of a brisk winter morning, Tommy might be sitting on a bench in the playground across the street, puffing on a stogie, his wide-brimmed fedora aslant on his grizzled and whitened head. Hunched forward, elbow on a knee, his free hand dangles at his side. With it, he clutches a rolled-up copy of the New York Post. He's waiting for Spring Lounge to open. Also known as the Shark Bar, it's the place with the painting of the shark guzzling beer on one of its outer walls, the image Gina passes every day. It opens at eight on the dot — yes, that's eight in the morning — and it stays open until four the next morning. Three-hundred sixty five days a year.

When hurricane Sandy whammed into the city back in 2012, flooding lower Manhattan, shuttering stores and shops all over the city, and transforming NoLita and SoHo into ghost towns, the bar remained open. The electricity was down, but that was no problem. People drank from beers in coolers by candlelight. Fifty-three people died in that calamity, but life went on as usual in the shadow of a stuffed shark sweeping past overhead, frozen forever in a pose of predation above each day's publican and his or her customers.

Jay presides over the Early Morning Drinkers Society — "the epitome of sophistication," as a sign under an illustration of dapper drinkers informs us. This is before Covid hit. A silver-haired mensch in his seventies, Jay is still as handsome as the actor he had been, first for the daytime soaps, and later with a role on the seventies sitcom The Jeffersons. Whenever a couple leaves — tourists, who'd never been in the bar before — he shouts at them, as they head out the door: "Same time next year, OK? I mean her" — pointing at the gal — "not you," pointing at the guy. It's always good for a laugh; not such a great joke, maybe, but Jay's timing is impeccable.

Restrooms are for customers only. But if some stray wanders into the bar and asks, "Is it OK if I just use your bathroom?" Jay replies, "Don't use mine; I live way up on the Upper West Side. Use this one here," and he points to the bar john. Again, maybe not such a great joke, but the timing and the smooth delivery win the day and the laughs. Jay is retired now, living with his wife in Florida. He bounced after Covid hit.

> **Jay presides over the Early morning Drinkers Society — "the epitome of sophistication."**

When the bar opens Tommy takes his perch on one end of the horseshoe bar, under an American flag and near the door. He orders his first combo of the day, a PBR and a glass of Jameson's. They go down quick and then it's on to the next round. He reads about his hero, Marmalade Mussolini, then the president of the United States, in the Post. Tommy has a fund of stories from his days as a prison guard. But he broke up with his wife and somehow lost everything along the way. His living situation is dicey. However, he expresses no regrets.

"When you have possessions, your possessions possess you," he says in his gruff, cigar-haggard voice. He almost sounds like a hippie, saying a thing like that. And there's a sign in the front window saying, "Hippies Use Side Door," but Tommy came in the normal way. By eleven he's three sheets to the wind, and the PBRs and the Jamos keep coming.

Ritchie camps on the opposite end of the horseshoe bar. This is years ago. He's in his eighties. He has a face like Popeye's, with a mashed strawberry nose, flabby jowls, a lantern jaw, and drooping earlobes that resemble dropped testicles. Sits there holding a cane with his china-blue eye flashing under a stocking cap pulled all the way down over his hairy, steel-gray eyebrows. Day drinker. He is garrulous and boring. Won't stop running his mouth. One day a barback jabs a wet mop at him and yells, "Shut up, old man!" Ritchie appeals to Jay: "Man's gotta talk. Man's gotta talk to someone, right, Jay?"

Ritchie is gone now. So is Jeff, the neighborhood uber-drunk. But now we're back in the day. He isn't allowed into the bar, except maybe to pee every now and then. He was once a tennis pro, the story goes, but then as another story goes, the man takes a drink, then the drink takes a drink, and then the drink takes the man.

Jeff panhandles outside the bar, slumping on the pavement in a filthy, inebriated heap. When someone give him a dollar, he fishes from his pocket a huge wad of bills, adds the dollar to it, and humbly says "God bless" to his astonished benefactor. Apparently Jeff's wealthy dad bankrolls him, and his drinking and panhandling. Or did.

Covid. The bar remains open, but you can't drink indoors by order of the New York City Department of Health. So everyone's arranged outdoors, seated at rickety tables under overhanging wood shelters lined with heaters going full blast. Why not just stay home? Everyone is stir crazy from Covid, and anyway, the bar's drinkers are nothing if not loyal.

Despite the misery the bartenders, mostly women, are a merry lot. Even through their masks you can tell that they are smiling. Today, as the wretched year 2020 runs out while the snow piles up, the publicans aren't really tending bar in the ordinary sense of the word but emerging

The Bar Is Open

every now and then from the empty, barricaded interior of the establishment to take fresh orders for alcohol, prescriptions that they will then fill back inside.

All of us are masked, many of us immiserate in our masks. Belled lepers, exiles, castaways on a Coney Island of the mind, a nightmarish, deserted stretch of beach where the sun never shines and the Atlantic Ocean has turned to ice. Still, life — which, remember, is short — goes on, and the Spring Lounge show must go on, too.

So the bartenders persevere, upbeat even if the clients are downcast. Their jolly dispositions in this season of snow and plague offer the promise of spring's green shoots and then the summer sun.

And suddenly it is summer. The snows are gone, and Covid is in retreat. The real Coney Island has reopened, and so has the inside of Spring Lounge. Summers are always best for day drinkers, because the days are longer and the longer the day is, the more you can drink.

The horseshoe bar under the ever-gliding stuffed shark is thronged. Conversation bombinates. Laughter bursts. The bartender is convivial, voluble, and sometimes bibulous. Strong sunlight slants in through the tall, plate-glass widows, but it never reaches much beyond the benches that line the far walls. If this is a cave, its patrons are spelunkers. It wants to be a dive bar but can't quite get there. It's too clean, and too spacious.

> **Conversation bombinates. Laughter bursts. The bartender is convivial. voluble, and sometimes bibulous.**

The framed pictures on the walls speak of an ever-more remote past. Hank Aaron swings for the fences. Jackie Robinson slides into home for the score. Jake LaMotta is in a crouch and giving you the ol' one-two punch. This is an old bar, with many past iterations. A black-and-white photo shows the bar as it was around the 1940s, when it was named Chappy's. A rotund gentleman in suspenders stands on the bar and takes a chug from a jug of wine while the bartender and other patrons, all men, salute him. I seem to hear a scratchy tune from an antique jukebox, a disc of vinyl sliding into a platter after a nickel is dropped into the slot:

Put another nickel in, in the Nickelodeon/ all I want is loving you and music, music, music …

Annie, Mercury in blue, of winged but aging feet, in her 70s, drops off the mail and grabs a hot dog — hot dogs, sometimes, and chips are on the Spring Lounge menu. Big, burly Hockey Tom, who once had an unsuccessful tryout with the Dallas Stars, is chatting with Paul, who frames pictures at an art gallery and creates his own art, figurative and abstract at the same time. Terry, an artist known for his unorthodox murals at venues around the city, nurses a beer. Later, a younger, hipper crowd will start filing in, and the Early Morning Drinkers' Society will formally adjourn.

Summer ebbs into autumn, which then again gives way to winter, often long and bitter in New York. During the depths of winter, around the time of the solstice, the light dies by 4:30 p.m. Do not go sober into that good night. Drink, drink against the dying of the light.

In general, joy is the order of the day at Spring Lounge. Of a day, someone announces — rather fatuously, it might seem — "Laugher is the best medicine." Laugh until your sides split, until your stomach aches.

Of another day, while there still are days to be had, Tommy complains that his stomach aches, but it isn't from laughter. The problem, he decides, is the PBRs. He's going to stop drinking the pisswater, and stick to straight whiskey.

Turns out the problem isn't the pisswater. It's the cancer.

When he returns from a hospital stay, he has a colostomy bag. He's going downhill fast, losing weight. He shrinks into a shadow of his former robust self. It is almost as if he is slowly being erased. He's in a nursing home, now. But on the phone recently, he sounds alert and chipper. He's a tough old bird. Still, the clock is ticking, the Doomsday Clock with its hands set perilously close to midnight.

Of a summer morning, Gina is across the street, seated on a bench outside a pizza parlor. She is sobbing uncontrollably. She rocks in her arms the bloody, mangled carcass of her dear little Rosie, whom she never put on a leash. Wild and free, just four years old, Rosie darted into traffic and was run over by a hit-and-run driver. Gina watched it happen. She is inconsolable. Soon she too will be confined to a nursing home. The summer of 1947, when she was crowned queen of the San Gennaro festival, now seems as remote in time as the War of the Roses.

Still, like Tom, she's hanging in there. A friend of hers reports that's she's doing well enough: "I get three meals and day and my snacks. What more do I want?"

Even so, her life — yours, too — is imploding downward and inward, with ever greater velocity toward a vanishing point that will end with one last twinkle of light — a final, scintillating protest against the onset of night everlasting.

Life is short. Drink early.

— David Misialowski

THE BAR IS OPEN

'Gentleman, the bar is open.'

How long I had waited to hear those words. They were spoken at the tail end of the plague year, at the entrance to Spring Lounge, by Dave the bartender. At long last, the interior of the bar was again open for business. But at the start of the disaster, on March 16, 2020, I was working as a bartender at The Athenian, a small Greek wine-and-

dine bar in the East Village. On that day, all the bars in New York City were ordered closed because of the spread of Covid.

Closing the gate behind us, I reached to shake the cook's hand and said, "See you at the end of April." I said it jokingly, but also sarcastically. He walked off in the direction of the nearest subway station and I headed downtown. The city was completely quiet. There were few pedestrians, traffic was light, and noise hazards

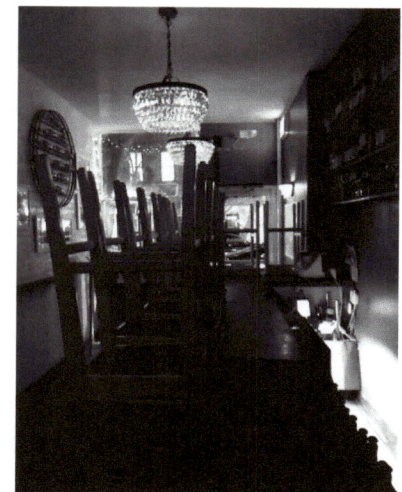

The Athenian in the East Village, on the day it was closed because of Covid. It never reopened.

had almost completely vanished. I couldn't even find an open deli to grab a Tall Boy for my walk home. But I thought, "I'll be back there by April. Nothing to worry about. It's all being overhyped." As it turned out, the Athenian never reopened, like many other businesses that permanently closed in the wake of the disaster.

Like everyone else in the city and around the world, I had no idea how serious Covid 19 really was. But the reality of the virus, and of death, hit home when I came

Continued on Page 14

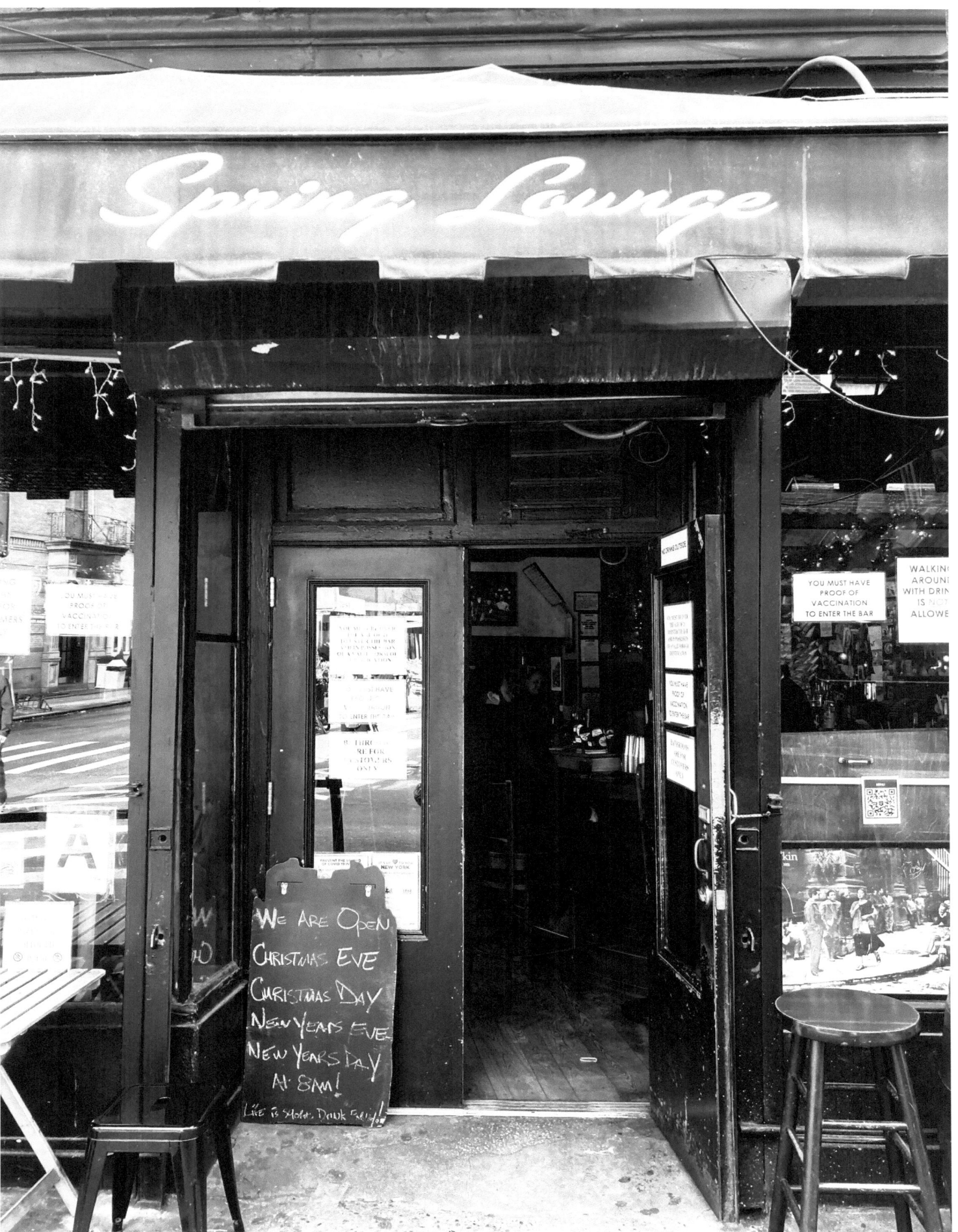

THE BAR IS OPEN

upon the bodies in orange bags in freezers, stacked on the street like discarded garbage. I had become familiar with death at a young age. I grew up in a working-class Hispanic neighborhood/barrio in the age of AIDS, when that deadly virus in addition to crack cocaine, crystal meth, gang violence and police brutality dominated our lives. Almost all of the fatherless children that grew up around me had peered down into an open casket at a young age, or had seen the dried blood on the street or splattered on a wall from a drive-by shooting that had occurred the night before. Now, once again, death was literally in front of me. The sky seemed to know, too. It was gray and foreboding and the mournful dirge of Nearer My God to Thee seemed to emanate down from the sullen clouds above.

By summer, some businesses had begun slowly and cautiously to reopen. Spring Lounge was one of them, though the interior remained off limits, and people had to gather around tables arranged outdoors. The bar had been a neighborhood fixture for decades, just north of Little Italy at the corner of Spring and Mulberry Streets. I first set foot in the place in 2008. Living not far away in Chinatown, every so often I'd go there for a pint and a shot. I didn't become a regular right away. I was just a kid who thought of myself as a writer, a poet, and I'd drop in at the bar whenever I had writer's block. I wasn't familiar with the Early Morning Drinkers Society, and didn't really know any of the colorful bartenders or the mischievous patrons. But I noticed there were long lines to enter the place almost every evening when I walked by.

In the late summer of 2020, I became one of a number of doughty drinkers who'd sit outside Spring Lounge at rickety tables drinking our beers and shots and devouring what we sarcastically called Cuomo hotdogs. We were irate at the then-governor, Andrew Cuomo, for ordering the interiors of bars and restaurants to remain closed for what we thought was an unnecessary length of time. Later when the inside of the bar finally reopened, great precautions were taken. Barriers were set up between tables and we'd have our temperatures taken and the results written down in a log book. We'd have to wear masks at all times, except of course when we had to lift them to eat or drink. With my phone I began taking pictures of the bar and its regulars. I began to meet them and developed a relationship with them. It was also when I got to know Dave Misialowski. The first time I saw Dave was years prior. Constantly typing on his laptop and going outside for a cigarette break every 10 minutes, pacing back and forth, being crushed by the world and the weight of his own genius. "That man is writing the greatest novel ever written," I thought. And as that year turned into four years we developed a friendship. Our interests in poetry, nihilism, and art motivated us both.

And not just him, but many others I now consider myself very lucky to know. Dave the bartender with his good looks, easy charm and "don't take shit" punk-rock attitude. Mike, another bartender, with his humor and down-to-earth nature. Someone who checks in on a person when he or she is going through serious withdrawals, just to remind them that they'll be OK. Kristen with her million-dollar smile and eyes strong enough to bring out the sensitive sides of the toughest Lower East Side skinheads. April, the kid sister of the bartenders whom I've never seen without a grin. Professor Tom, with his nostalgic memories of concerts and the records of all of our youth. And Jen. The boss lady. The mother to all of us who were outside of the closed bar in early hours and freezing weather. Tough as a stack of kegs and she can knock down a wall of stacked bottles of booze without messing up her hair, that's how Jen comes off to me. She can take any obstacle like a global shutdown and make sure her staff and regulars are taken care of. The Future is Women. Jen, go after em'.

The only one missing was Jay Hammer. But the stories that the patrons and staff told about him every day made it seem as if he were still behind the bar endlessly cutting limes instead of living it up in Florida.

Such a dark time we went through. With the other members of the Early Morning Drinking Society we witnessed the city go through a tragic state of disarray. We'd all wonder, what's next?

In the summer, during the depths of the plague, when we thought things couldn't get worse, the riots started. We were again seeing the country tearing itself up because of a senseless death, this time of George Floyd, a death, like so many others, having to do with race. And instead of protesting peacefully, the way the civil right leaders of the 60s had preached, these protesters used Floyd's death as another excuse to trash the same kind of working-class neighborhoods from which many of us had proudly come. The civil rights leaders' message of confronting hate with love, and stupidity with intelligence, went unheeded.

Some four years on from the Covid disaster, life has returned to normal for many of us. There are always new stories to be told and new people to meet. New endeavors, new jobs, new relationships. Ups and downs. A prescription of pills to help you get through the upcoming year, with a round of shots called red-headed sluts to chase them down. We will face new challenges, new obstacles. We will just ask someone to hold our beer as we take them on. There will be more pictures to take and more books to write. But always, there will be only one Spring Lounge.

Gentlemen, the bar is open.

— Feo

Publicans

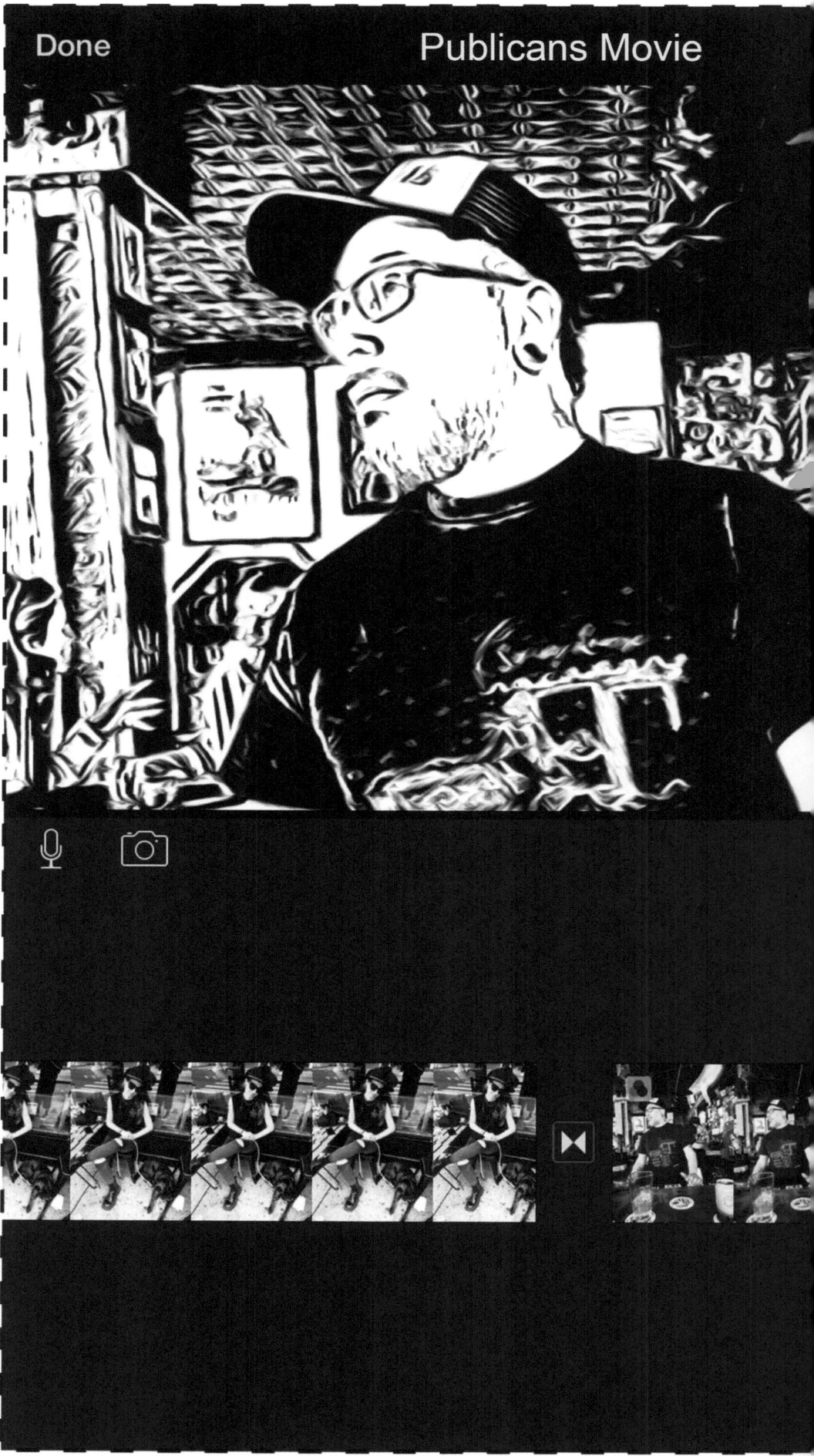

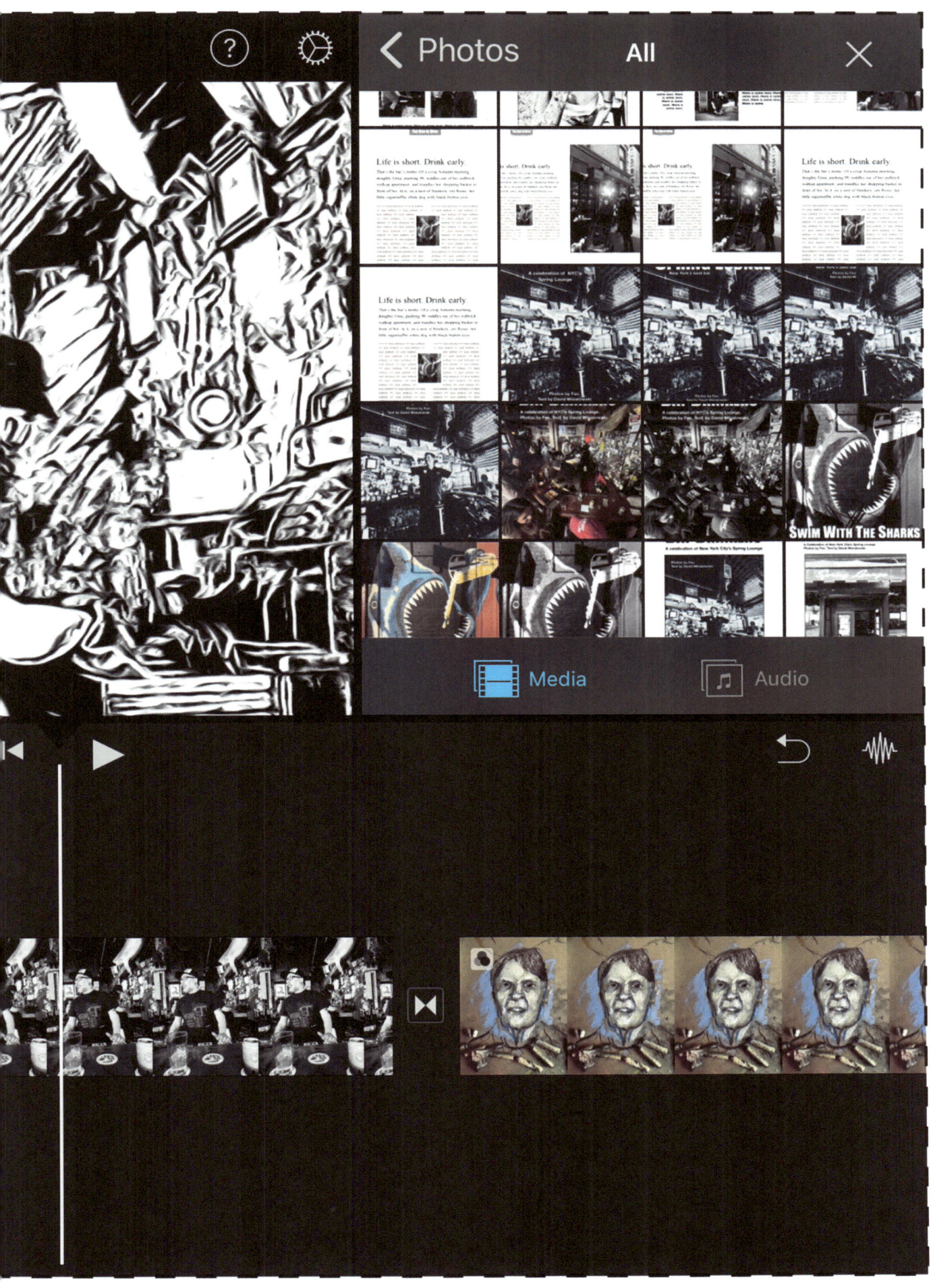

The Bar Is OPEN

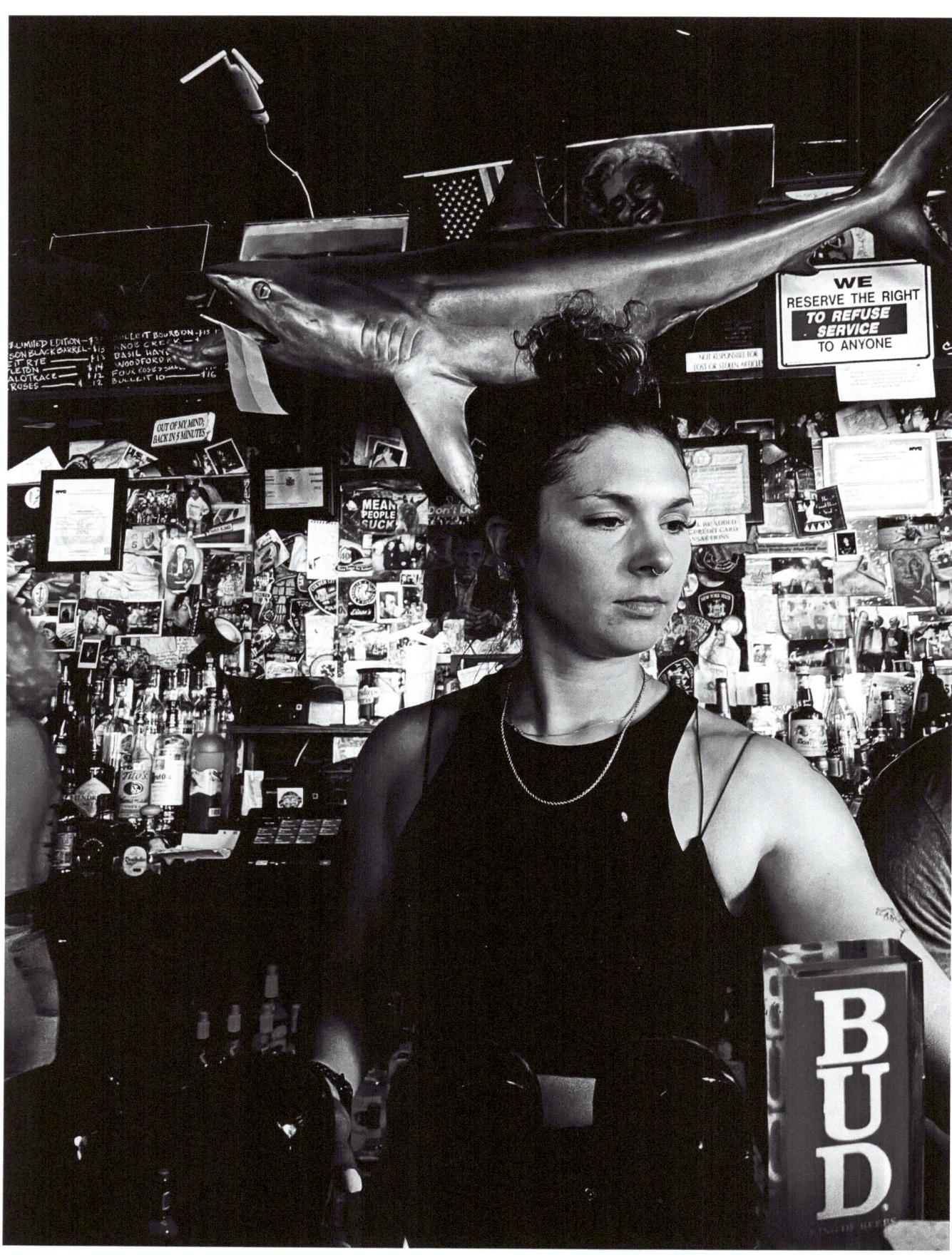

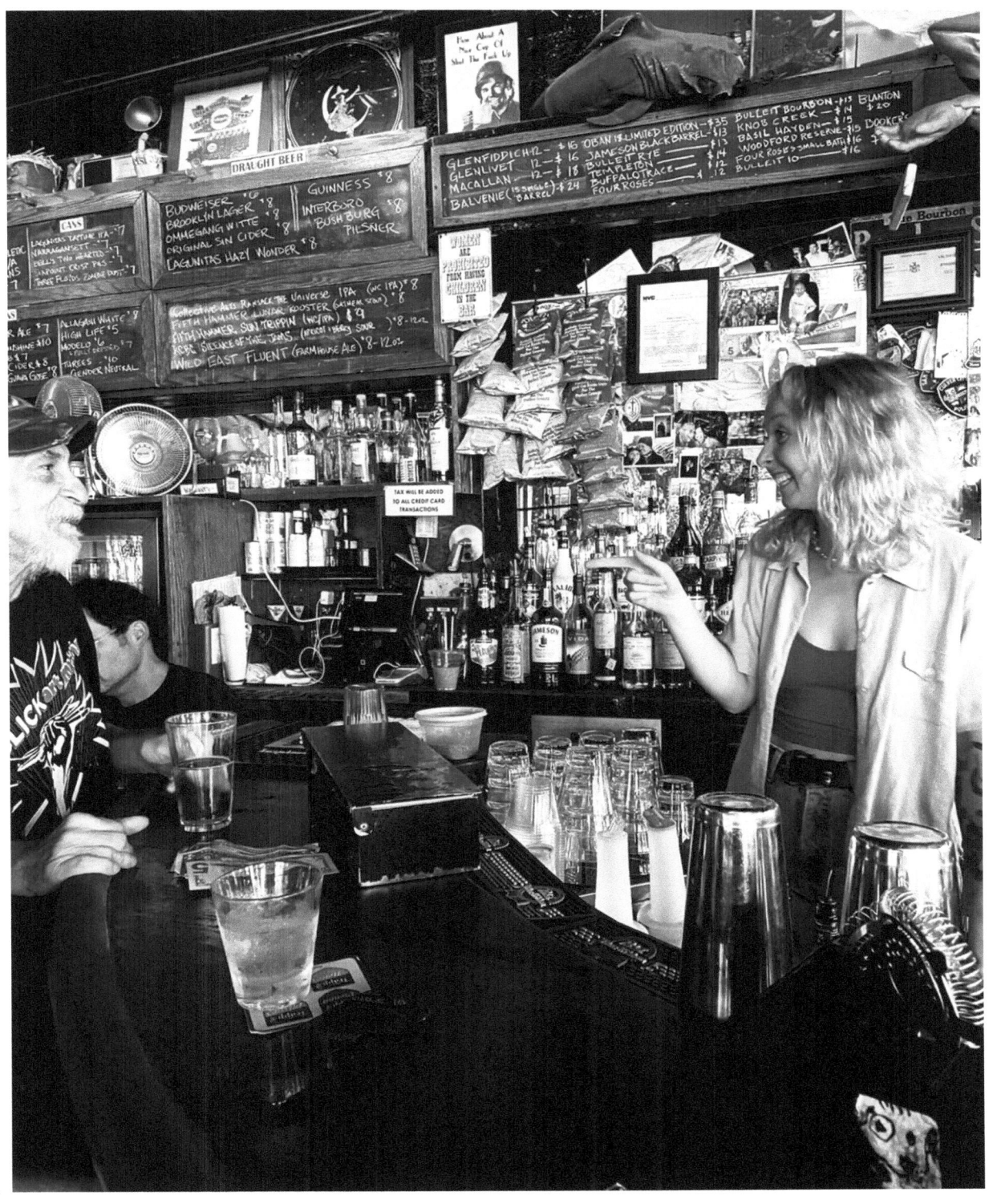

Anna, left, a bartender who works the afternoon and evening shift, after the Early Morning Drinkers Society has adjourned for the day. Above, Sarah, another afternoon bartender, jokes with Terry, an artist and a Spring Lounge regular.

THE BAR IS OPEN

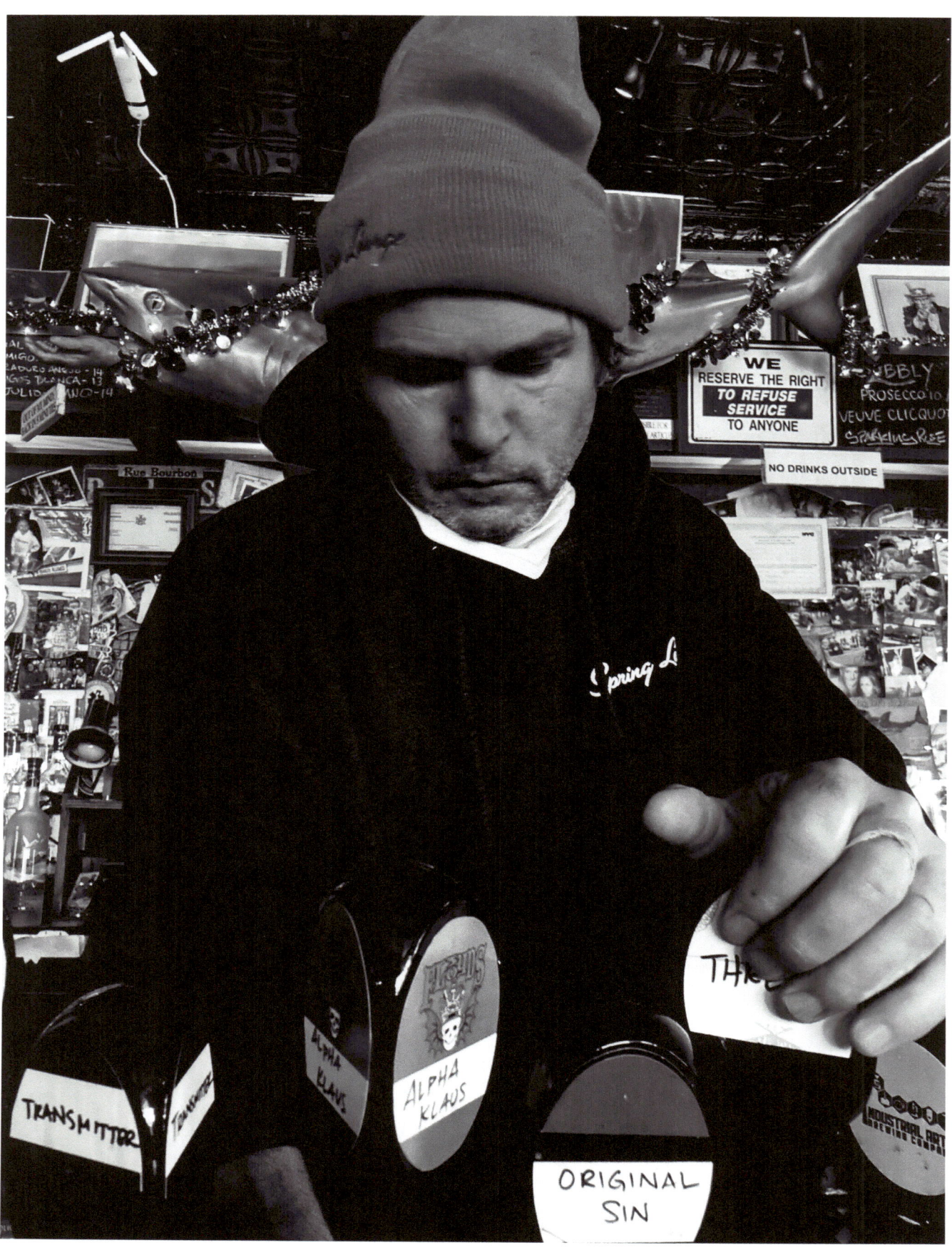

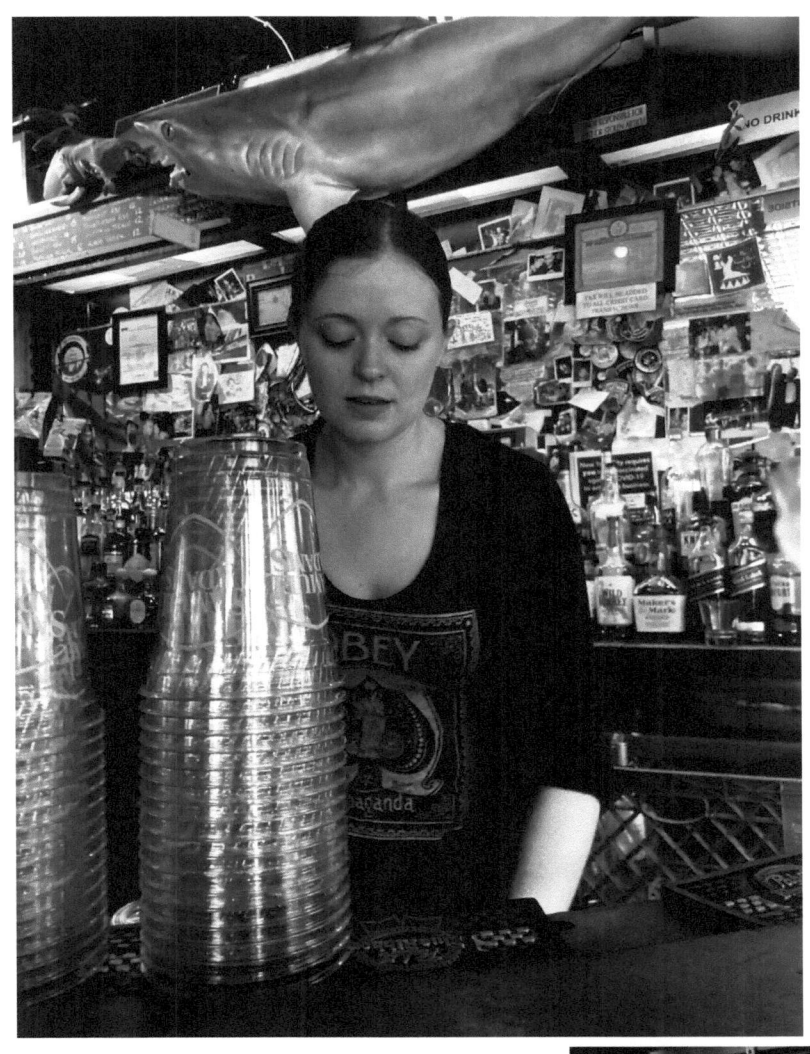

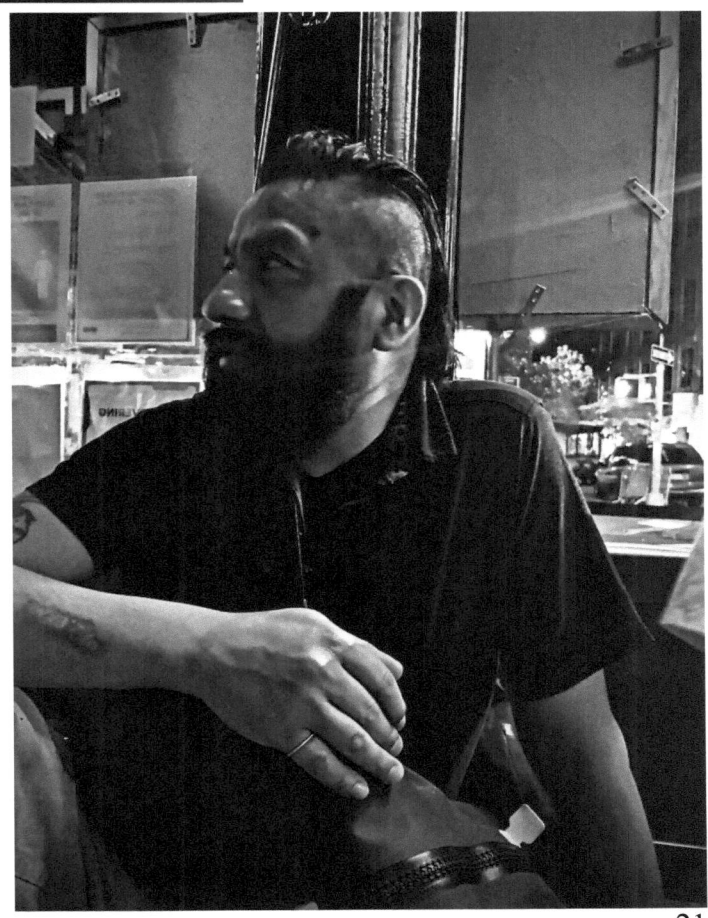

Professor Tom, left, so called because his voluminous knowledge of music is practically professorial, works the taps in full Lounge regalia. Above, April, another afternoon bartender, and, at right, Abraham, a veteran barback.

THE BAR IS OPEN

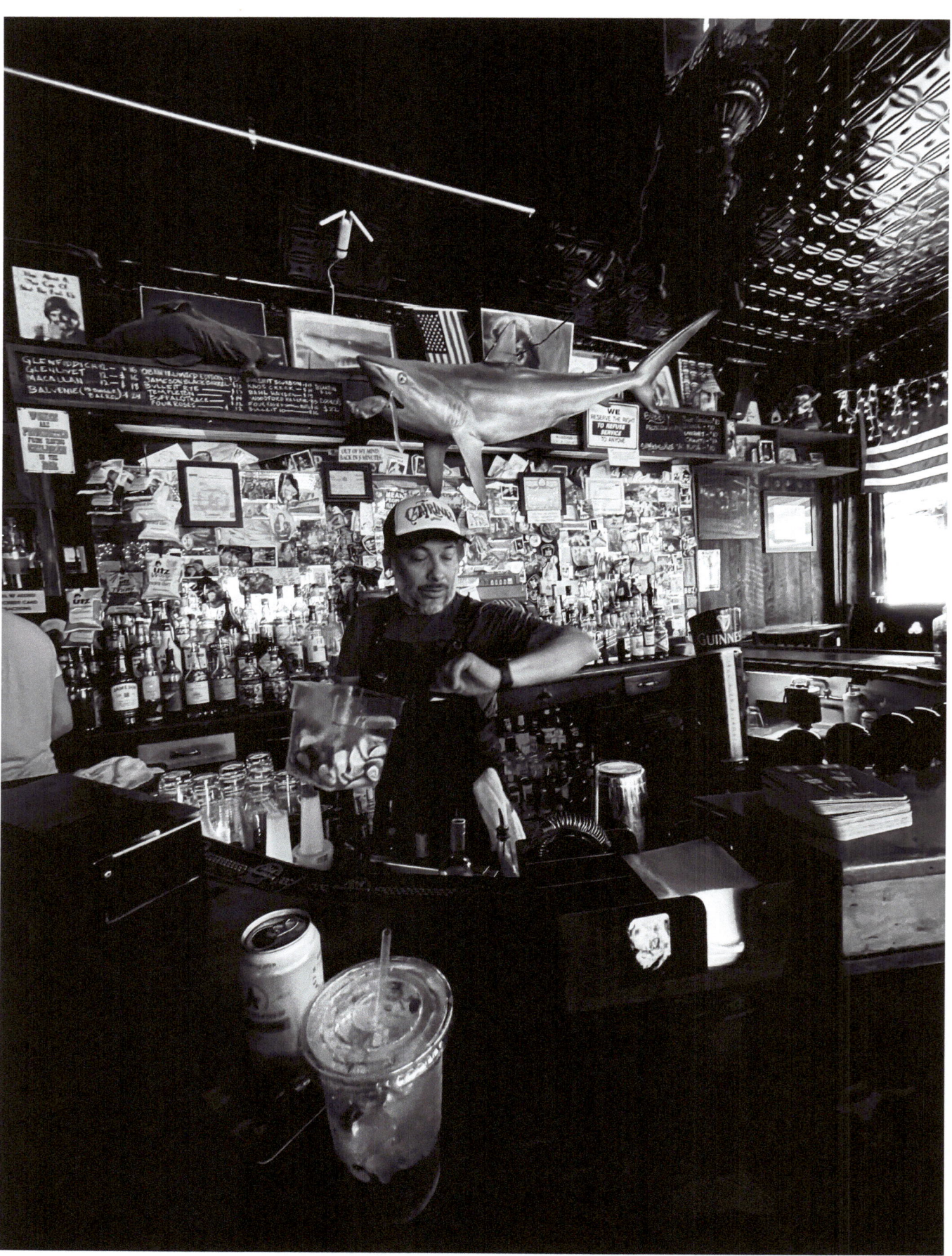

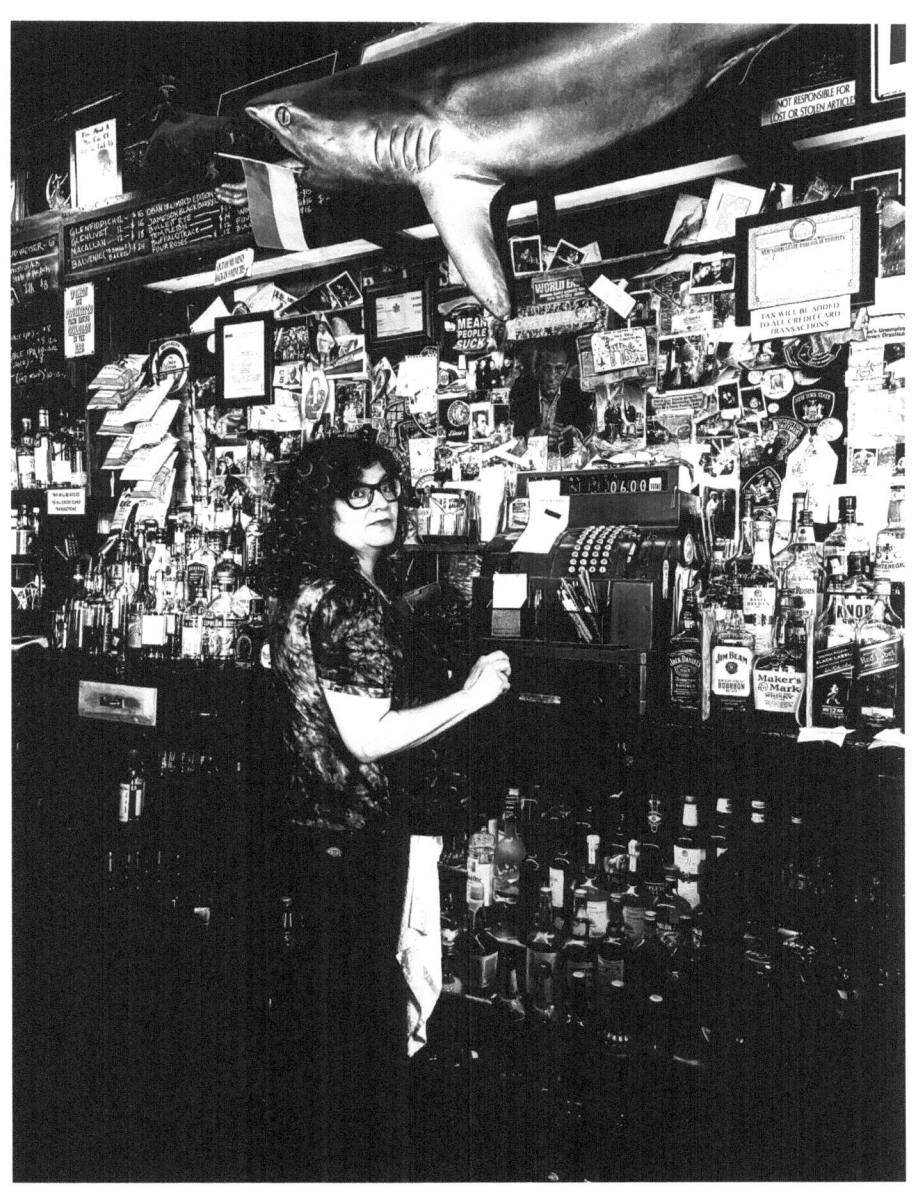

Motorcycle-riding Victor, left, who works as both a barback and a bartender, as he checks his watch while preparing for the late-afternoon rush. Patricia, above, a longtime Lounge bartender, and Stephanie, right, who was steadfast serving patrons indoors but mostly outside during the Covid shutdown.

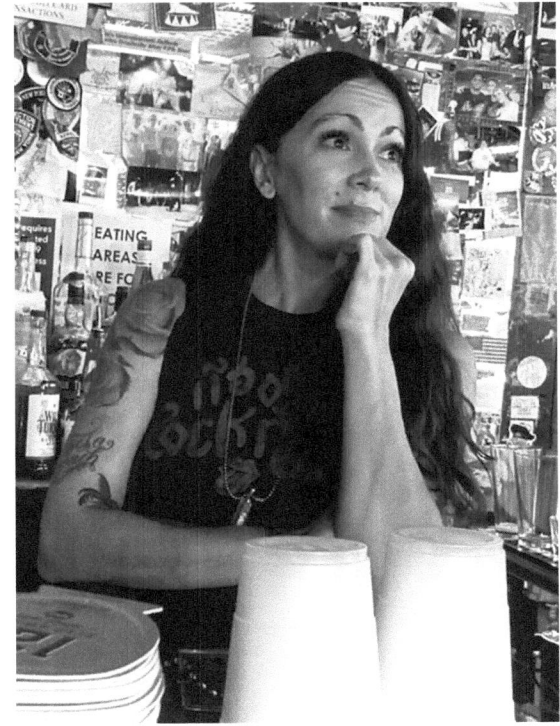

The Bar Is OPEN

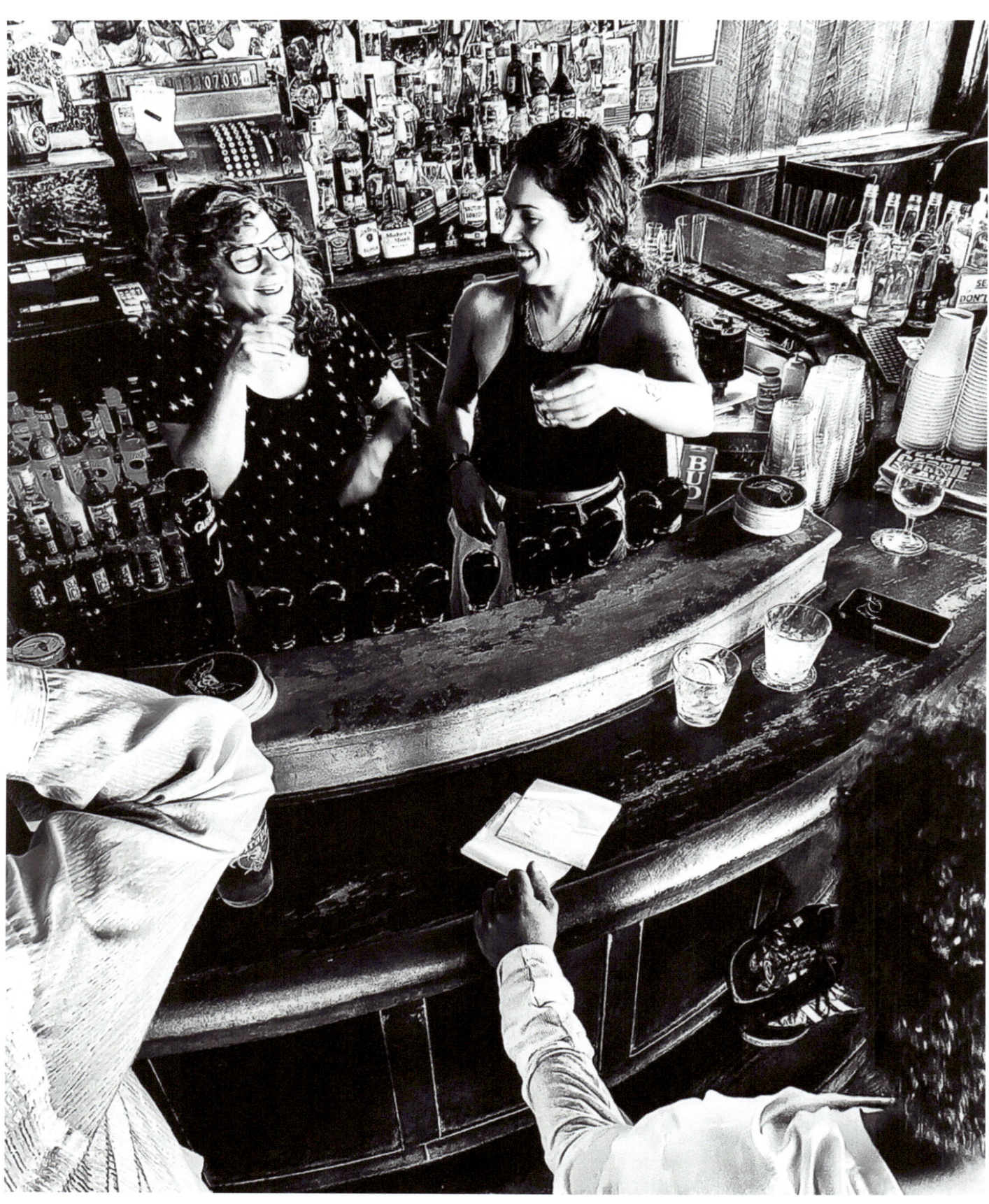

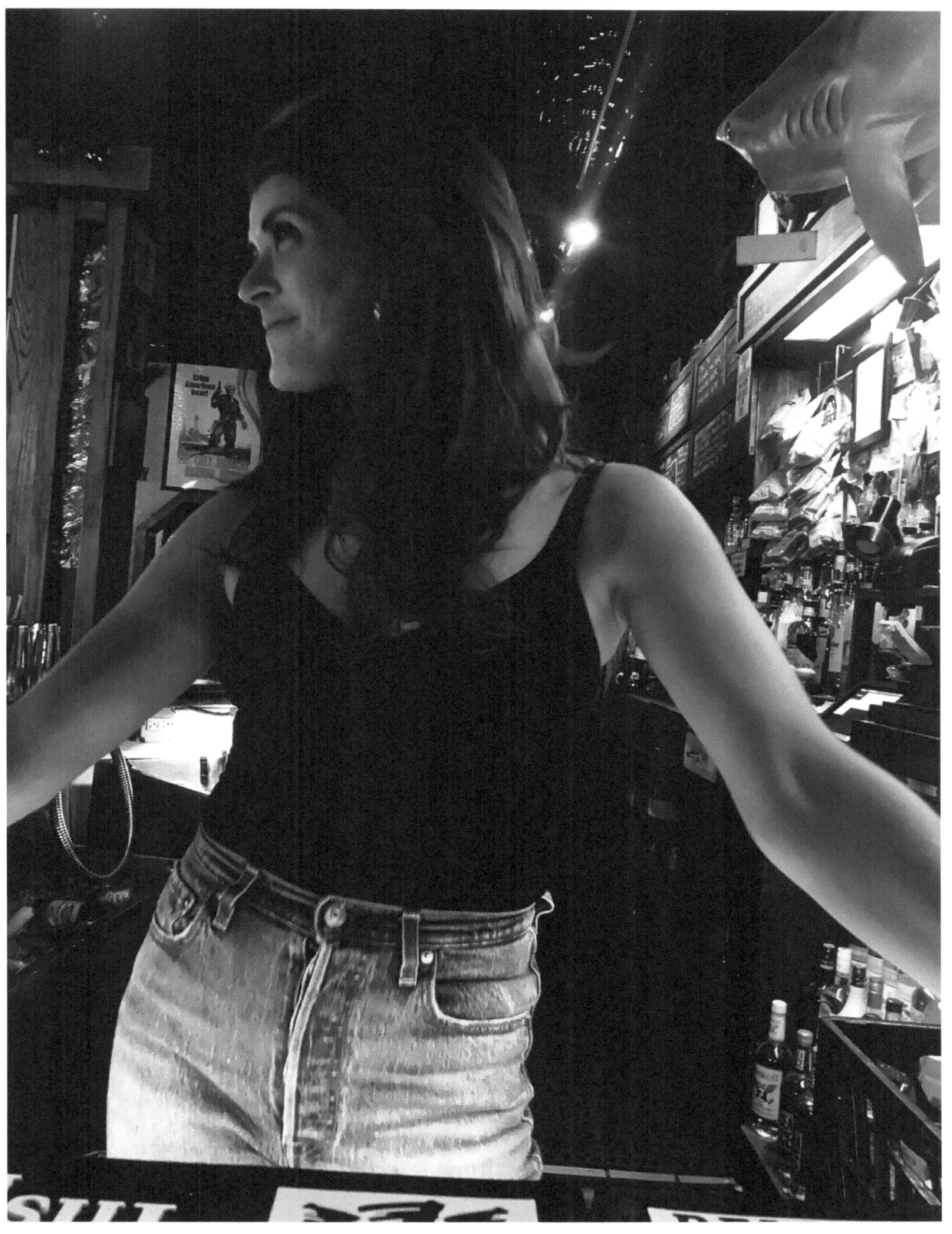

Patricia and Anna, with two regulars, toast the start of the weekend. Above, Kristen, whose captivating smile was mostly concealed under a mask during the Covid era, is seen in more recent and happier times.

THE BAR IS OPEN

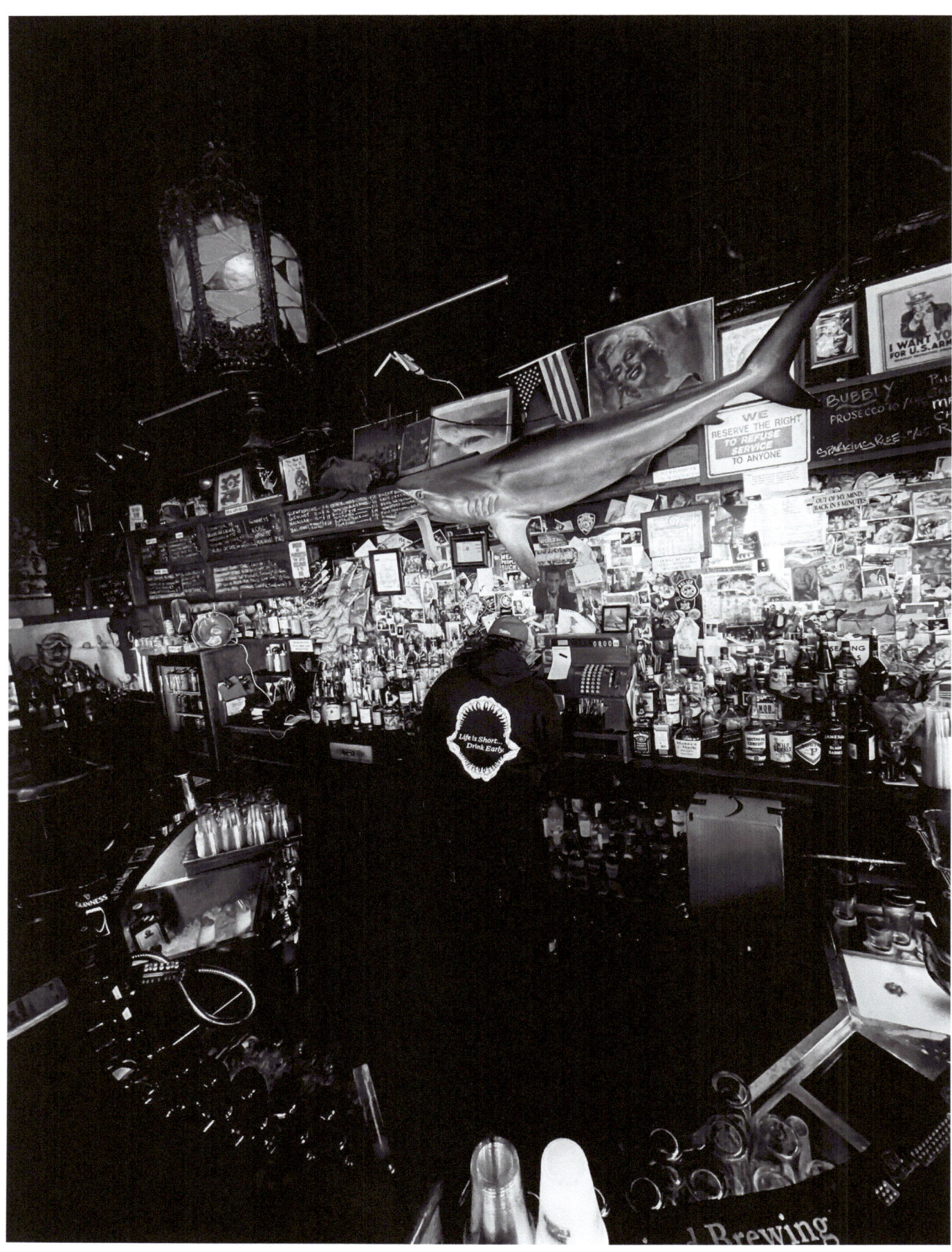

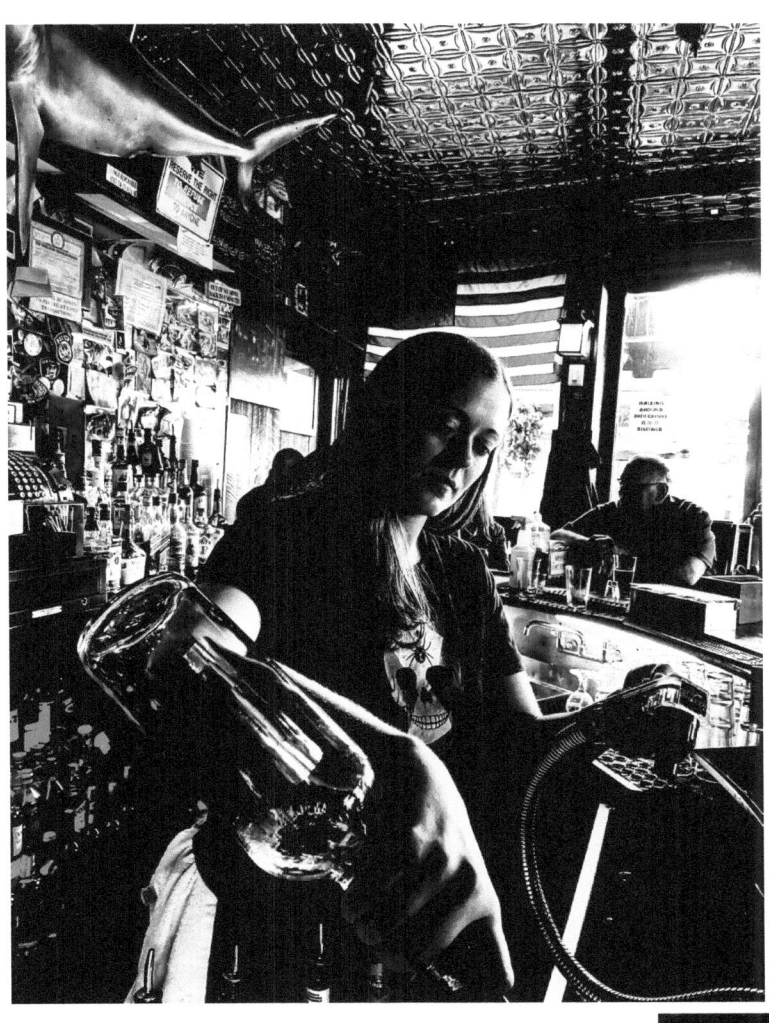

Behind the counter, the bar's most prominent stuffed shark, one of three, is frozen in mid-swim over Mike, at the cash register. April, above, hard at work, and Sarah, right, who hails from Ireland, and always greets her guests effusively.

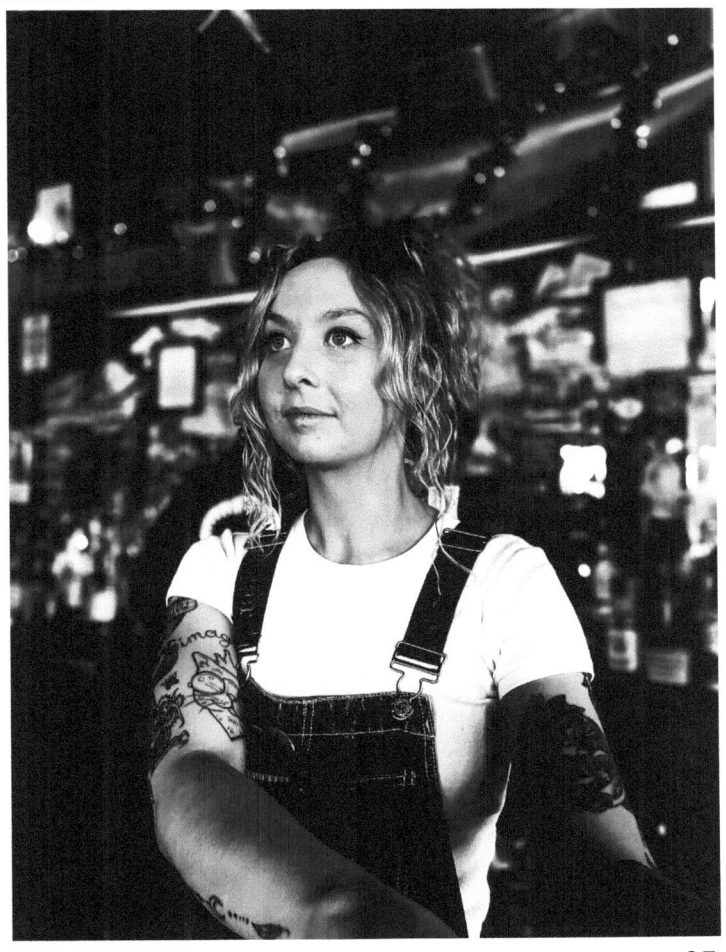

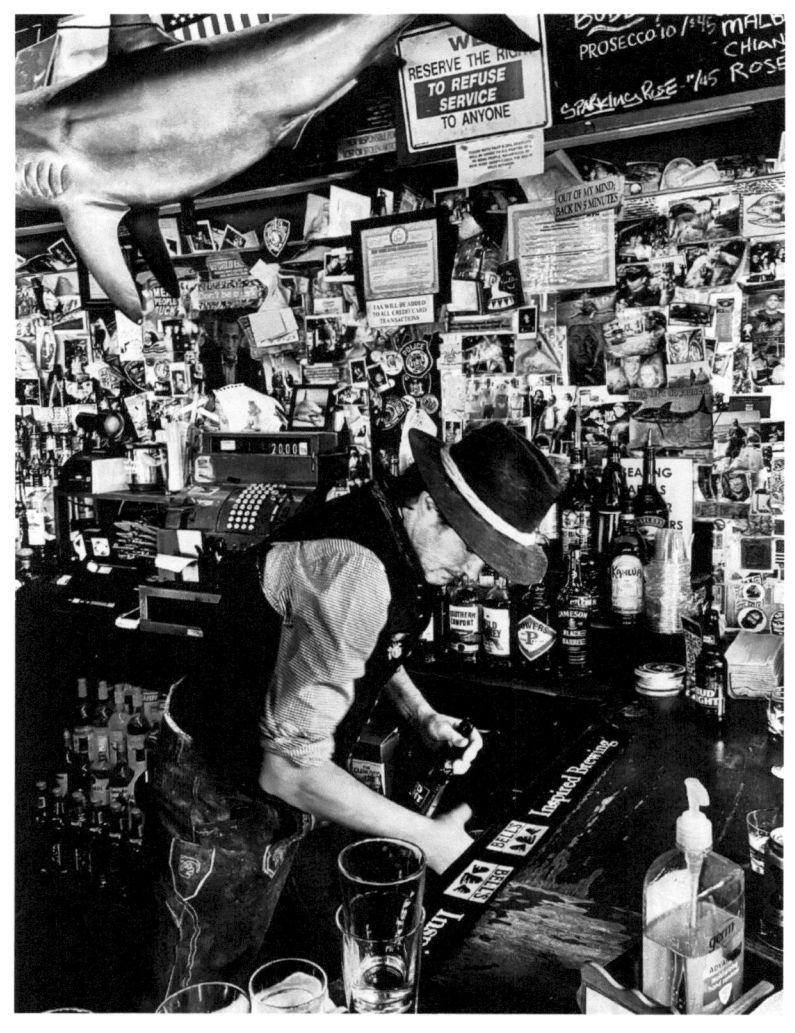

Tom, above, is dressed up for Oktoberfest. Natalie, right, an actress on stage and an avid Simpsons fan, in a characteristically light-hearted pose. Opposite page: Natalie, rear, and Anna during a rare quiet moment at the lounge.

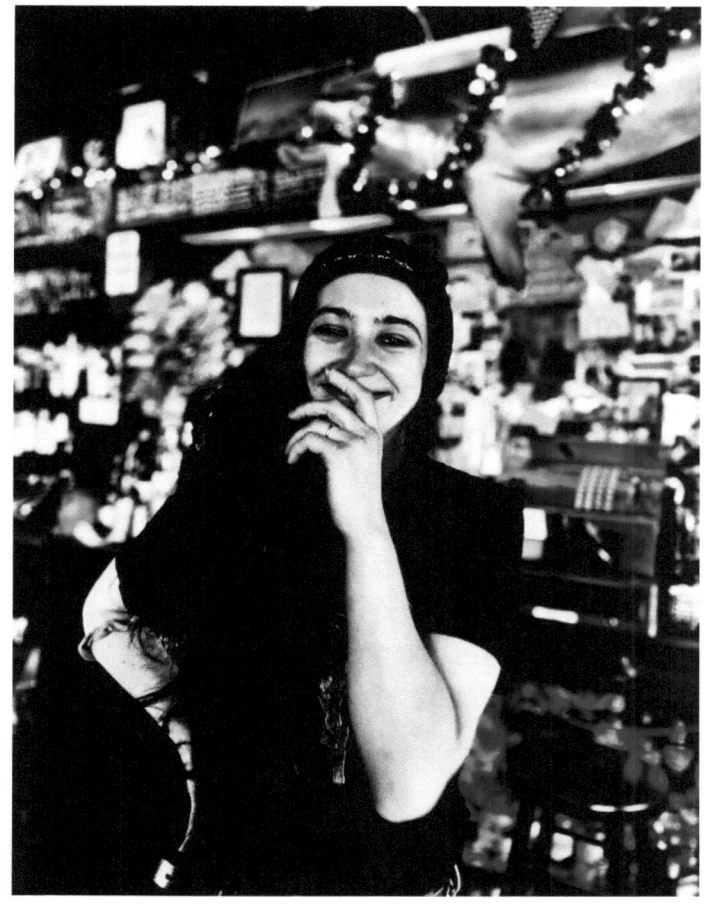

The Bar Is Open

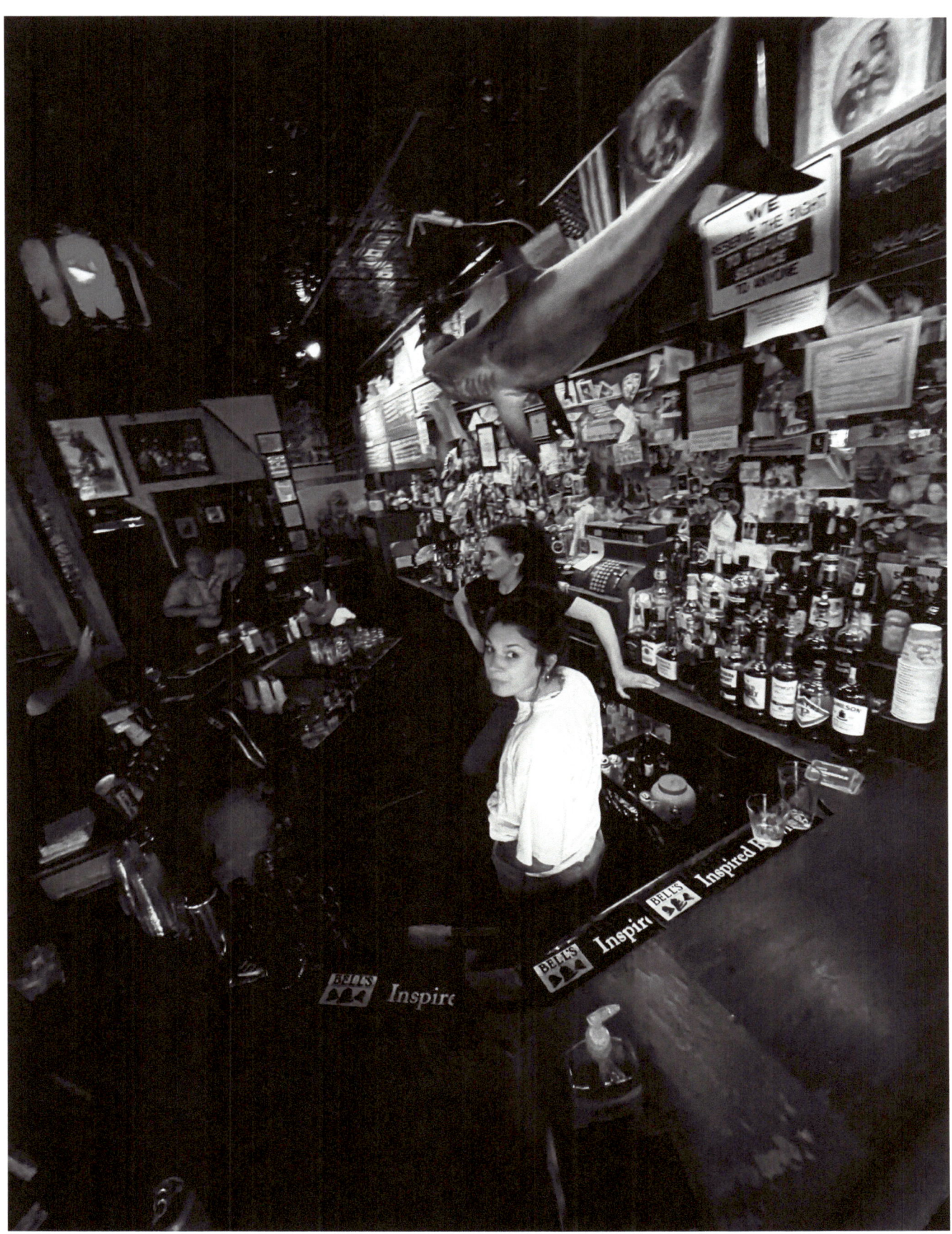

PATRONS

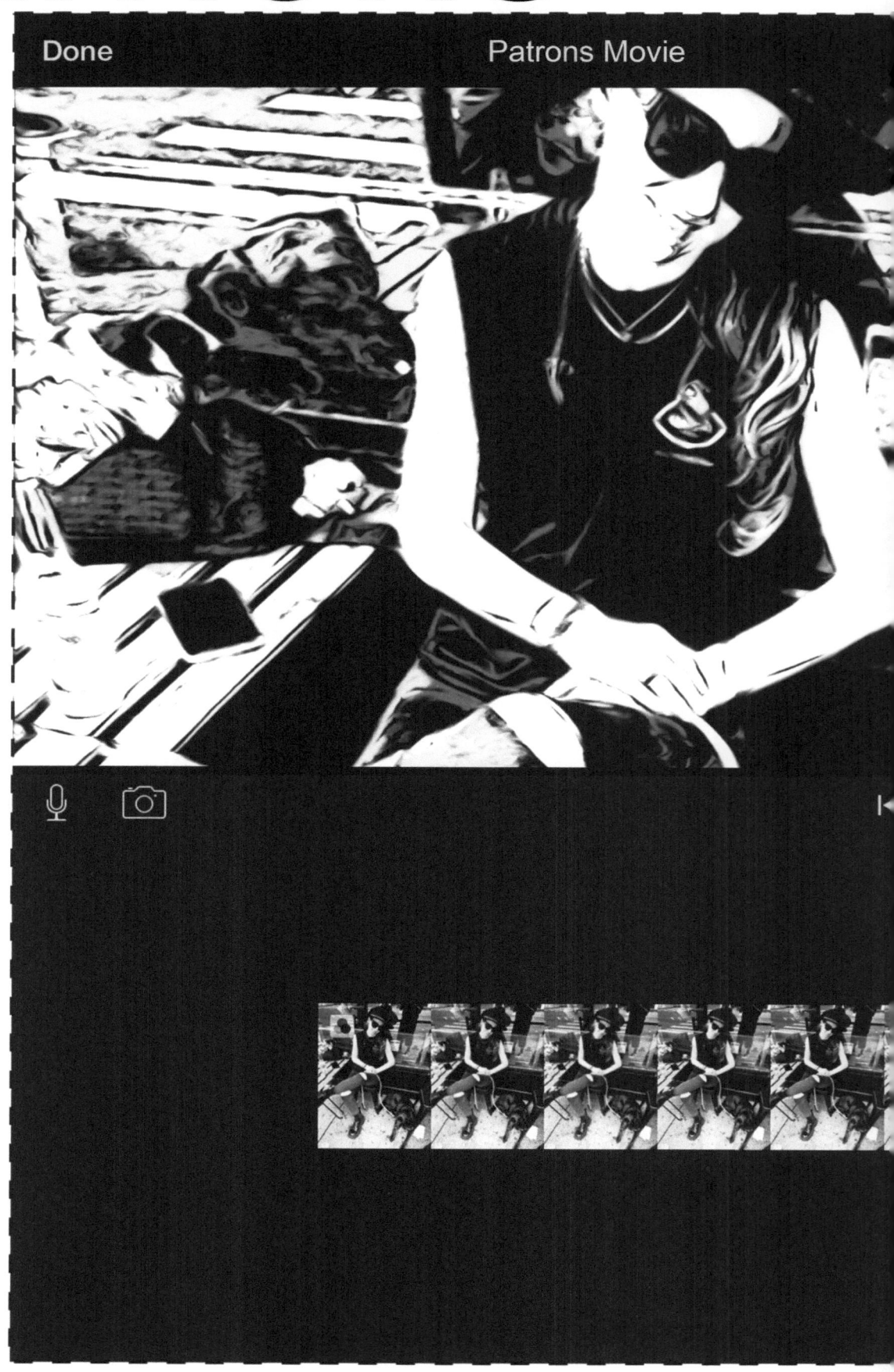

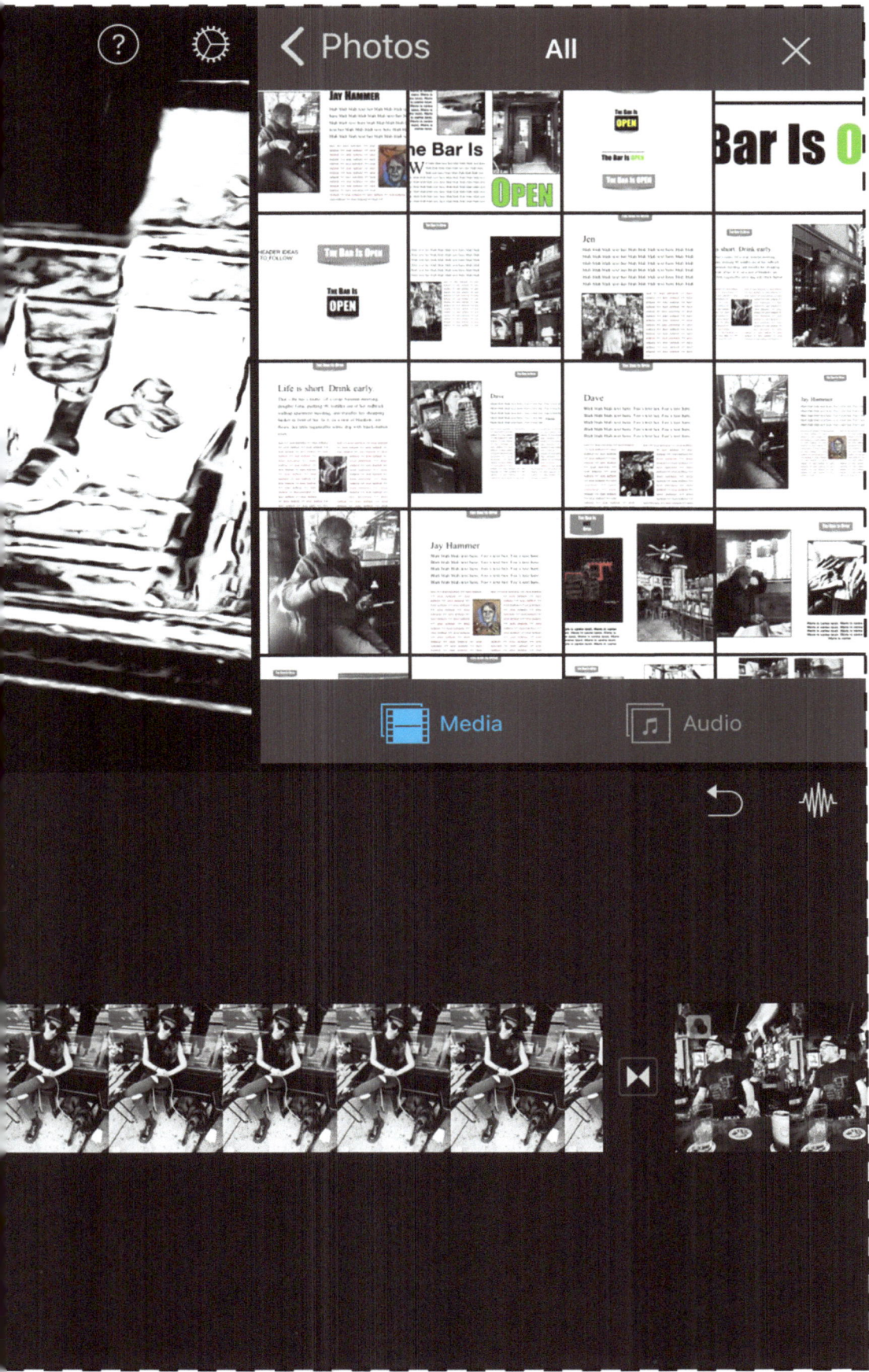

The Bar Is Open

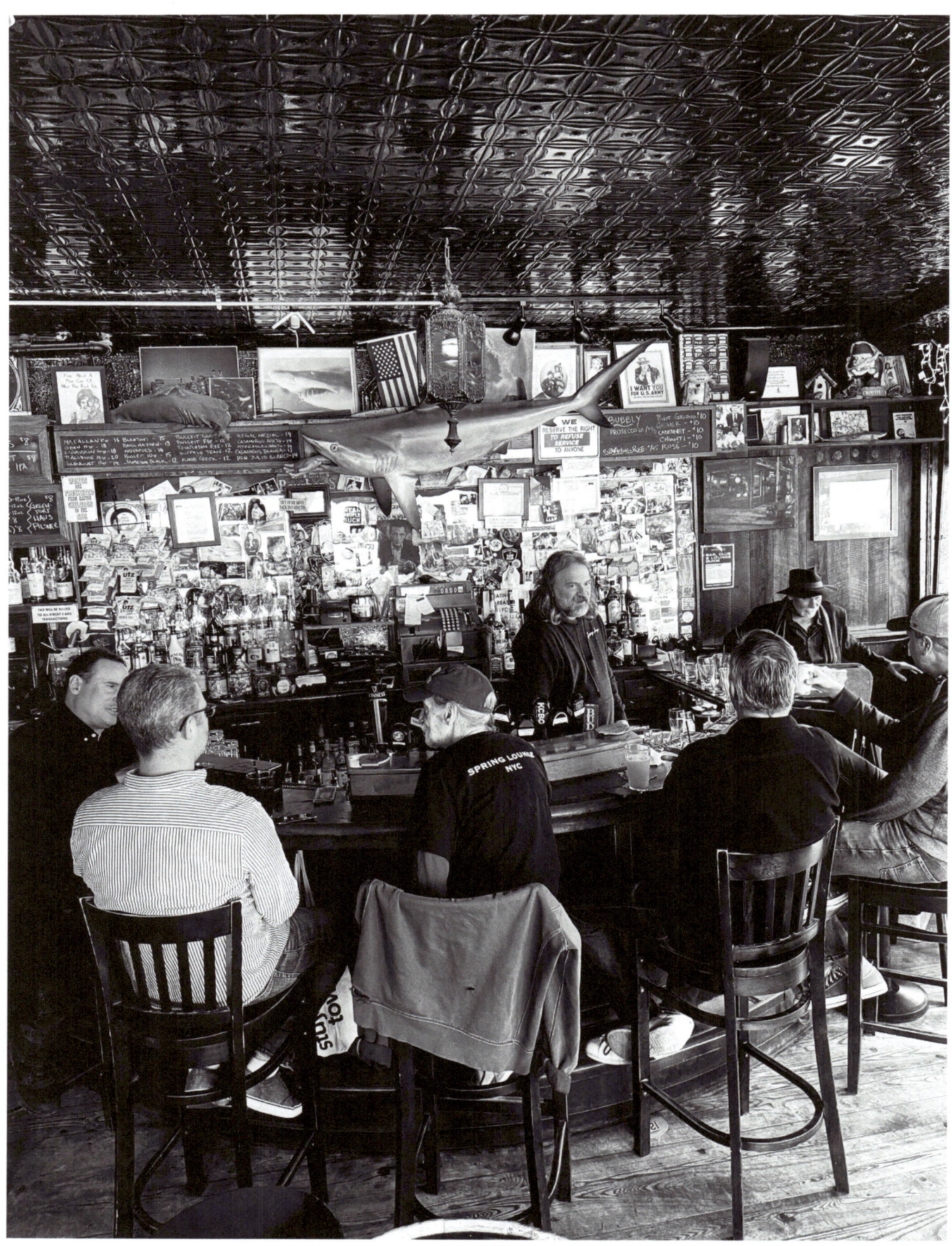

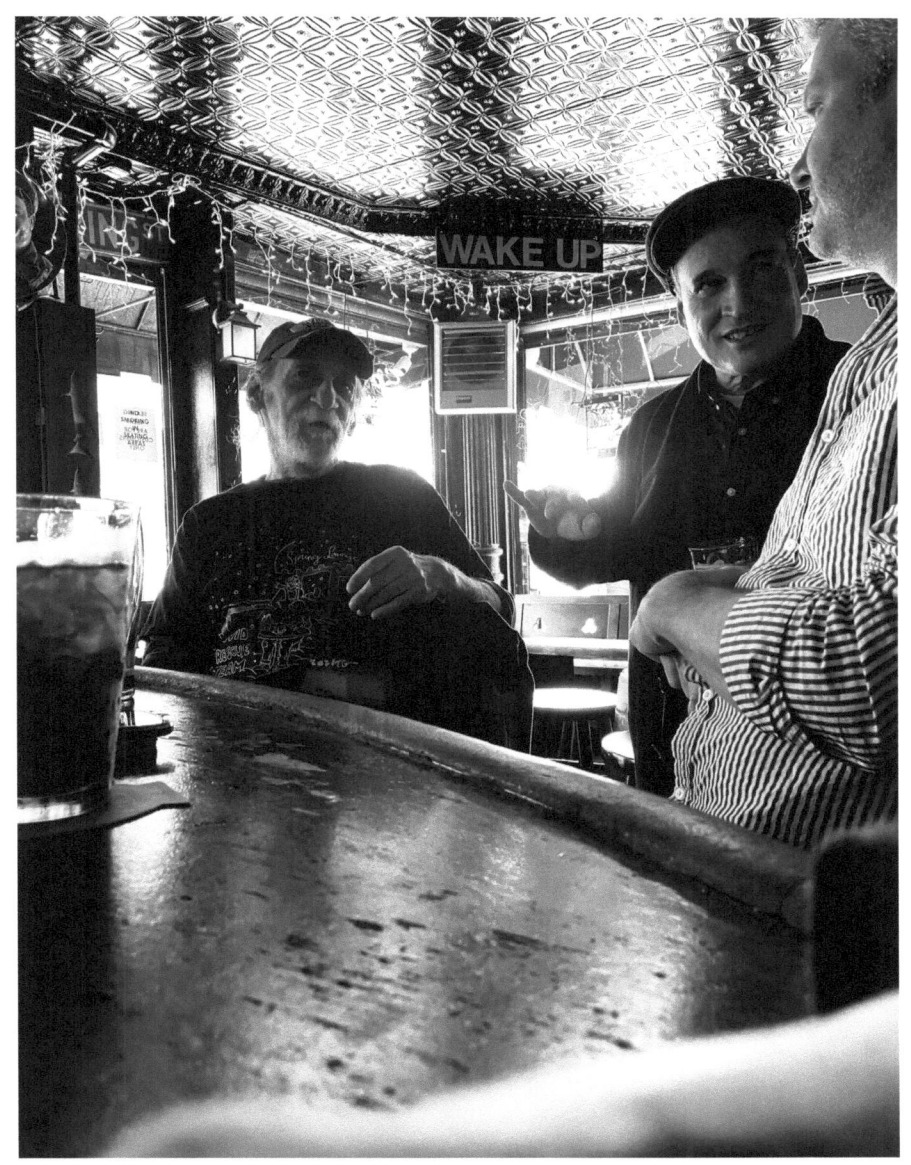

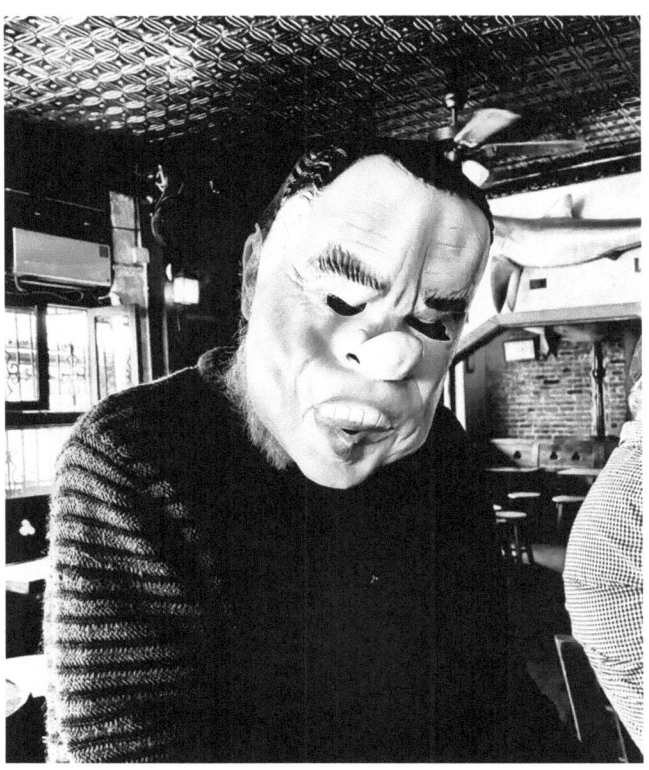

Some of the regular day drinkers of the Early Morning Drinkers Society, including some goober wearing a Nixon mask.

THE BAR IS OPEN

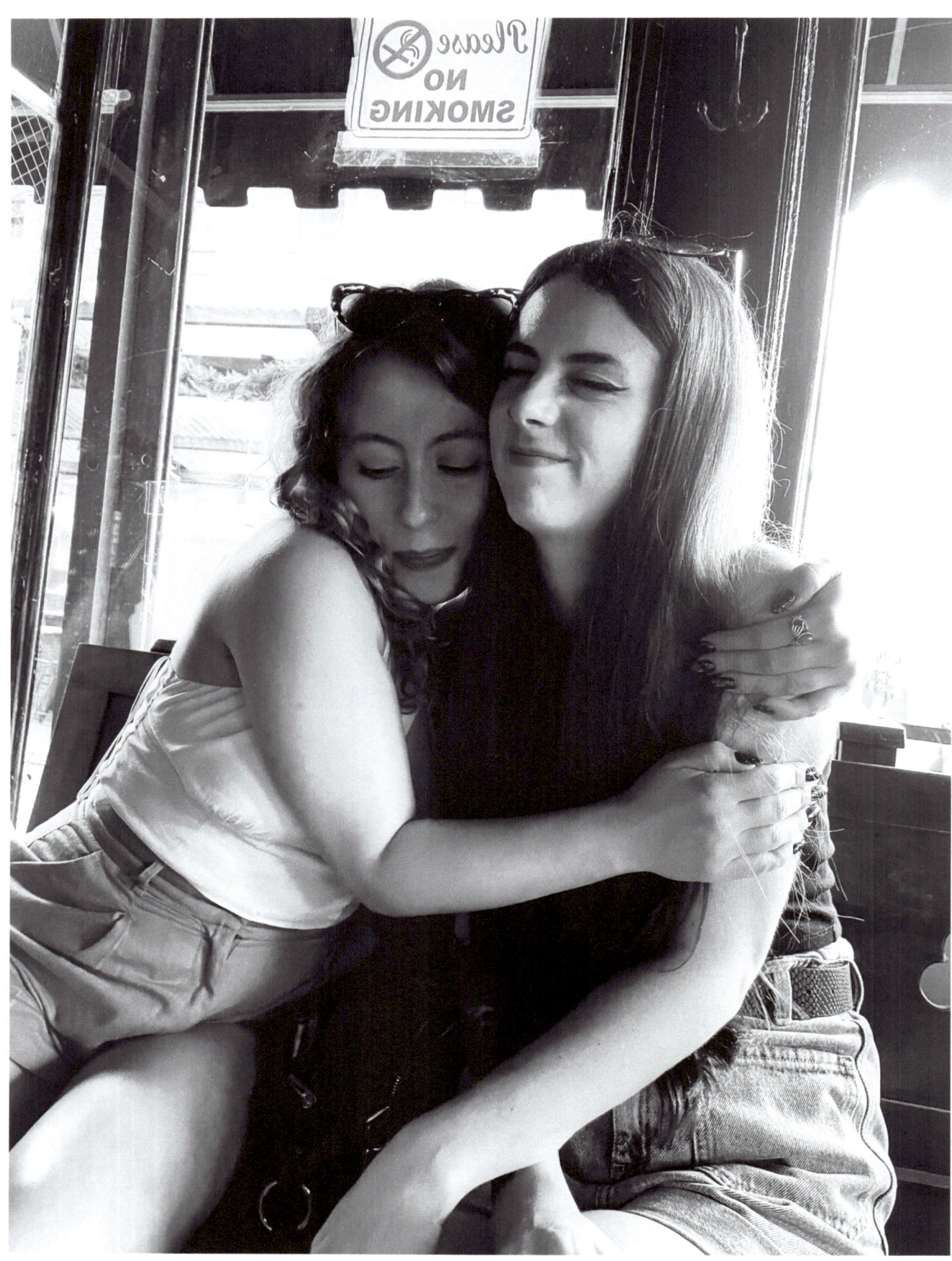

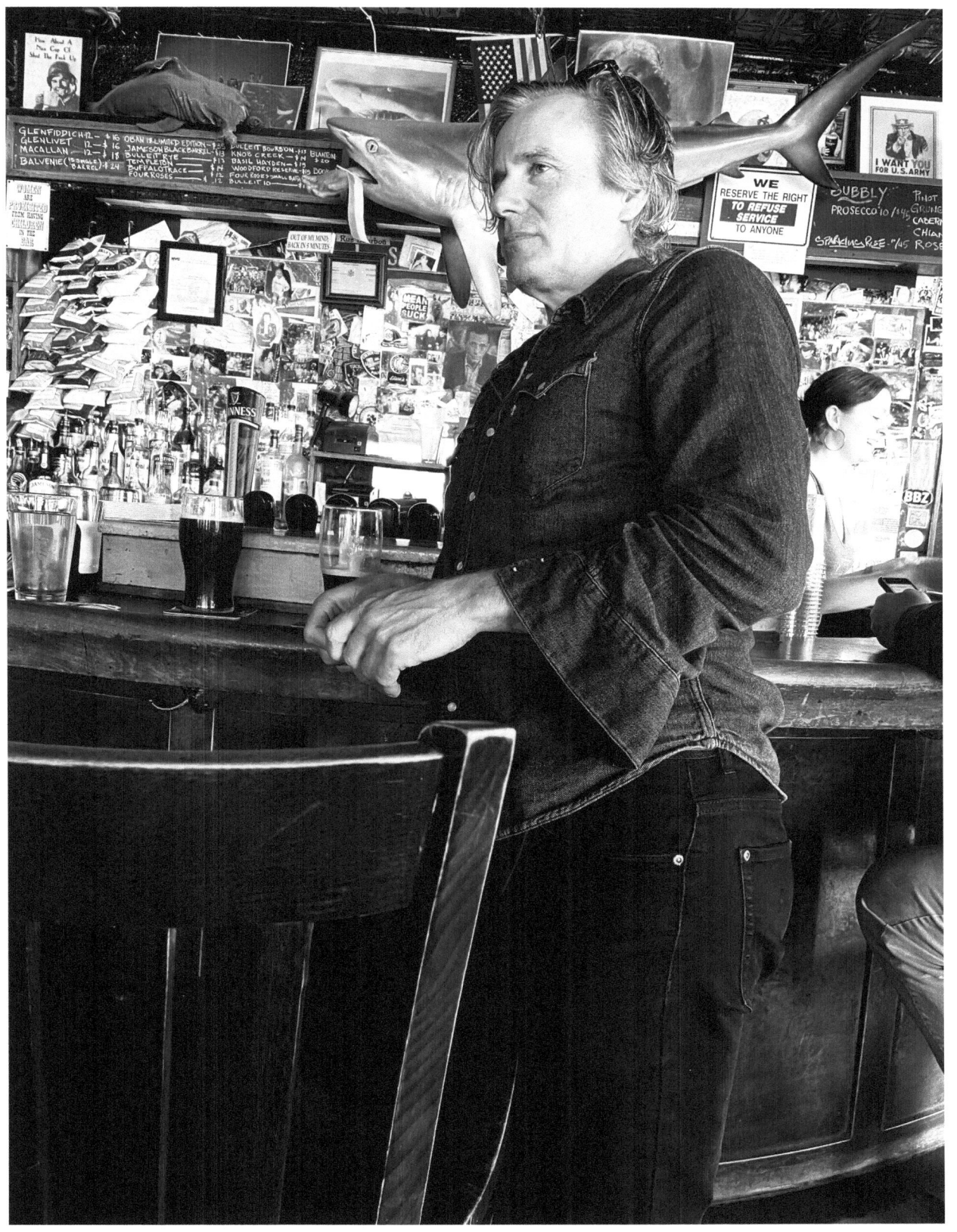

Pearl, left, and Emma, two friends visiting from Scotland who dropped into the bar and quickly got cozy there. The bar attracts and wows a lot of tourists. Above, Greg, a regular at the bar when he is not staying in Europe.

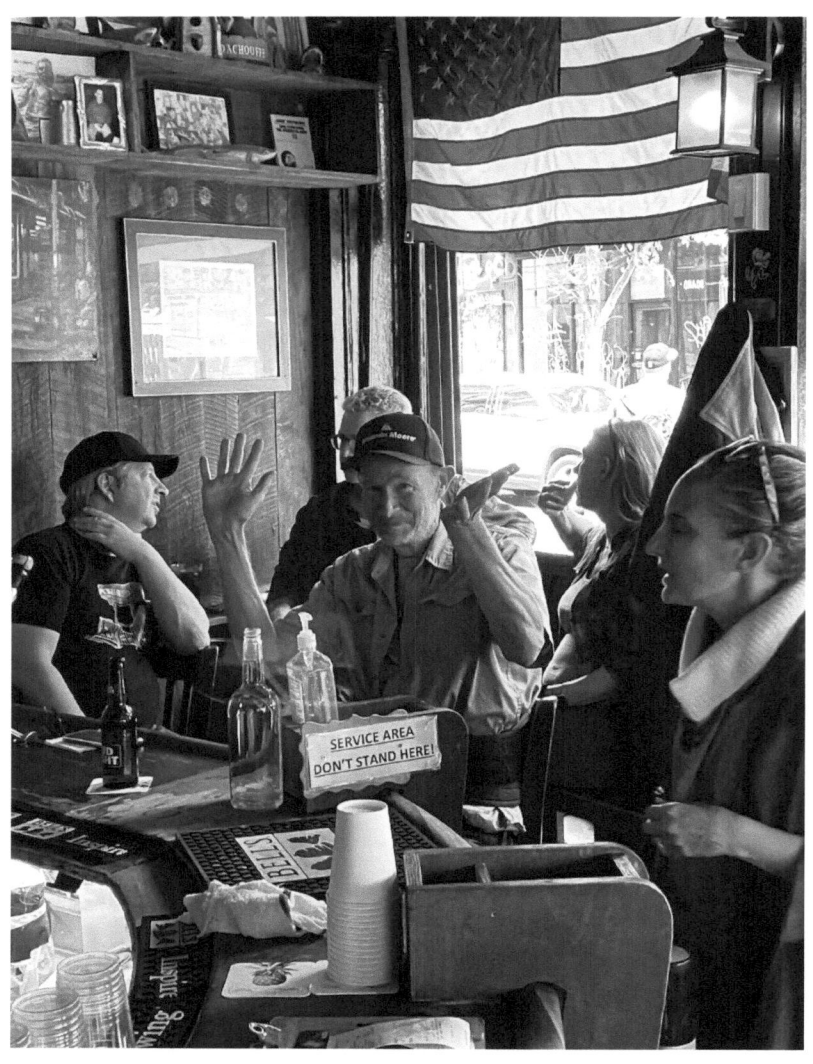

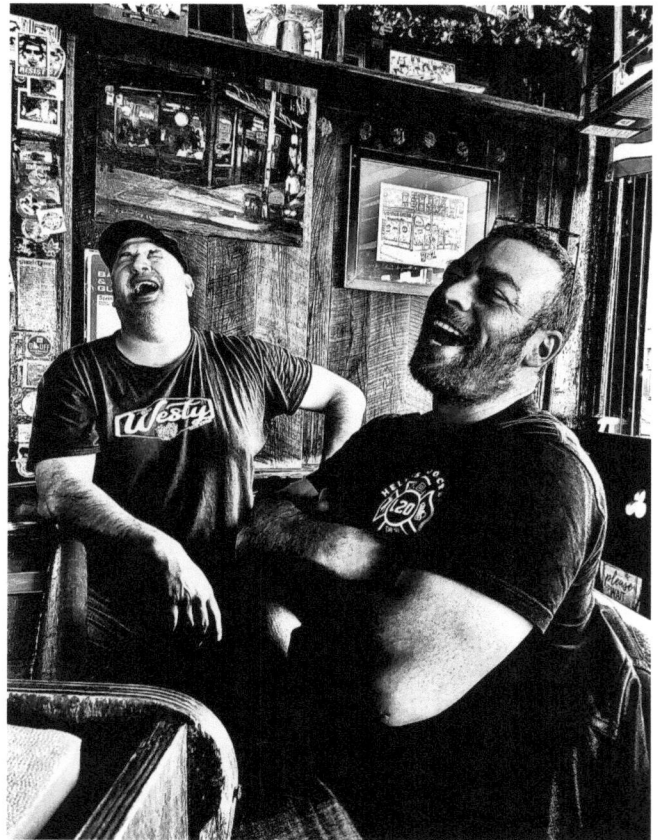

Above, Garth, another frequent day drinker, clowns for the cameras while hanging out with friends. Slap Shot Tom, a onetime hockey player, left, and fireman Johnny share a laugh. Far right, the interior of the bar from afar, the famed shark in mid-glide over a shaft of light.

The Bar Is OPEN

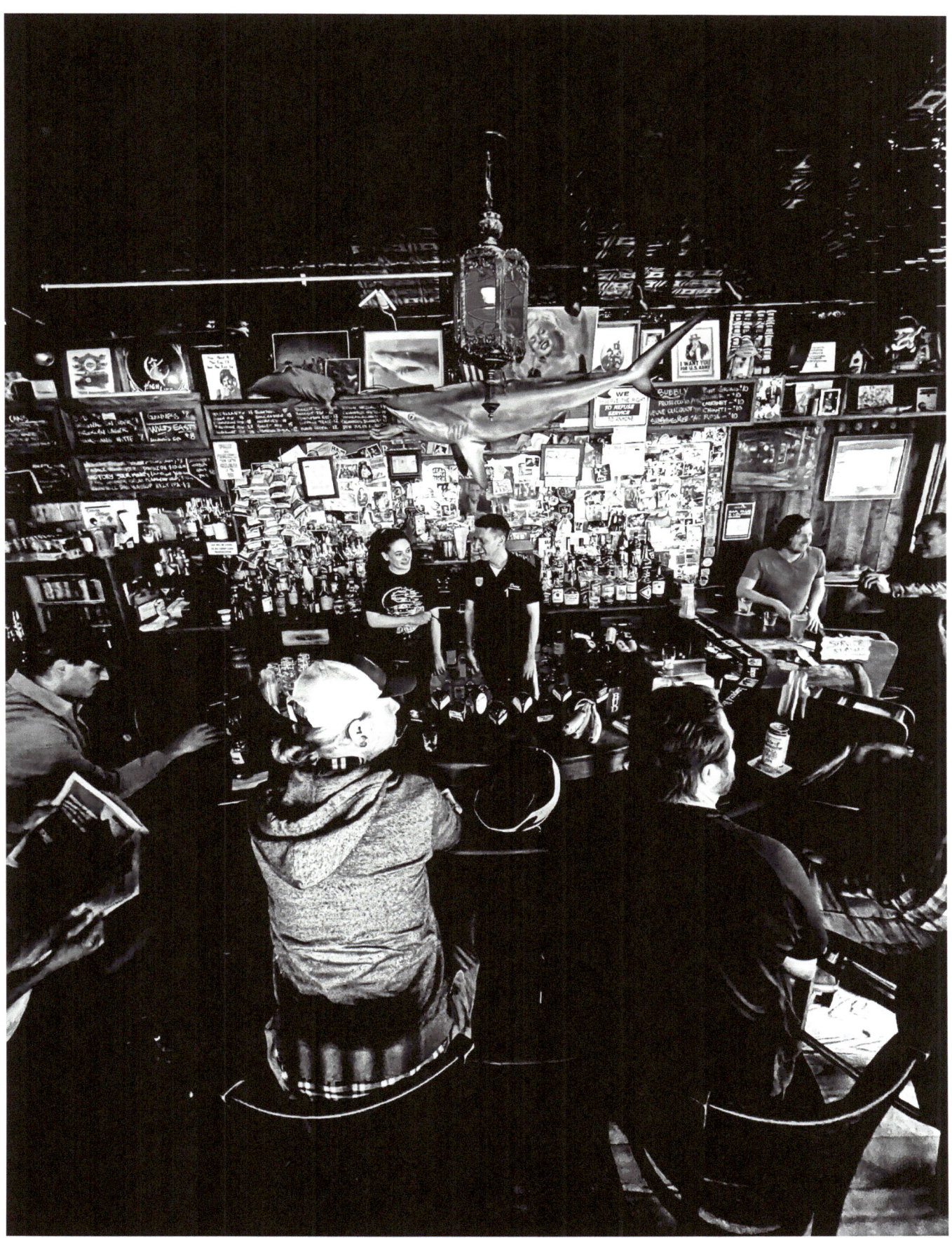

The Bar Is Open

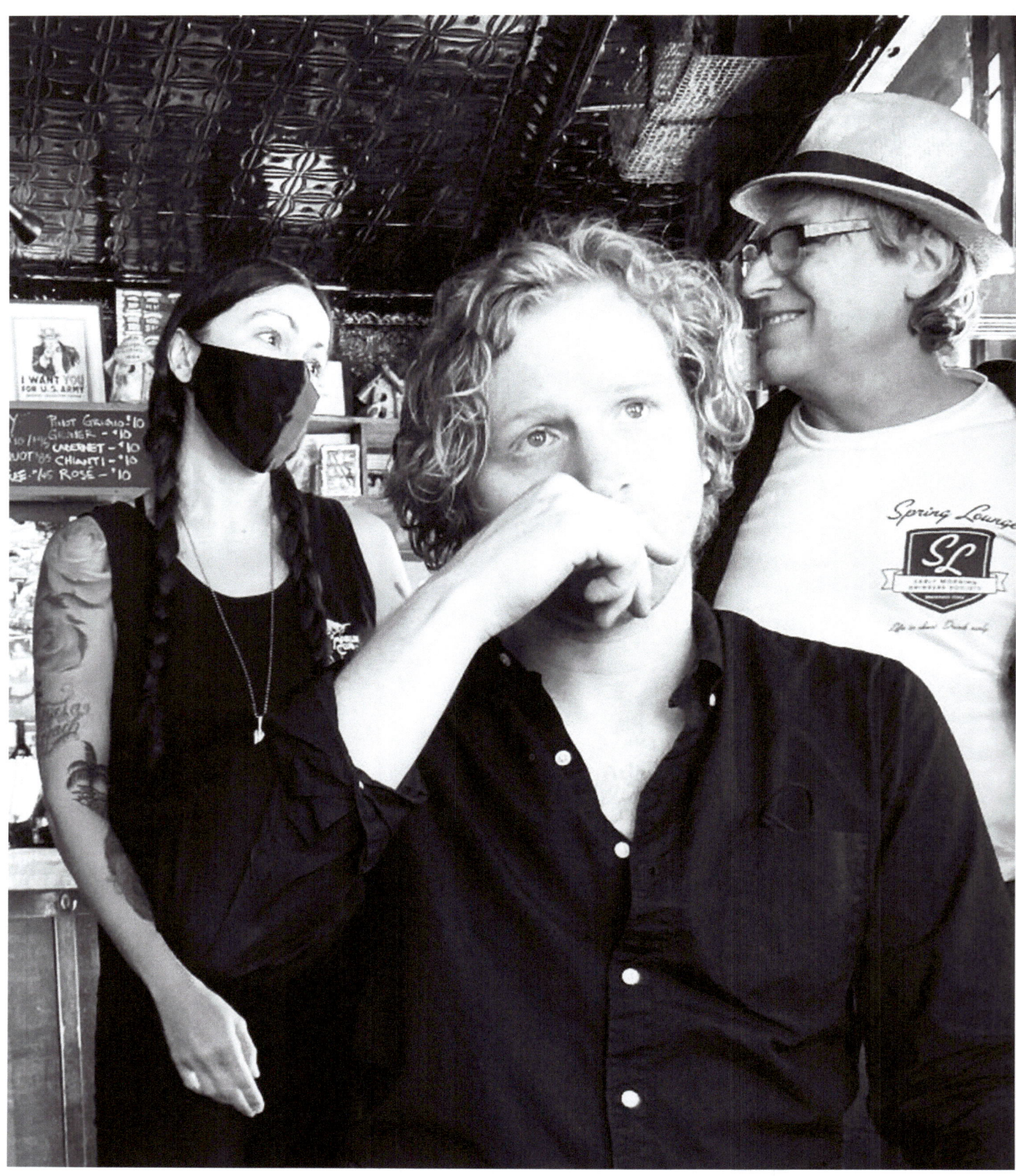

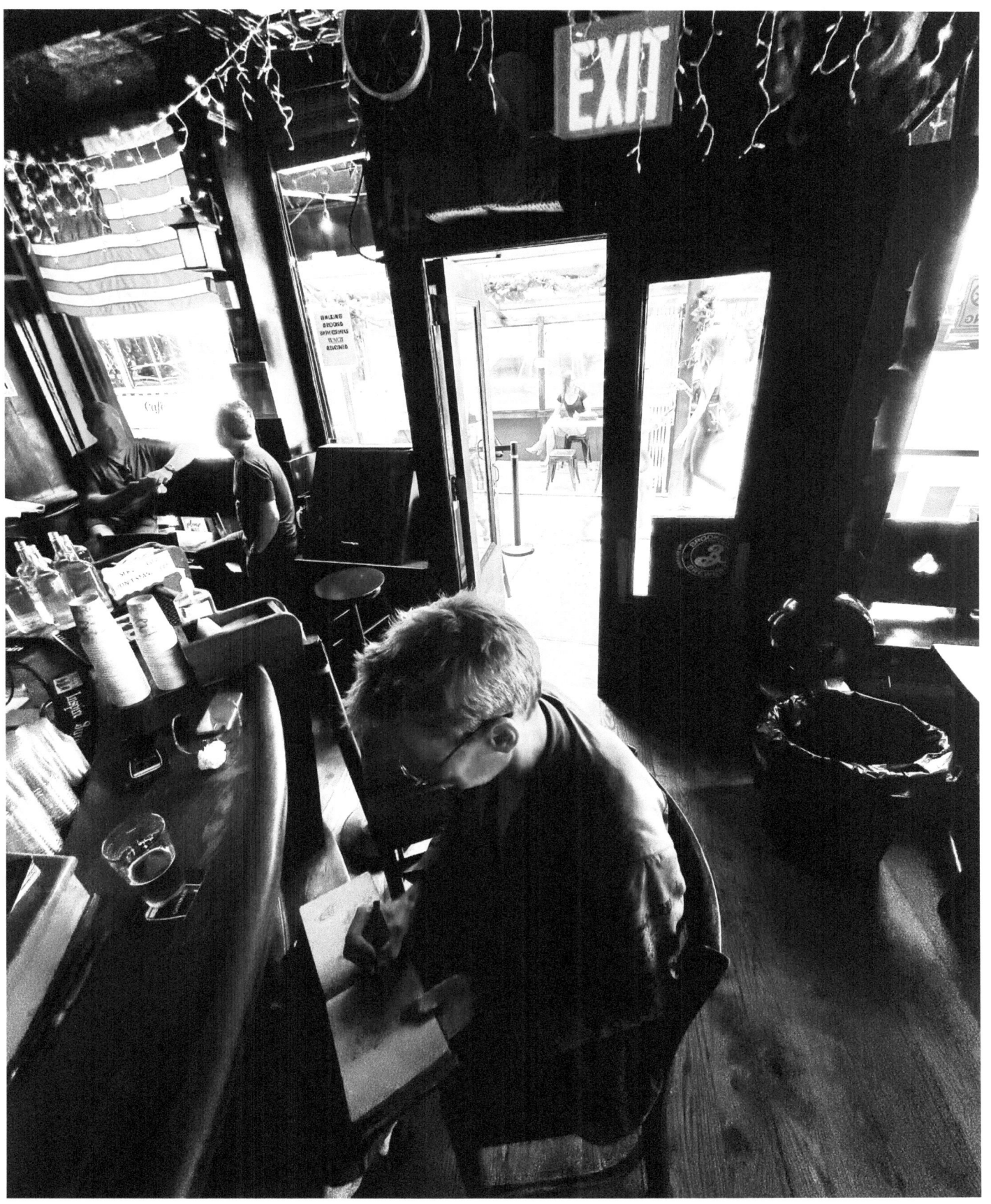

Left, a variety of expressions, from thoughtful to amused, and still the occasional mask even in the aftermath of Covid, are found among the patrons. Above, Monte, one of several artists who hangs out at Spring Lounge, is hard at work in his sketchbook.

The Bar Is OPEN

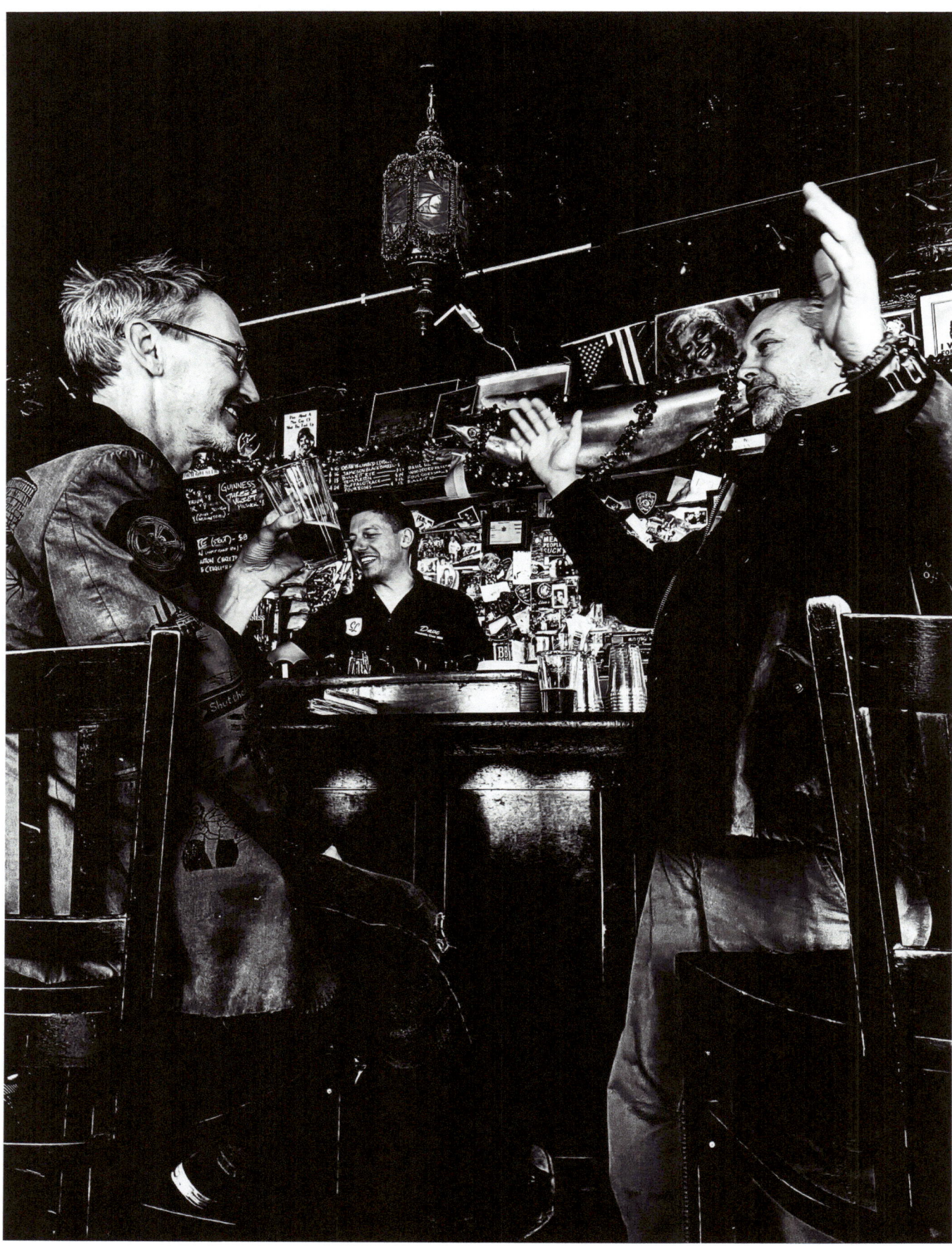

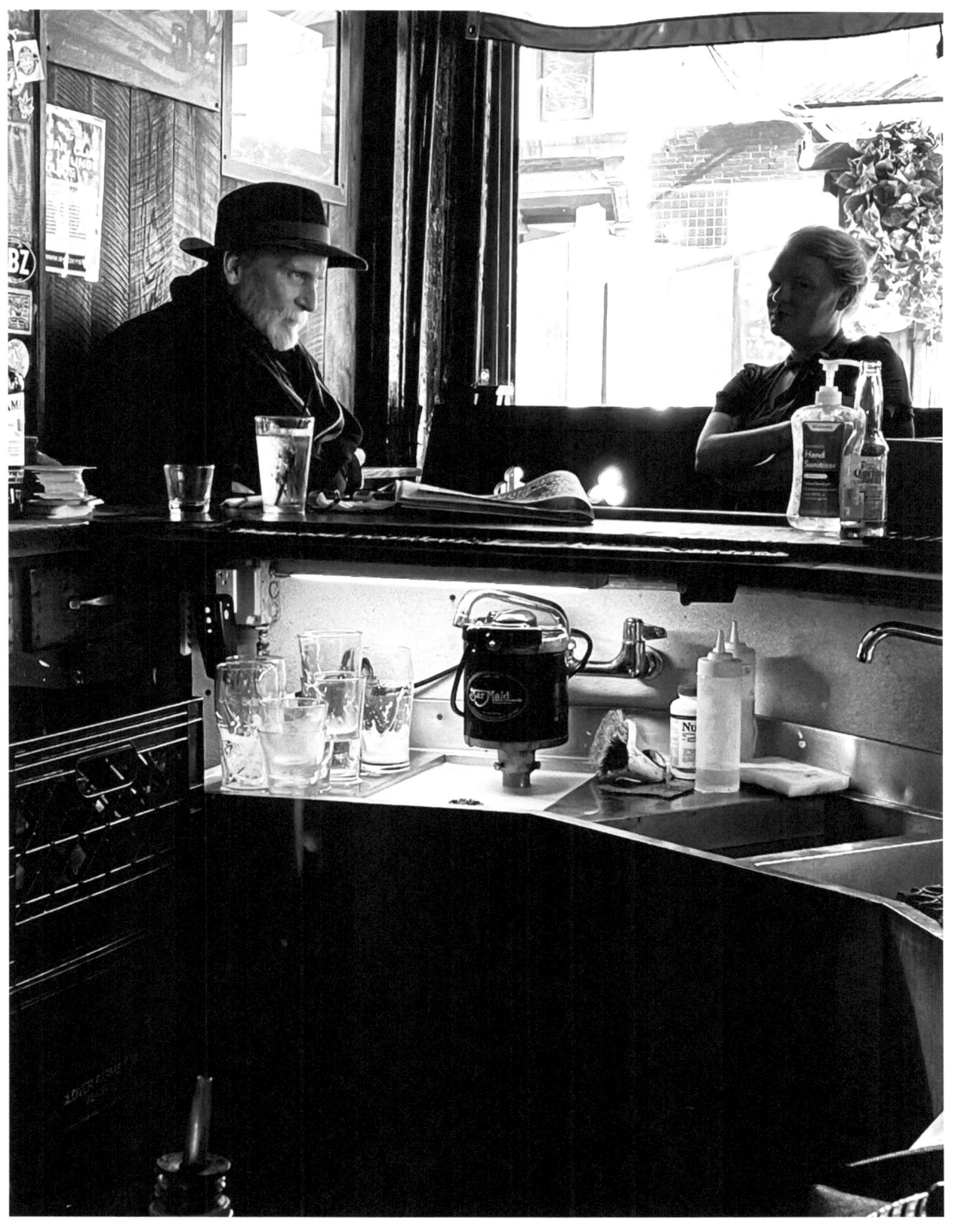

Left, laughter is the order of the day at Spring Lounge, especially after a few bracing libations. Above, Tom, a court police officer, wearing his fedora and in a characteristic pose in his favorite corner.

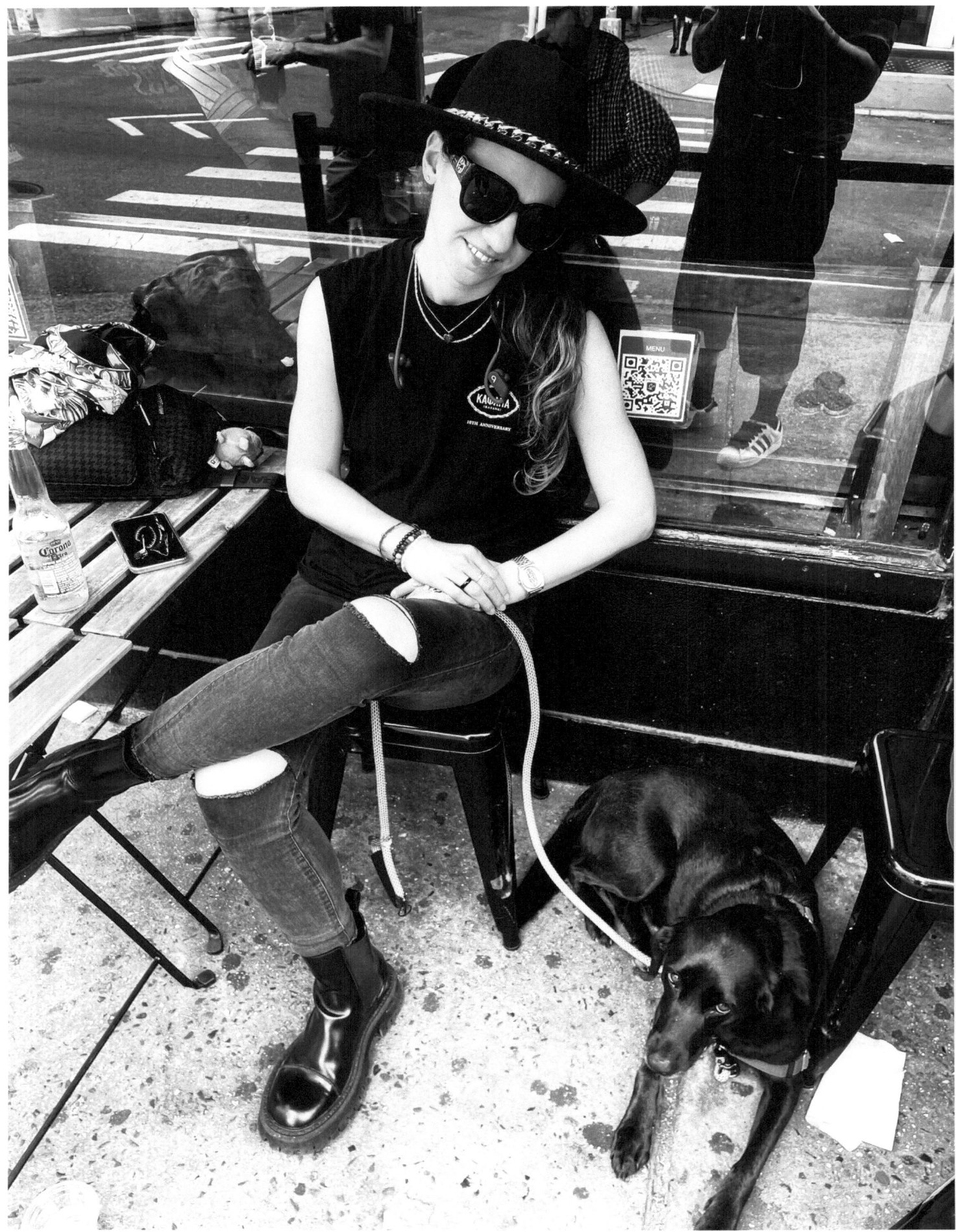

The Bar Is OPEN

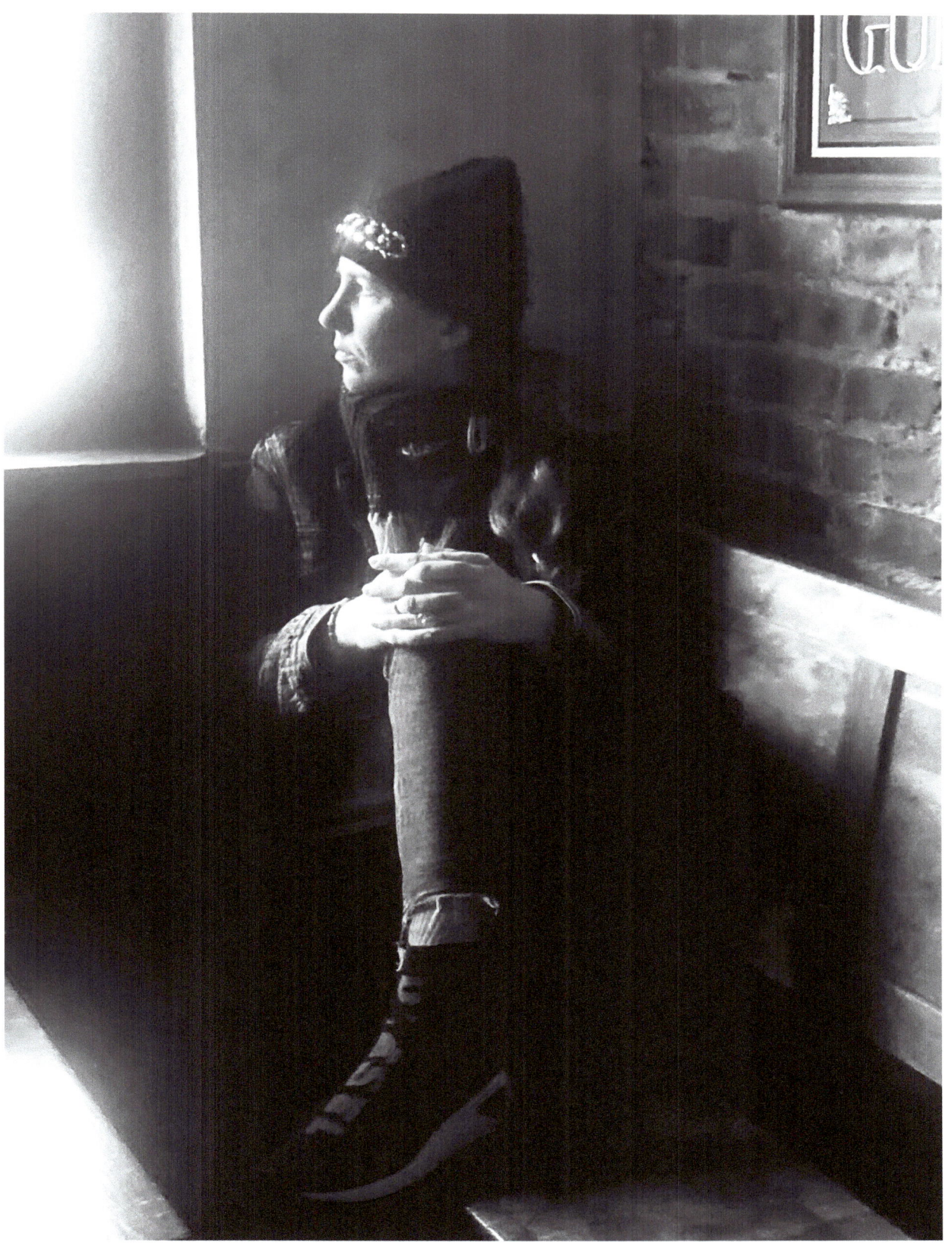

Two views of Maya, another regular who often relaxes outdoors with Lucy, whose sweet nature and placid temperament make her a bar favorite.

THE BAR IS OPEN

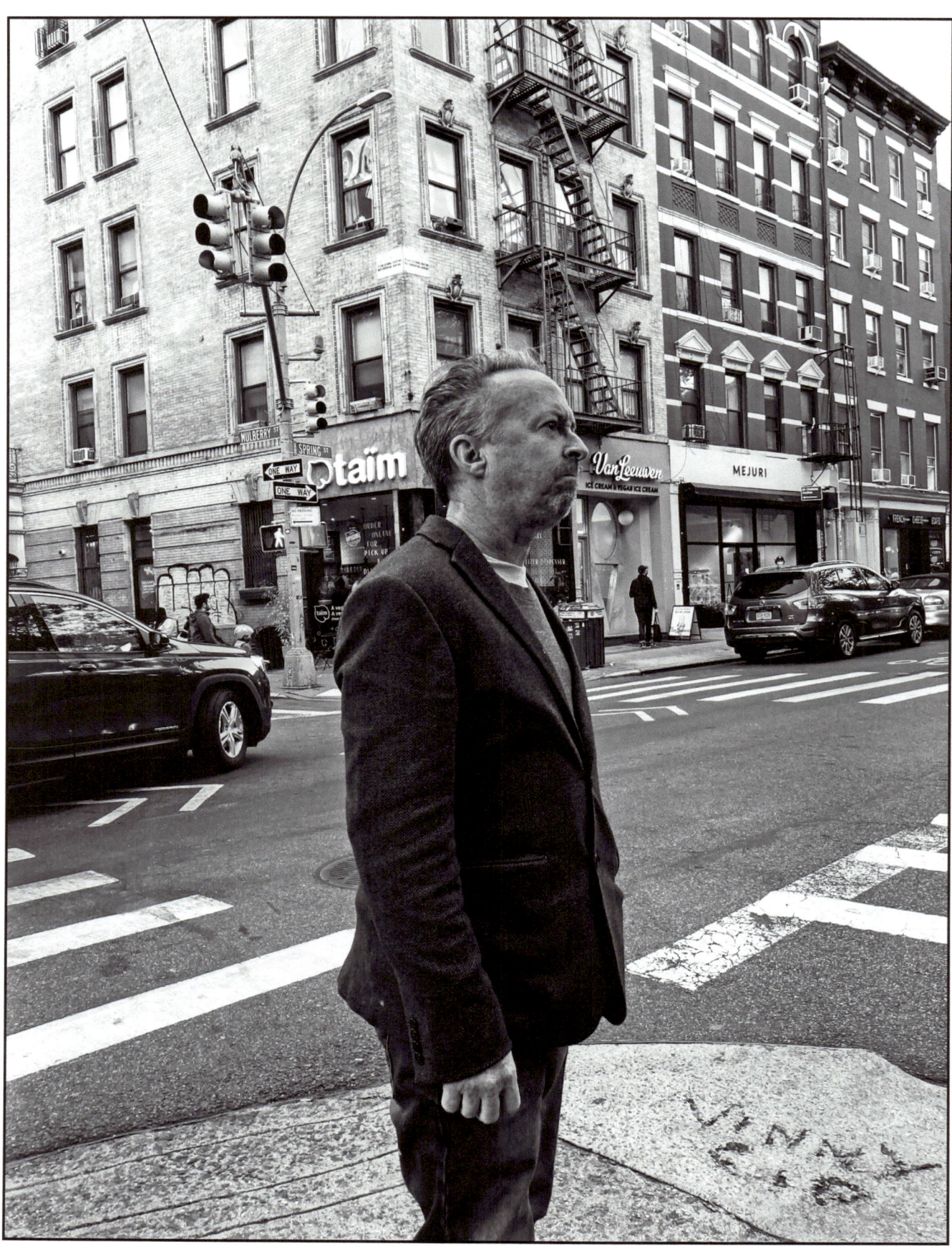

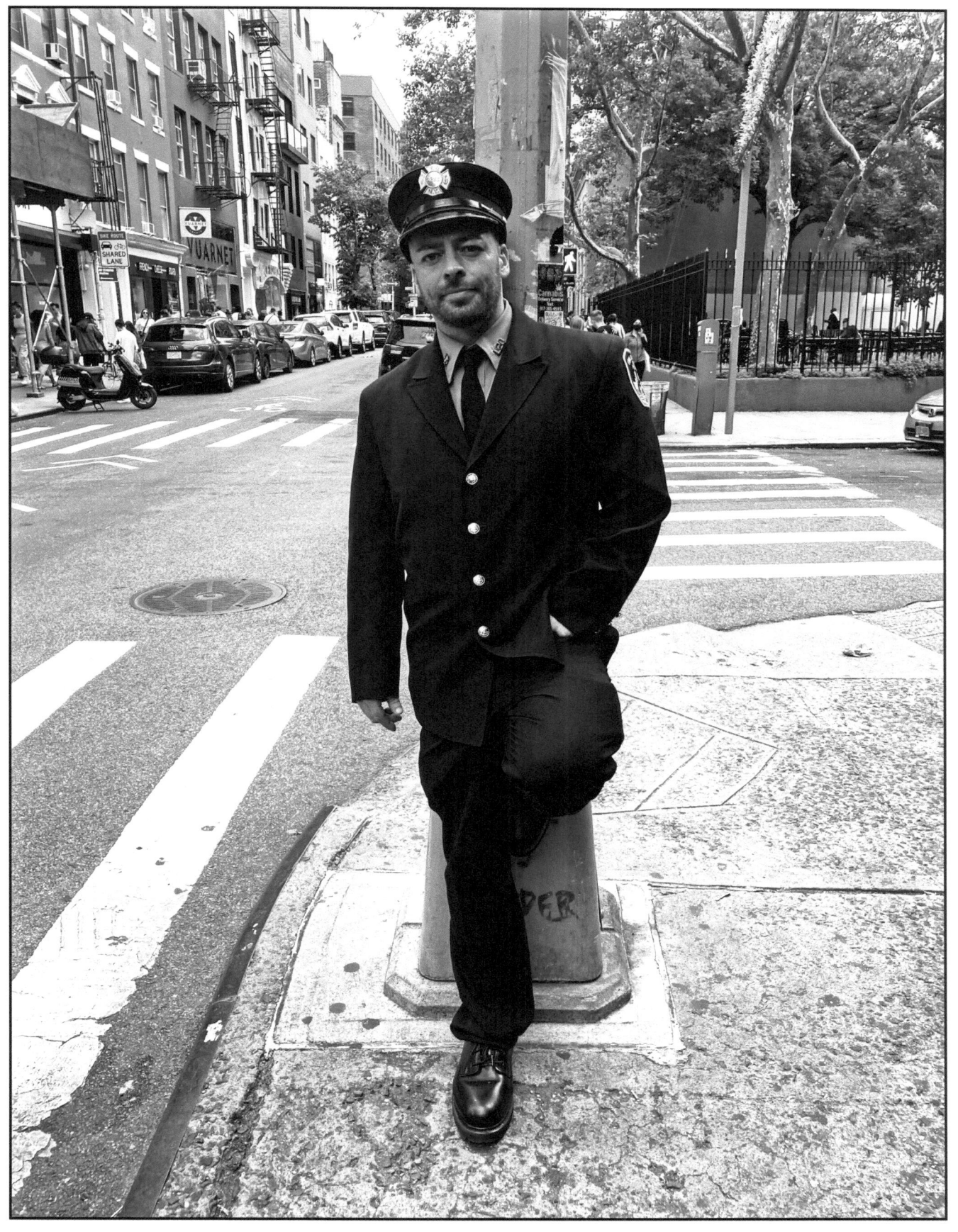

Paul, left, who works for art galleries and is a collage artist in his own right, and fireman Johnny, in full uniform on the 20th anniversary of the September 11, 2001 attacks on the twin towers.

THE BAR IS OPEN

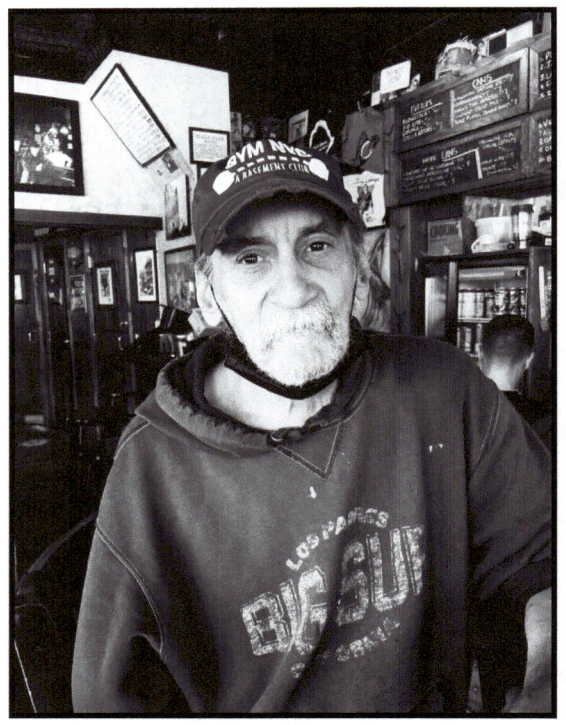
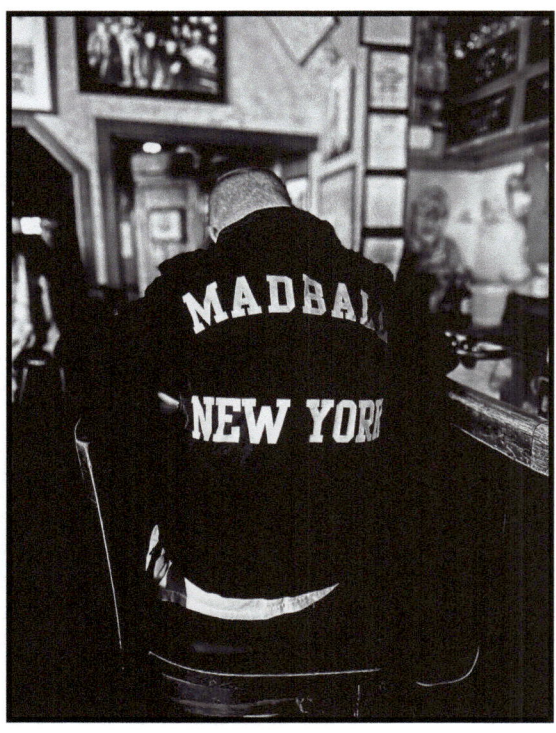
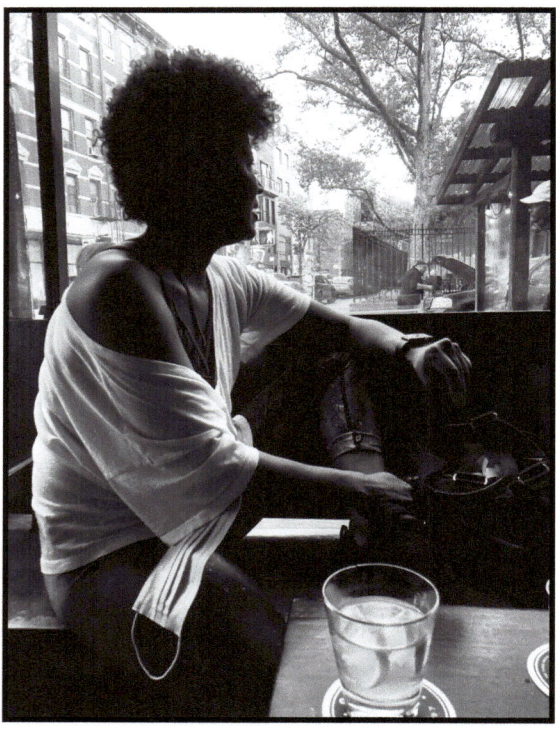
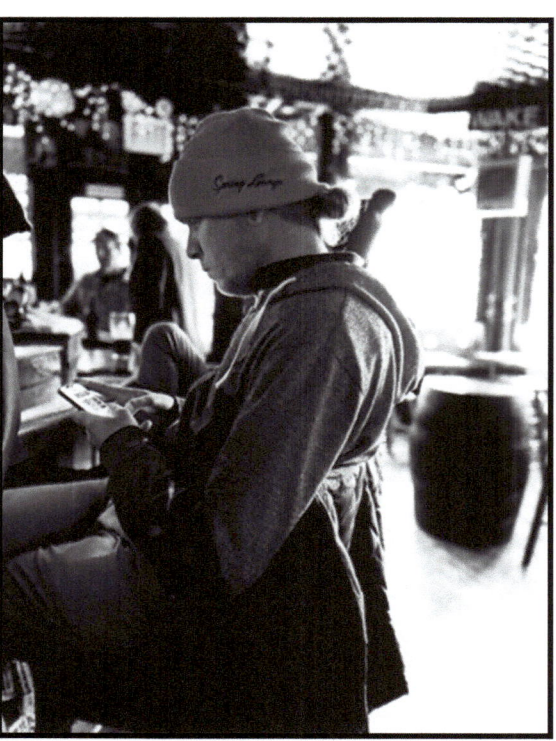

Right, an out-of-town visitor who studies photography, poses for her own portrait in the outdoor seating section erected in response to the closure of the bar's interior because of Covid. Above, clockwise from top left: Terry, an artist; a patron wearing a jacket promoting Madball, a local Hardcore band; Dennis and Kim, two more members of the Early Morning Drinkers Society.

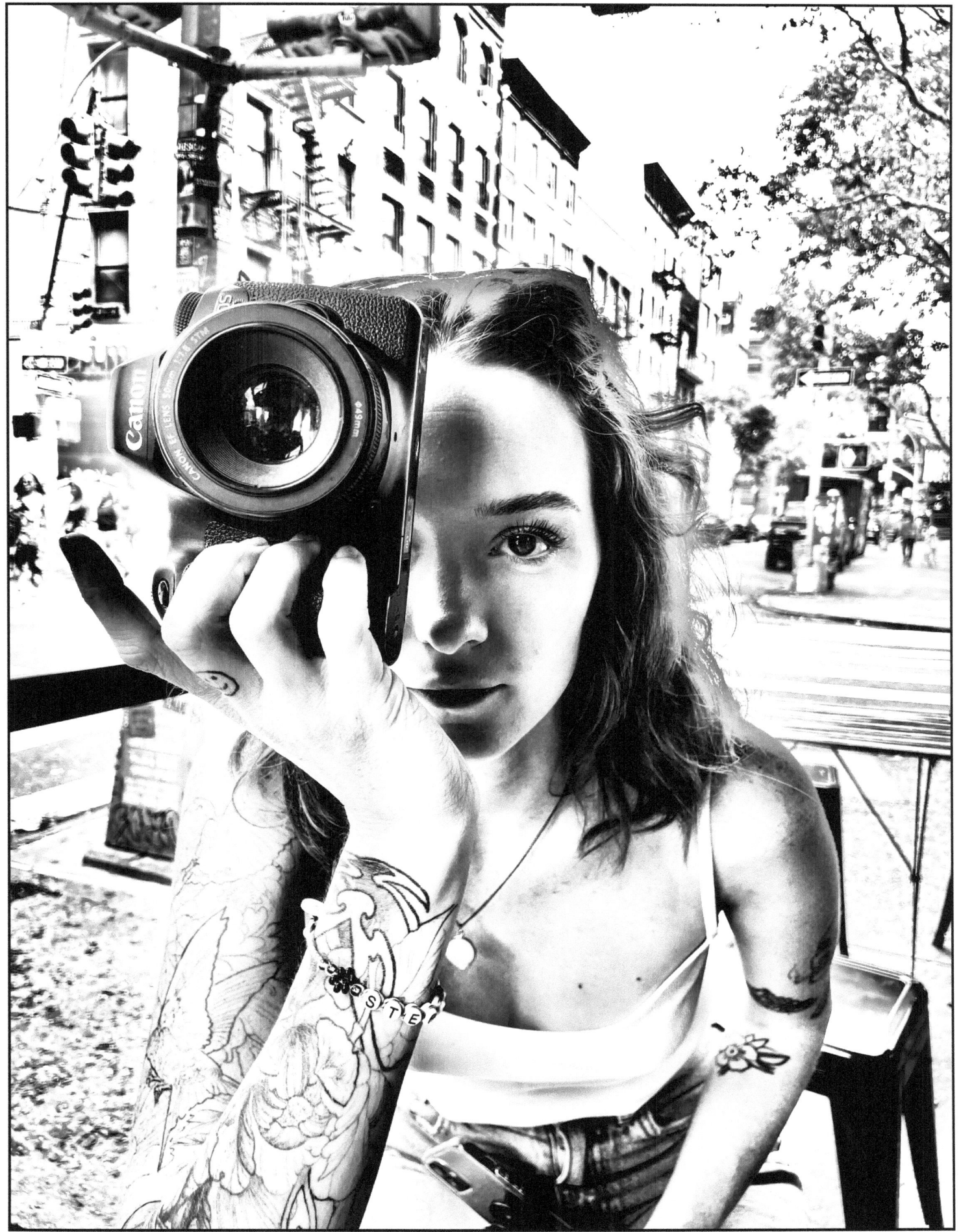

The Bar Is OPEN

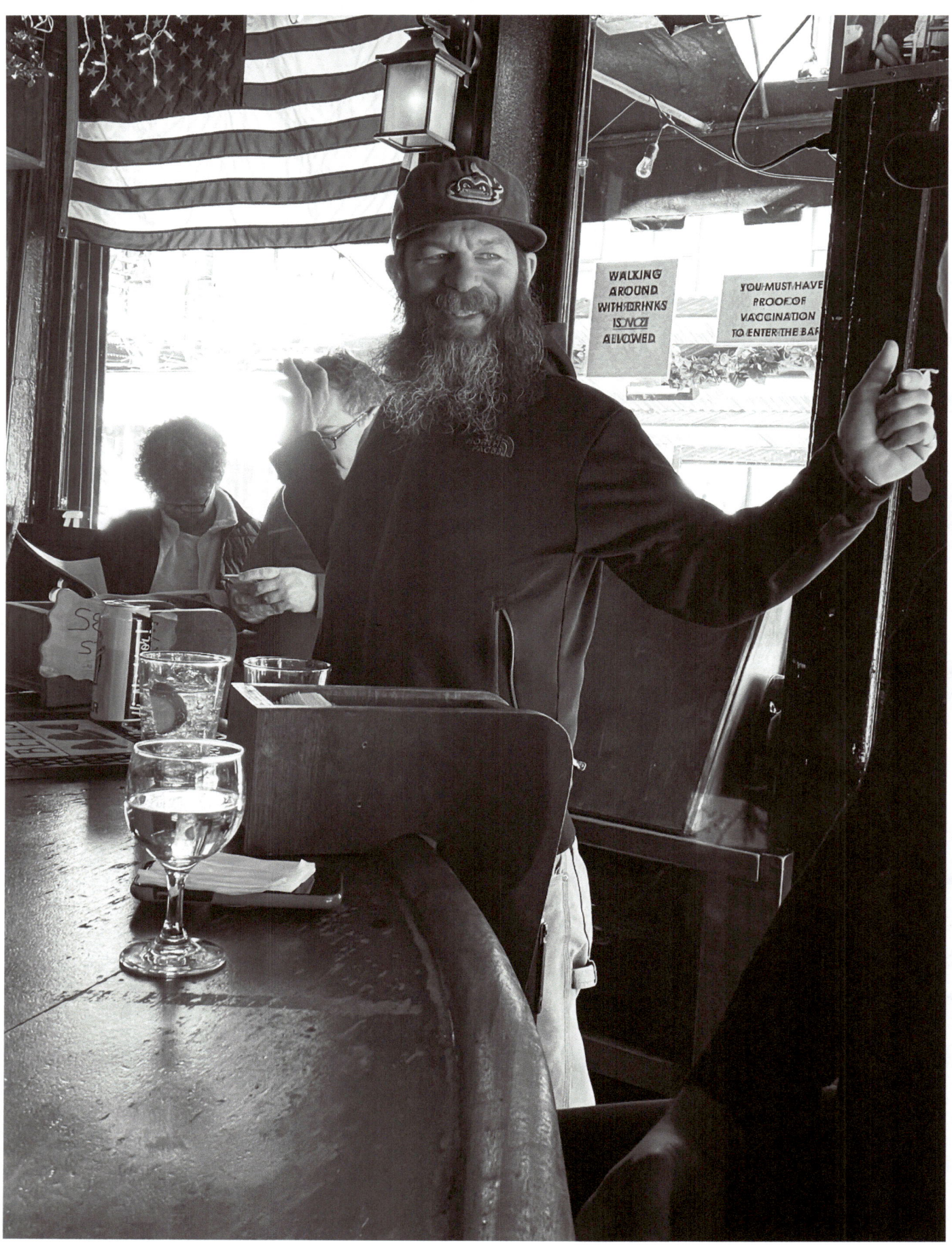

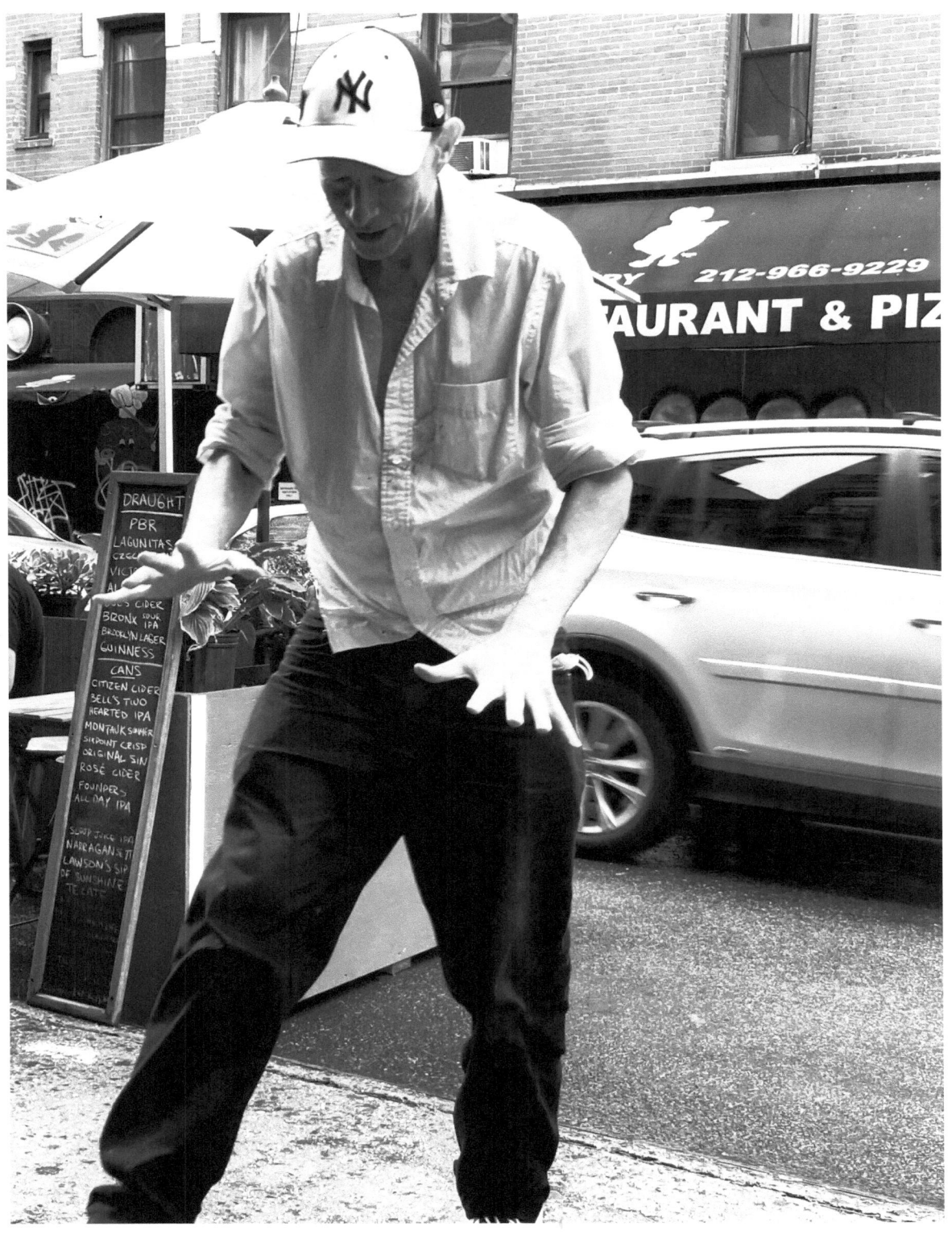

Keith, left, known as Appleseed for planting sunflower seeds all over the city, and Garth express the enthusiasm that comes with patronizing a bar where everyone knows your name.

THE BAR IS OPEN

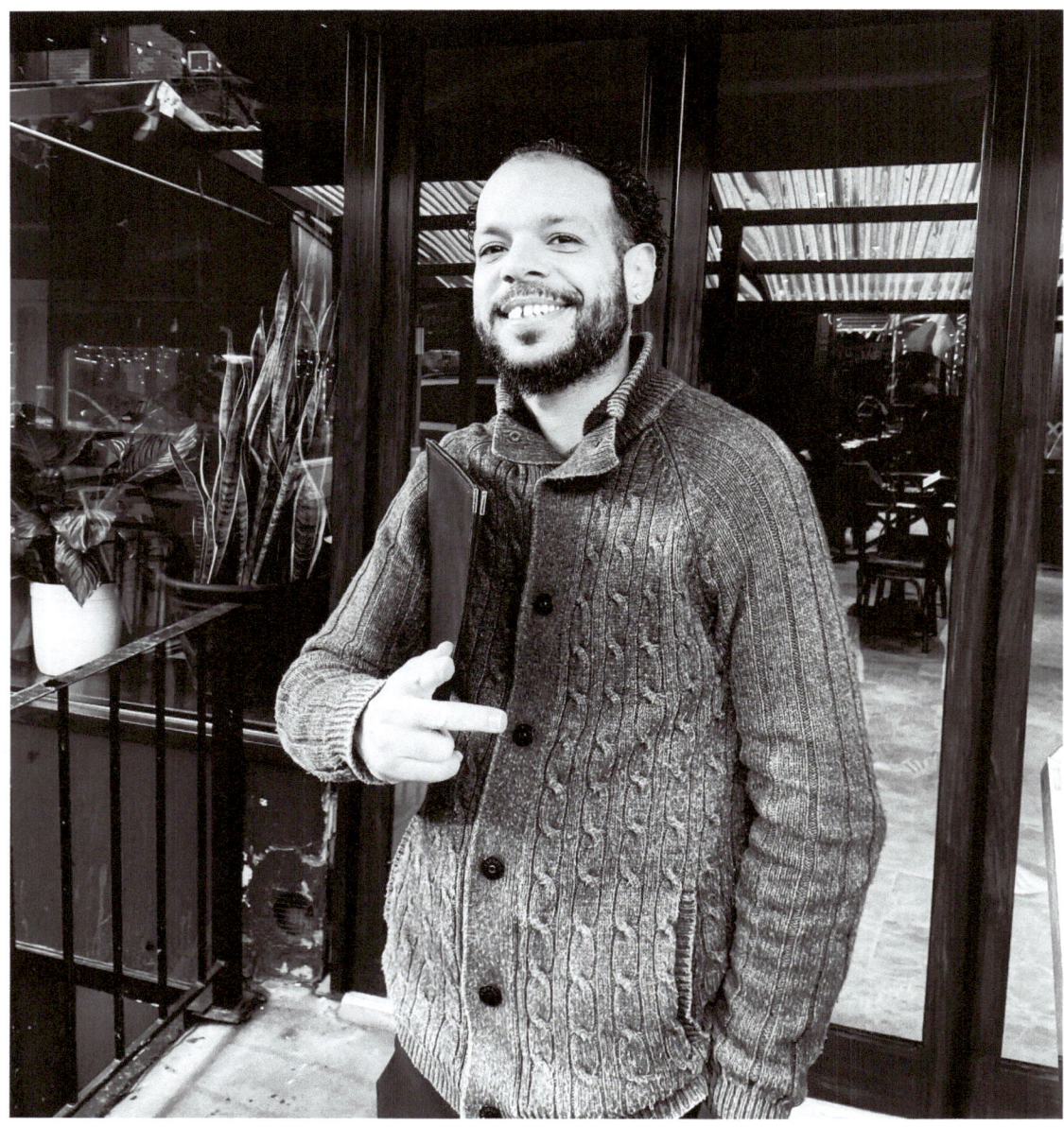

Above, Alex, who can be found outside Little Italy restaurants luring passers-by in for dinner and drinks and who repairs to nearby Spring Lounge after his shift is over. Marc, left, and Greg are roommates who live in NoLita (North of Little Italy) and make the bar their regular watering hole.

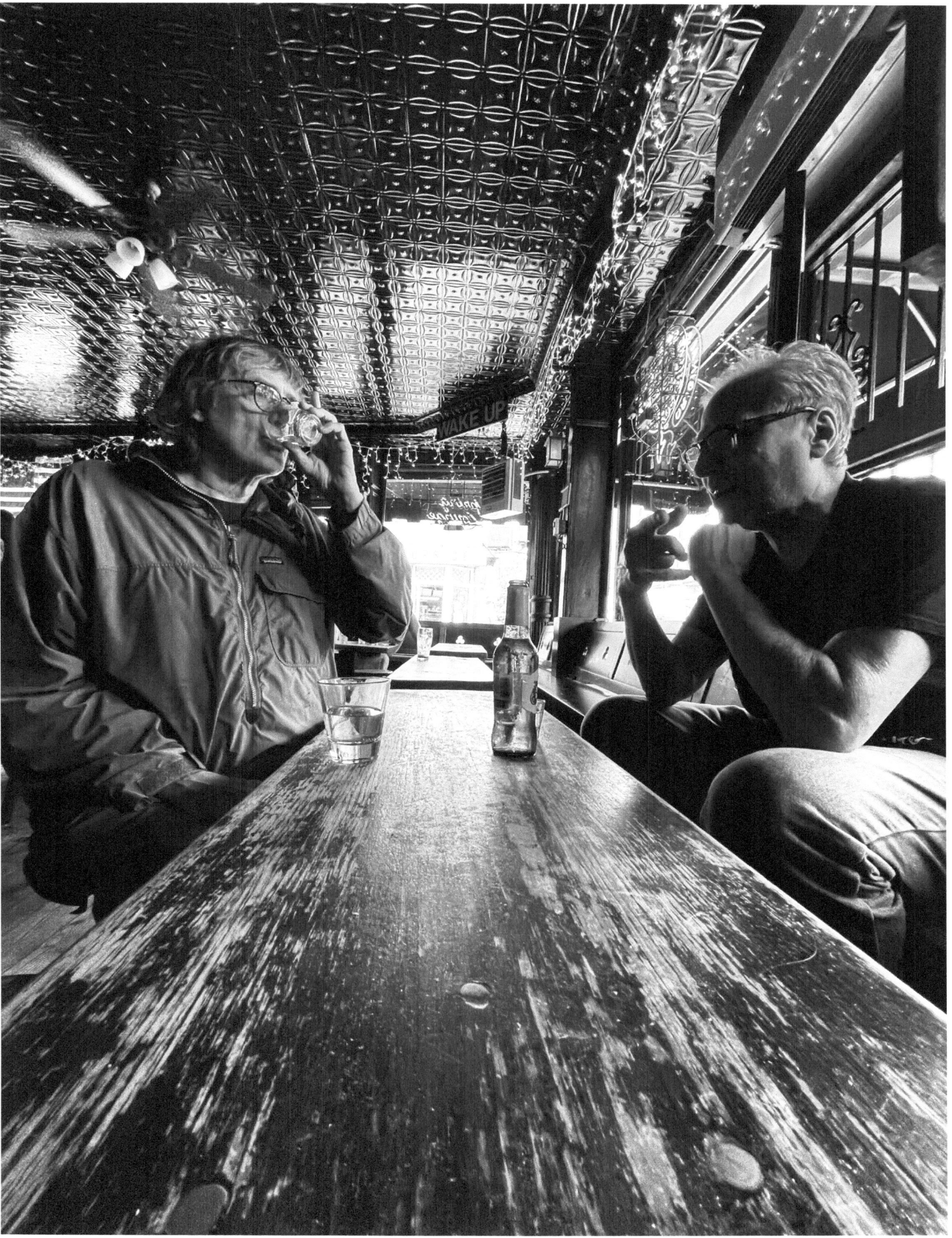

Right, Jen, the bar's general manager, wears a T-shirt jocularly critiquing the chili of the winner of the bar's annual chile cook-off. Below, Patrick, a voluble Detroit native, and, far right, Jen and Annie the mail lady, in her mid-70s, whose signature saying is, "Oh, hell no!"

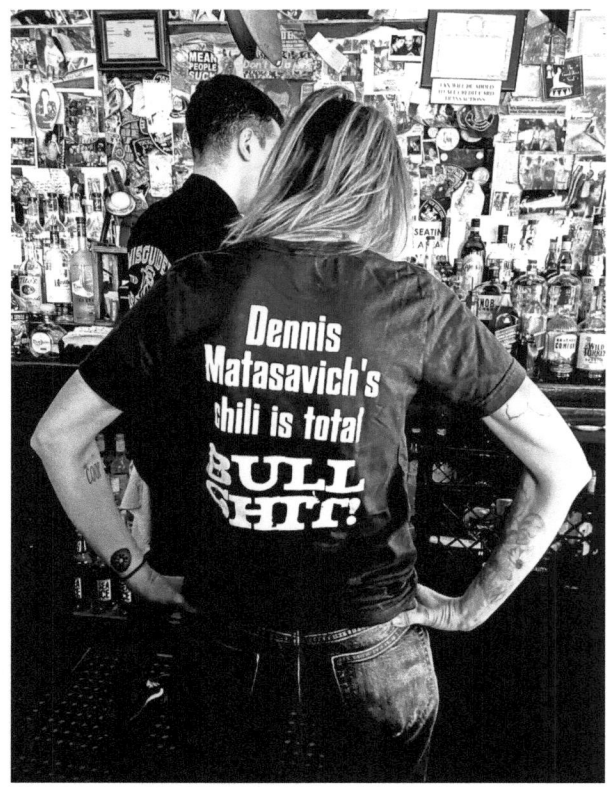

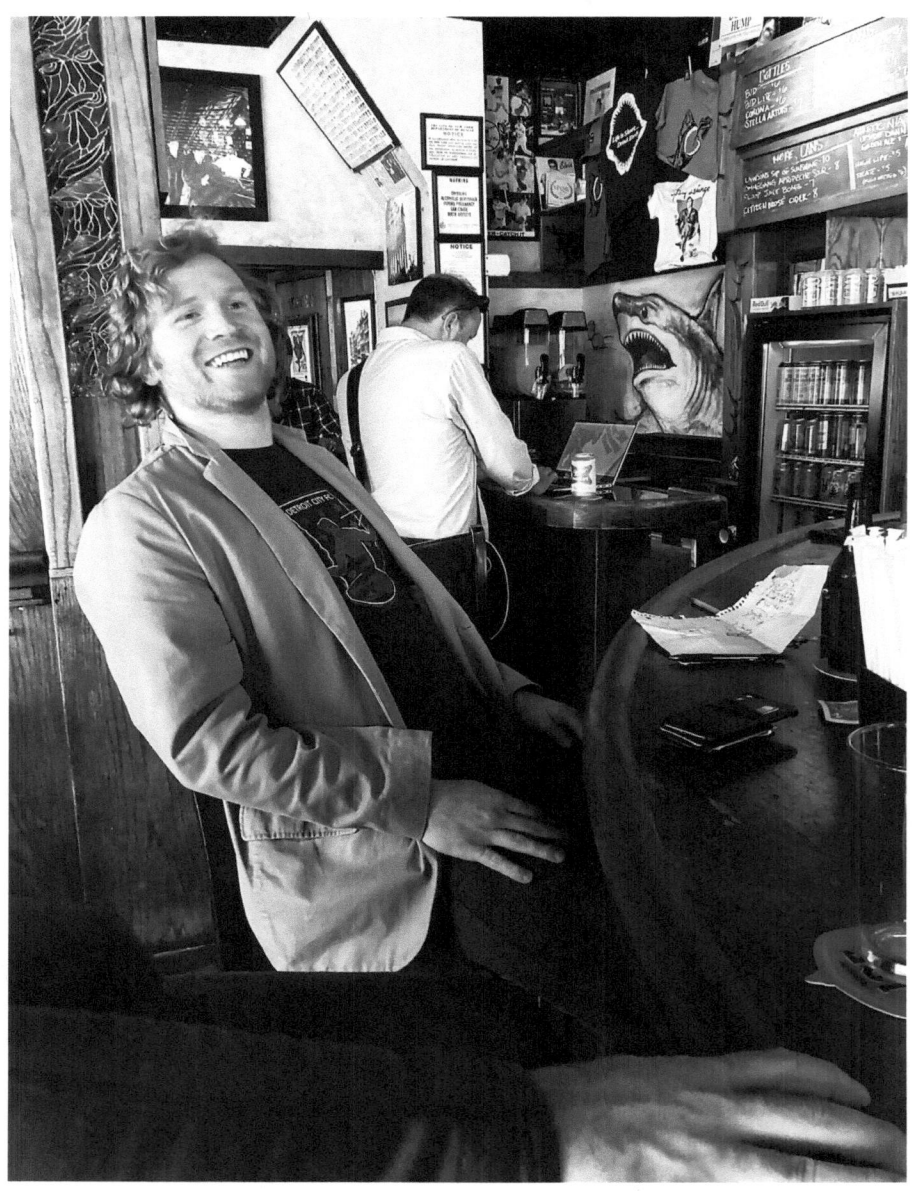

THE BAR IS OPEN

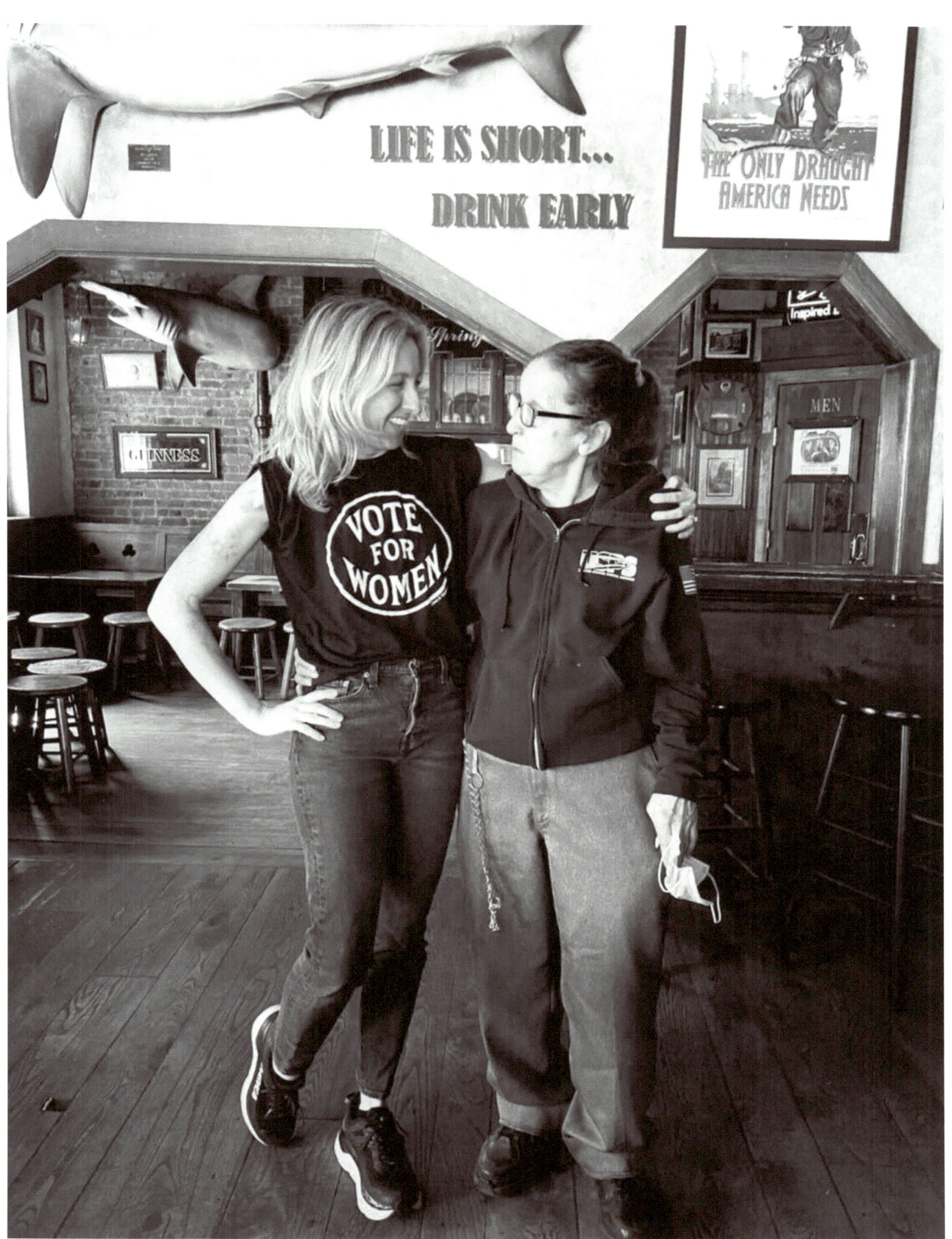

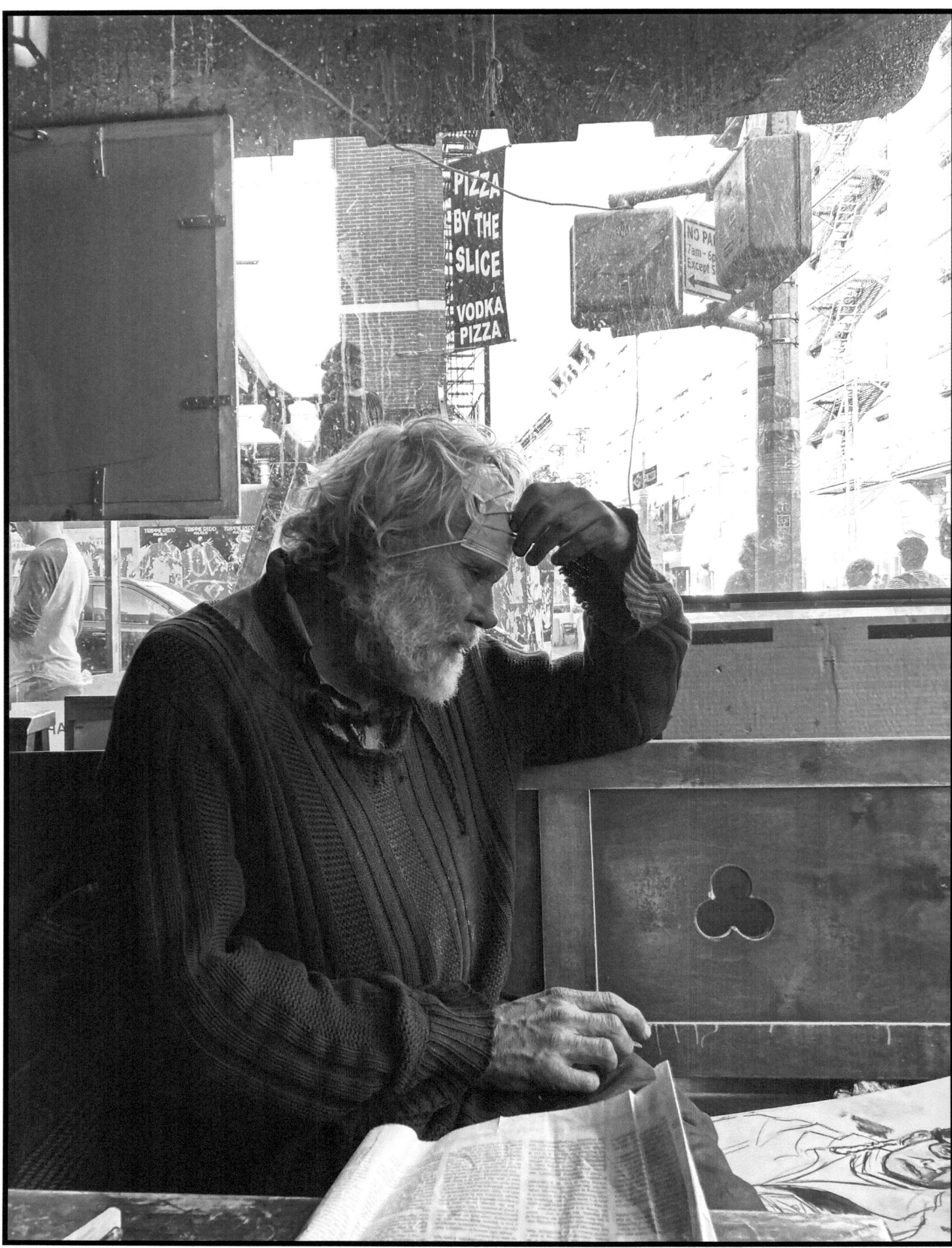

THE BAR IS OPEN

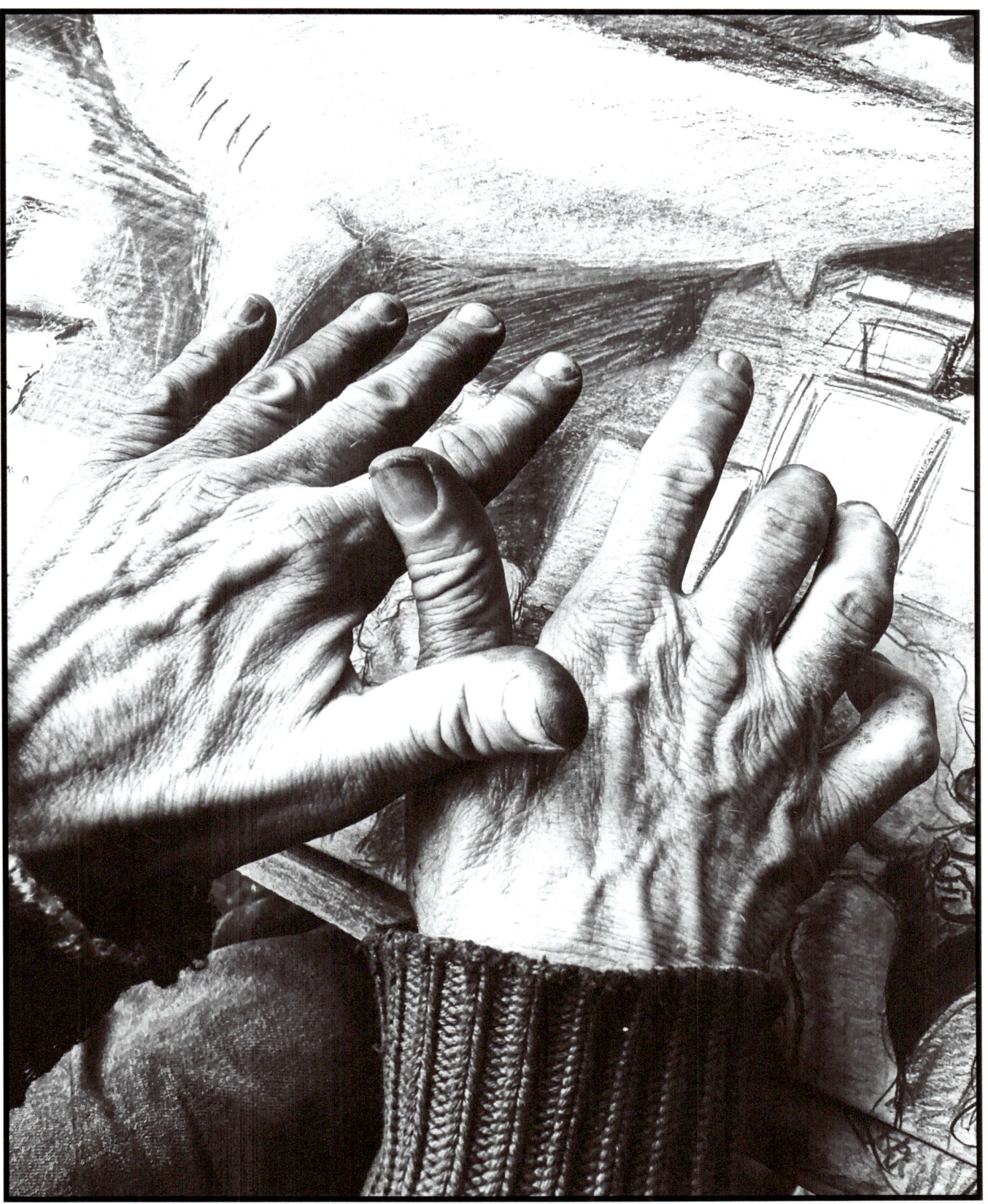

Dave, a writer, editor and artist who was a key player in producing this book, ponders over a drawing. Above, a closeup of the artist's hands hovering over one of his works.

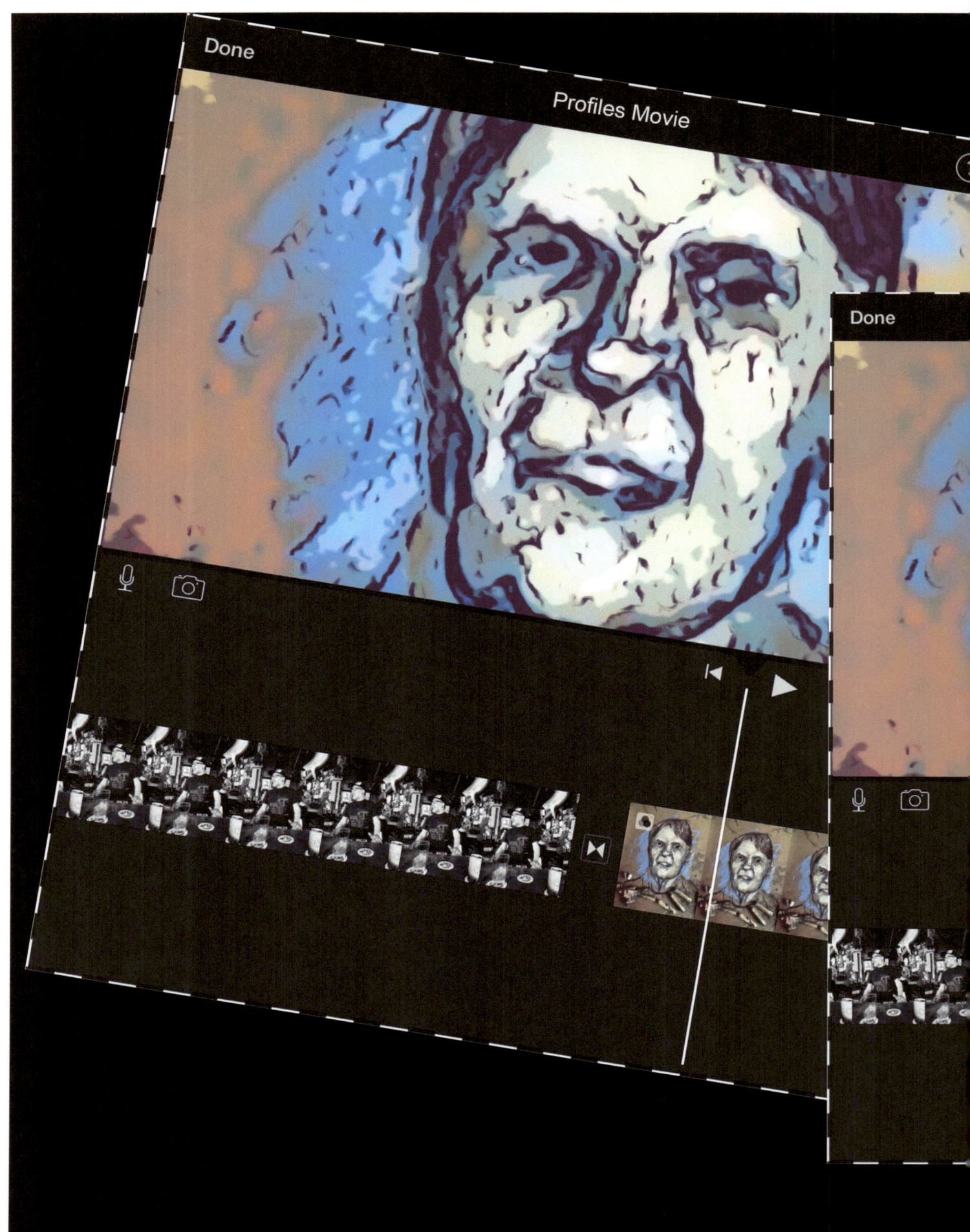

PROFILES

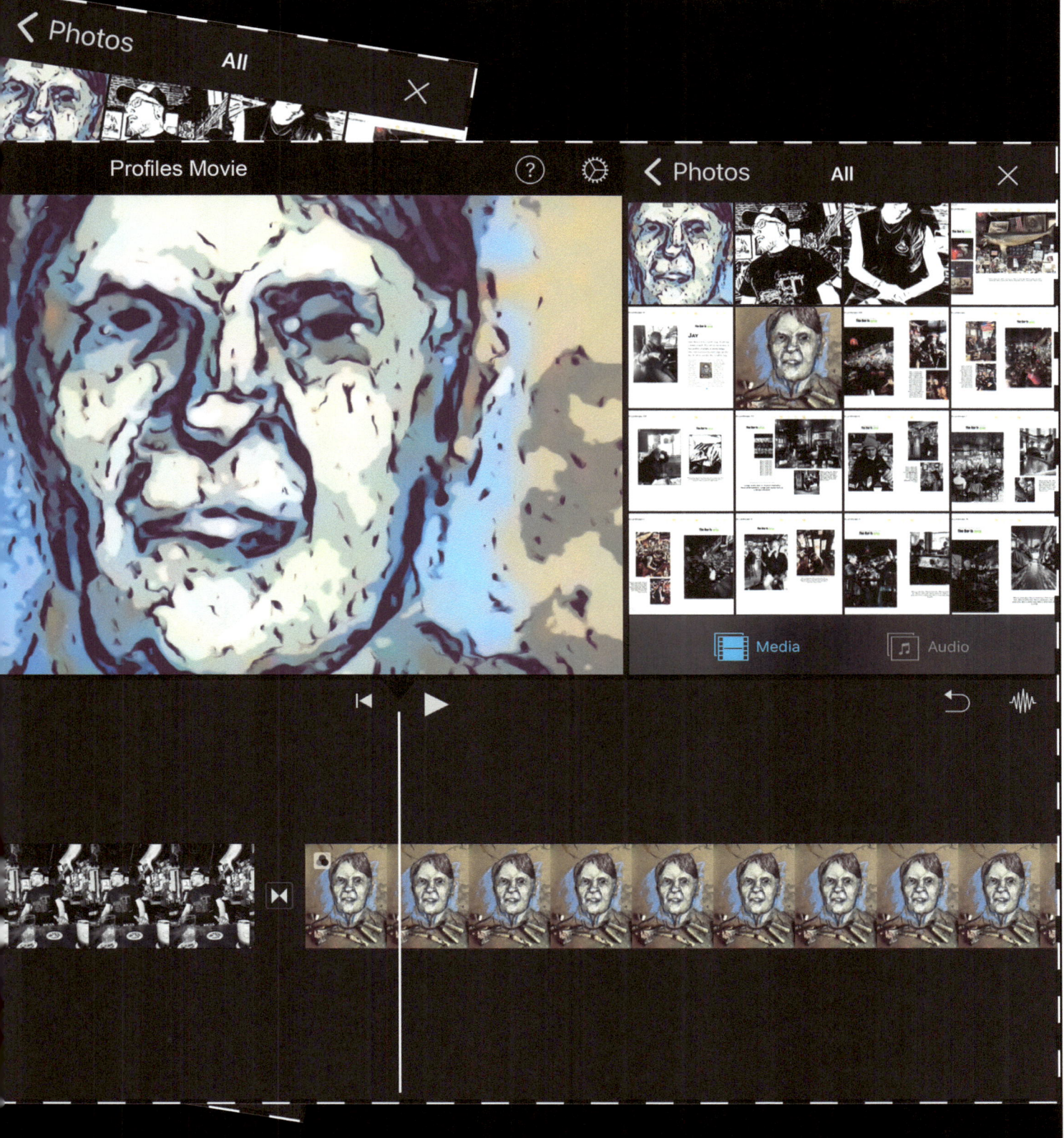

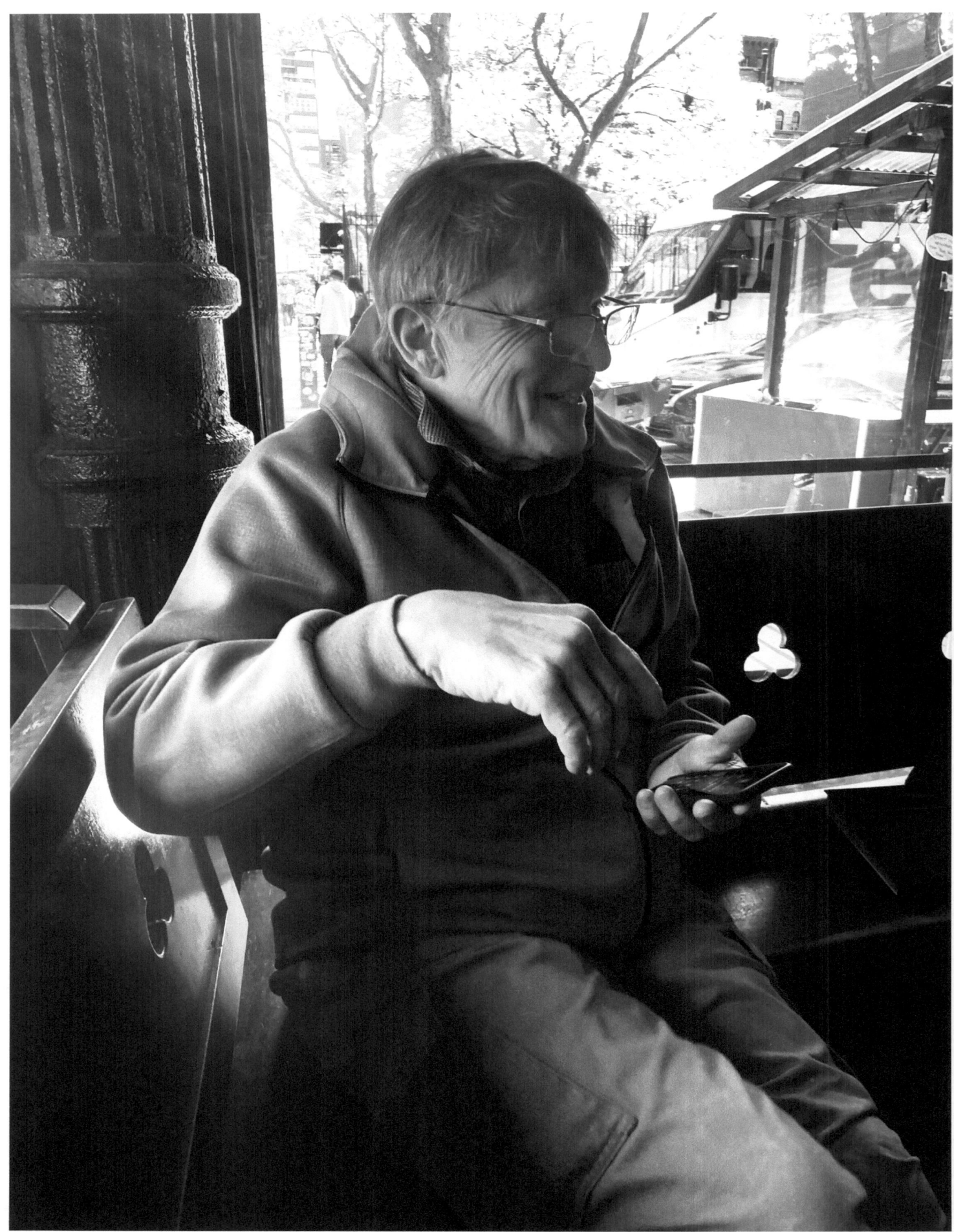

The Bar Is Open

Jay

This ain't journalism, thank God — we're not even printing last names, to protect the innocent — but rather impressionism, or maybe poetry of a sort. So these profiles won't be giving you dull stuff like full names and quotes.

Still, I wrote a bit about Jay in my intro, describing when, in the days of ago, he tended bar at Spring Lounge. His well-timed jokes and sardonic aplomb carried the day every time.

For this lime-cutter extraordinaire and raconteur nonpareil, for he who played Pandora music ranging from big band and be-bop to disco and hip-hop, a few journalistic details of his colorful past ought to be included, just because they are colorful.

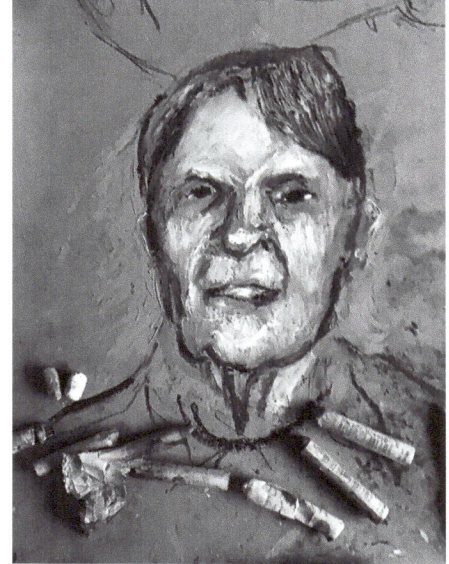

Before bartending, he was a star on the daytime soap Guiding Light, for which he also wrote, and later he had a key role on the famed 70s sitcom The Jeffersons.

He also had roles on Mannix, Kojak, and Adam 12, among other dramas, before gaining fame in his most demanding role of all, that of the main Spring Lounge morning publican who, after he retired, left us all laughing when he was gone.

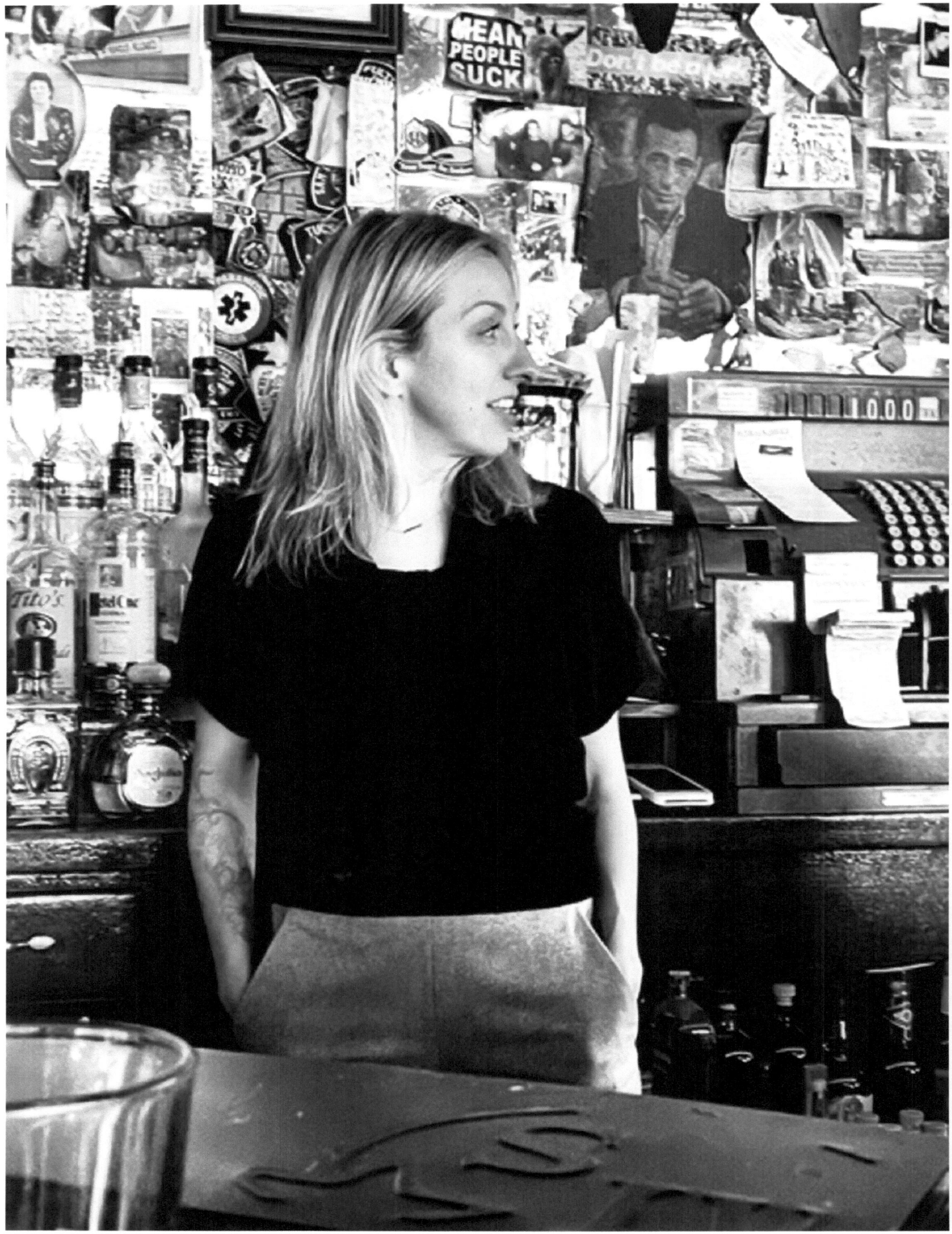

The Bar Is Open

Jen

She's the boss, the big wheel, the general manager of the joint. But she's not just sitting around in some remote office pushing papers or watching numbers scrolling on a computer screen.

Often she'll get behind the bar and work the taps. Or she'll do repairs. Or she'll haul around kegs, string Christmas lights, sweep the floor, chat up the patrons — whatever it takes to run an old-timey bar in the modern world.

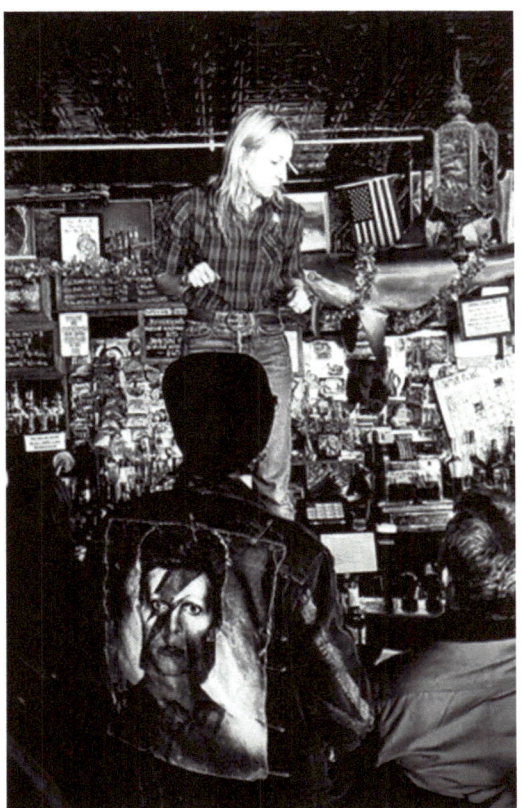

She started working at Spring Lounge as a barback during the San Gennaro festival of 2003. Each year, she loves to preside over two sessions of a chili cook-off, one version featuring the best chili recipes from beer distributors and the other pitting customer against customer. She also pioneered Kegs 'n' Eggs, a periodic Tuesday favorite featuring beer and free breakfast. The creator of these blowouts is her husband, who has worked as a chef in New York City restaurants for more than 20 years. It isn't slop that's served up — it's stuff like fajitas, eggs mixed with veggies, tortillas, kimchi, sometimes poached eggs, muffins, various kinds of hot sauces, the works. She and her husband have a young son and Jen is an assiduous promoter of "beer culture" — the Lounge taps are a craft-beer cornucopia.

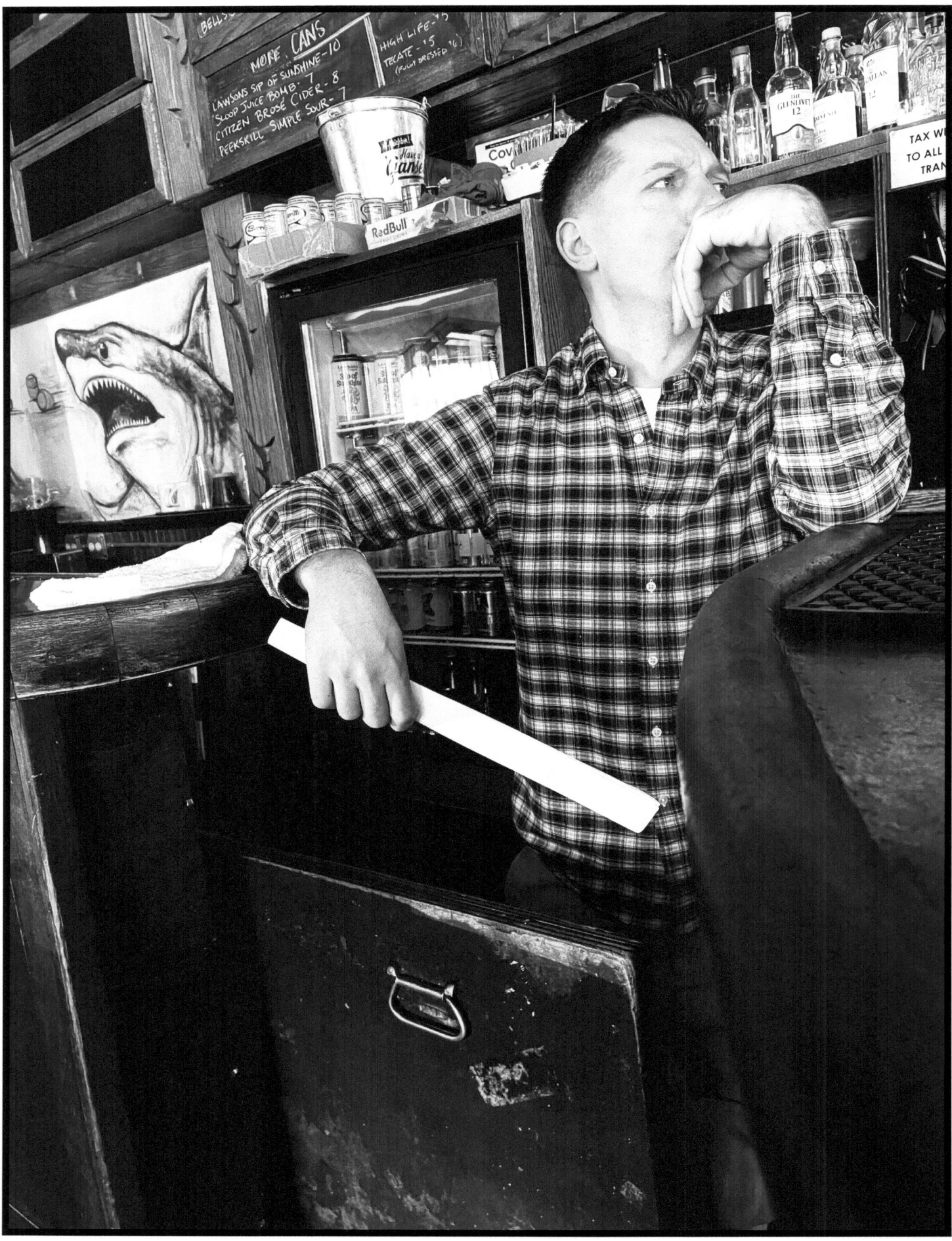

The Bar Is Open

Dave

He's one of the mangers, under Jen, and tends taps two days a week. Befitting his role, he's mean and tyrannical, a cruel task master who often flays his minions and even some of the customers with the steel rod shown at left. Nah, just kidding.

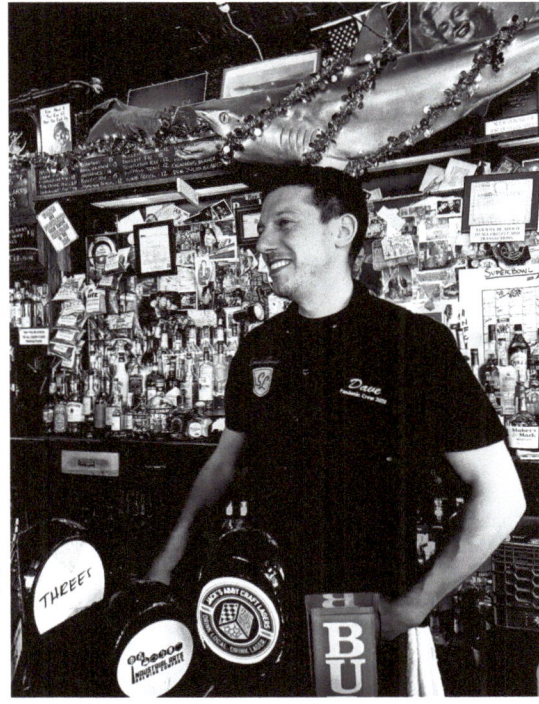

Dave plays in a punk-rock band and recently got hitched, and he and his wife are expecting their first daughter. Pandora punk generally pervades the place when he's behind the taps.

Round the horseshoe bar he's got a retinue of regulars on the mornings when he works — always mornings, for most of the bartenders pictured in this book preside over the fabled Early Morning Drinkers Society, with the taps turned on promptly at eight and shut tight at 2 p.m. What follows are the more conventional afternoon and evening crowds.

Dave was on duty and on the TV news in March 2020 when Covid closed this and practically every other business in the city, expressing fear for the future of the bar. He soldiers on during the post-plague prosperity.

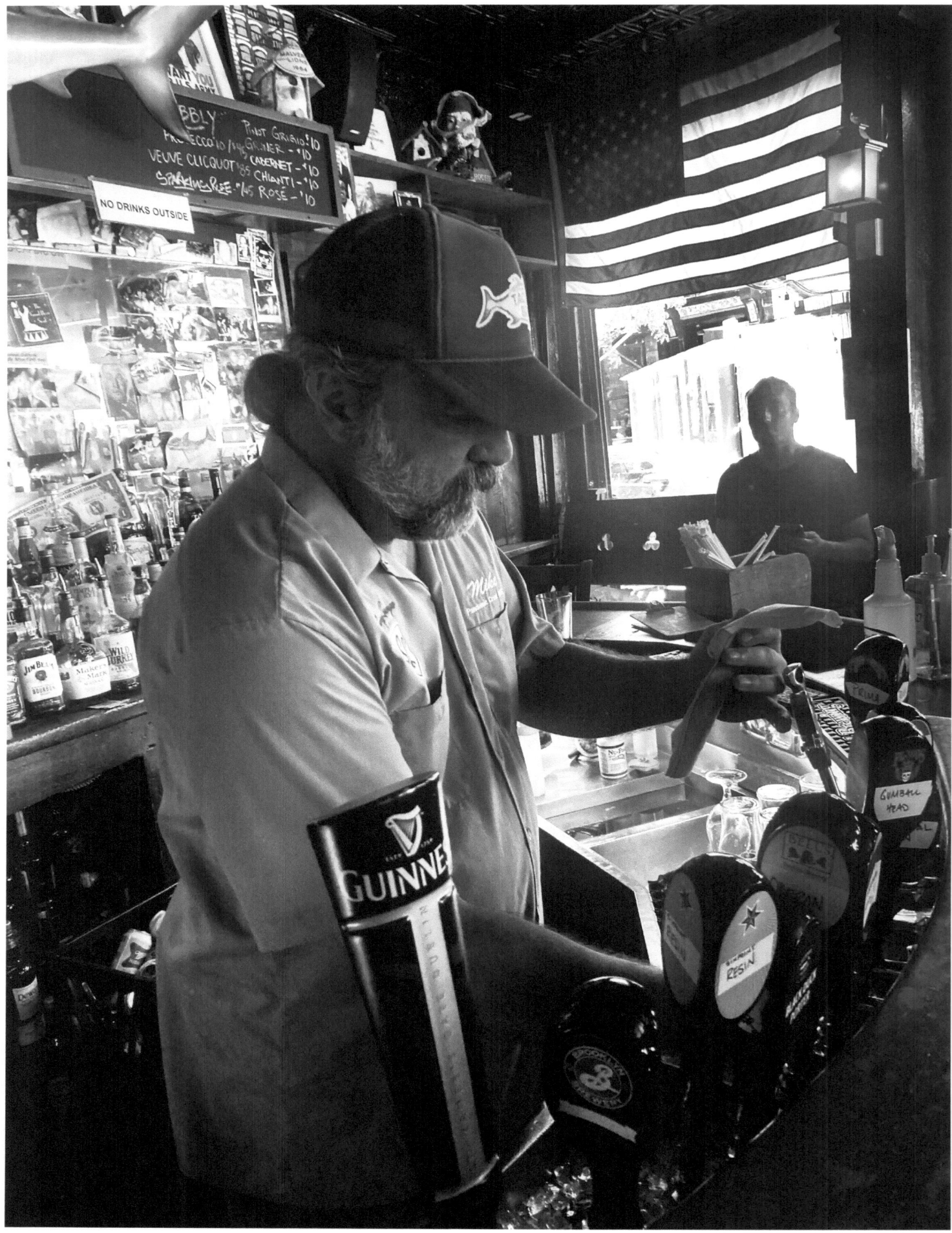

THE BAR IS OPEN

MIKE

When I think about Mike, I think about boats and Wednesdays. It seems strange that two such disparate nouns can go hand in hand, but they do, like fish and chips.

That's because Mike works the taps only on Wednesdays, and then the rest of the week he's off overseeing the other bars that he actually owns when he's not plying the waters and fishing from his boat.

His boat is named St Joan, and I created he sign and the artwork that was painted on the side of it. Mike isn't religious that I know of — the "St. Joan" in question was a jocular swipe at a holier-than-thou relative, I believe — but he does

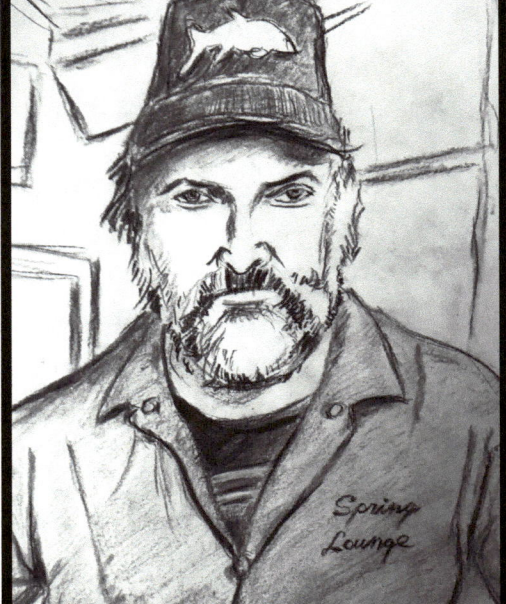

have a thing, if not exactly worship, for 70s rock, some of it the easy-listening variety that clashes rather spectacularly with the punk that seems to dominate the tastes of most of the other barkeeps the rest of the week. In the old days, before Pandora and the internet, bar customers got to drop quarters in a real juke and play their own music, but those days are long gone. Such is "progress."

Mike also wears a red cap with a fish silhouette on it — see my drawing of him, at left.

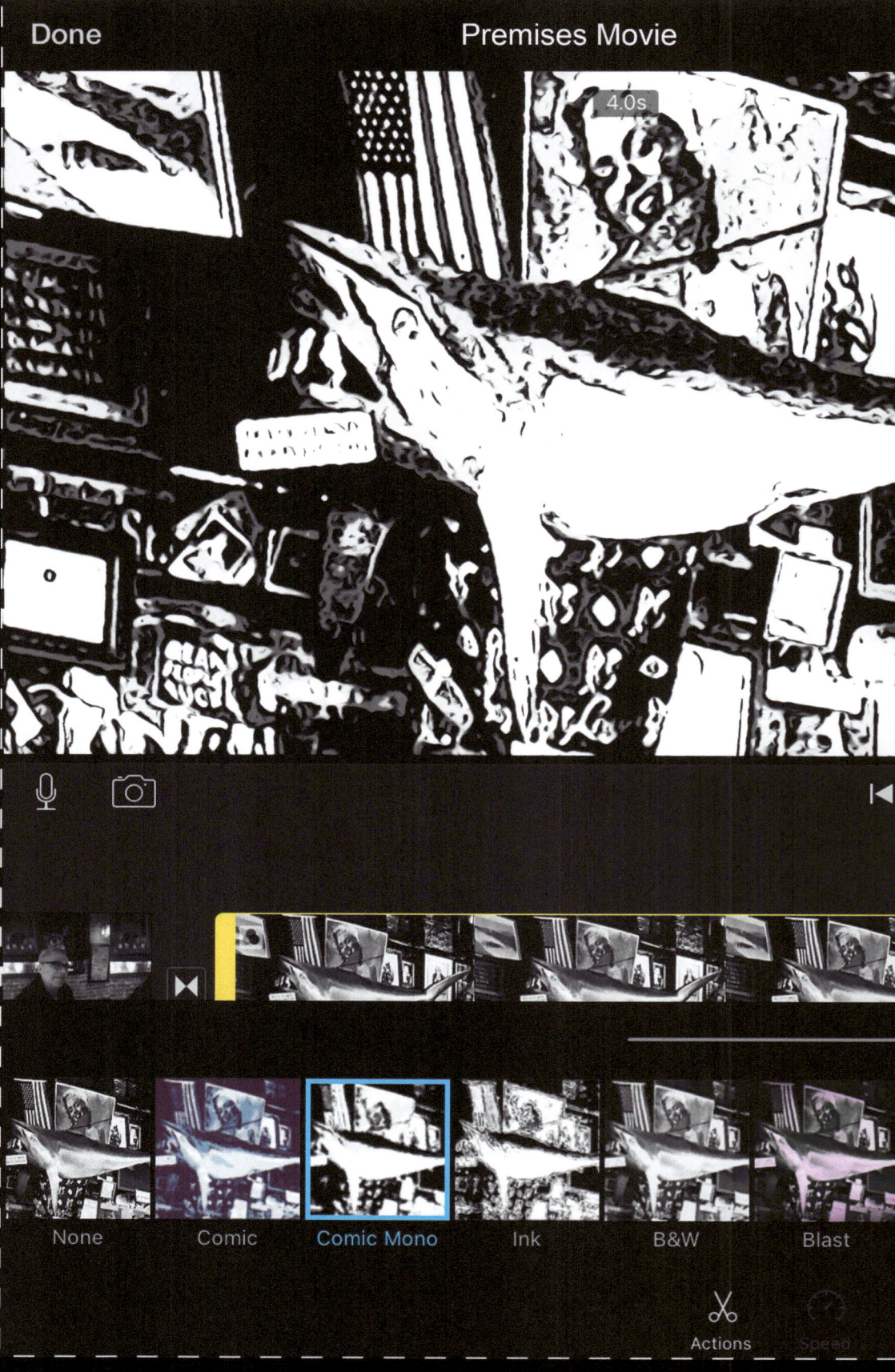

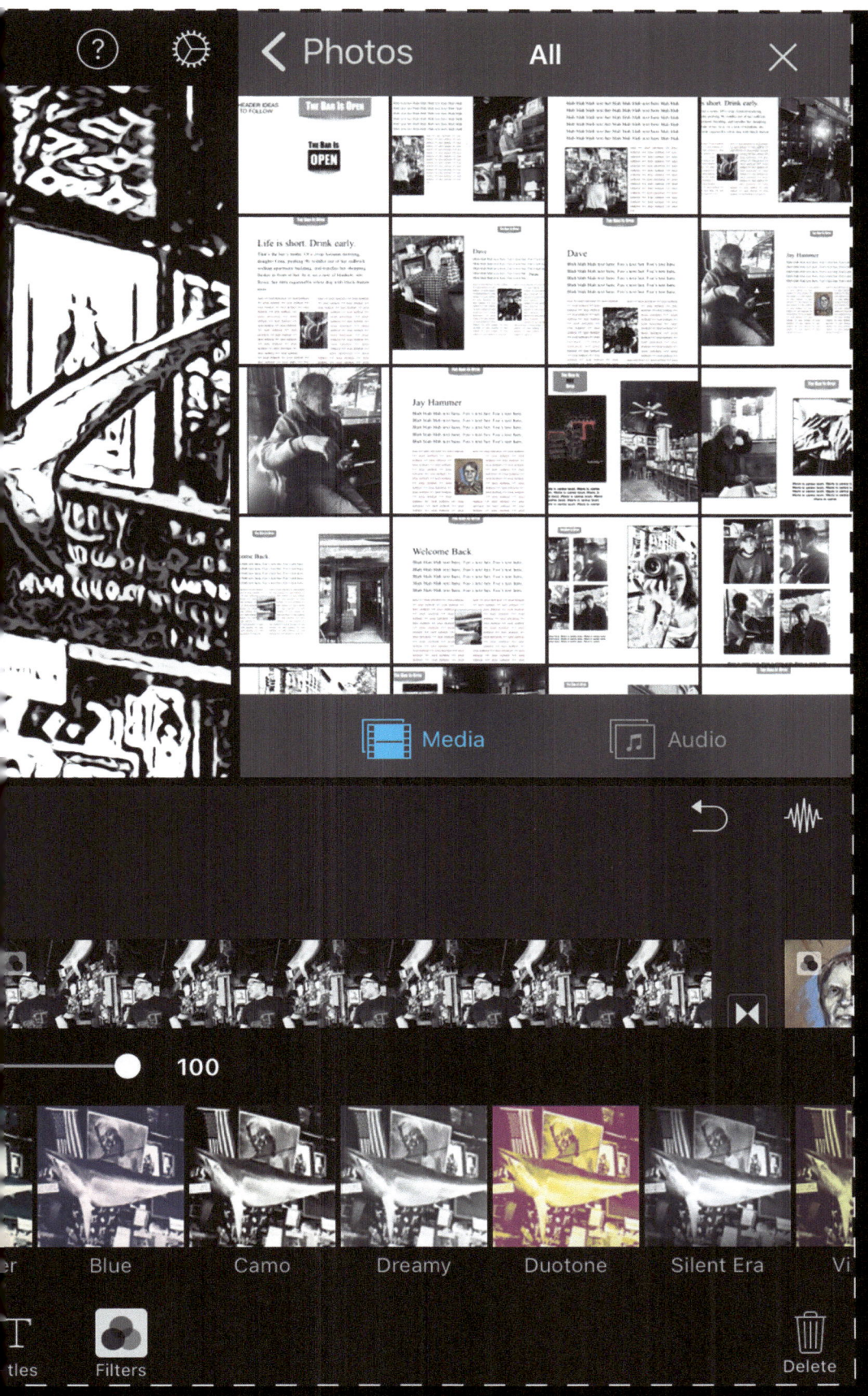

PREMISES

The Bar Is Closed

Right, a common and depressing sight around the city in the early days of the Covid pandemic in 2020. Restaurants, bars and other retail establishments all over the city were shut down for months as the authorities desperately struggled to control a virus that was killing increasing numbers of people.

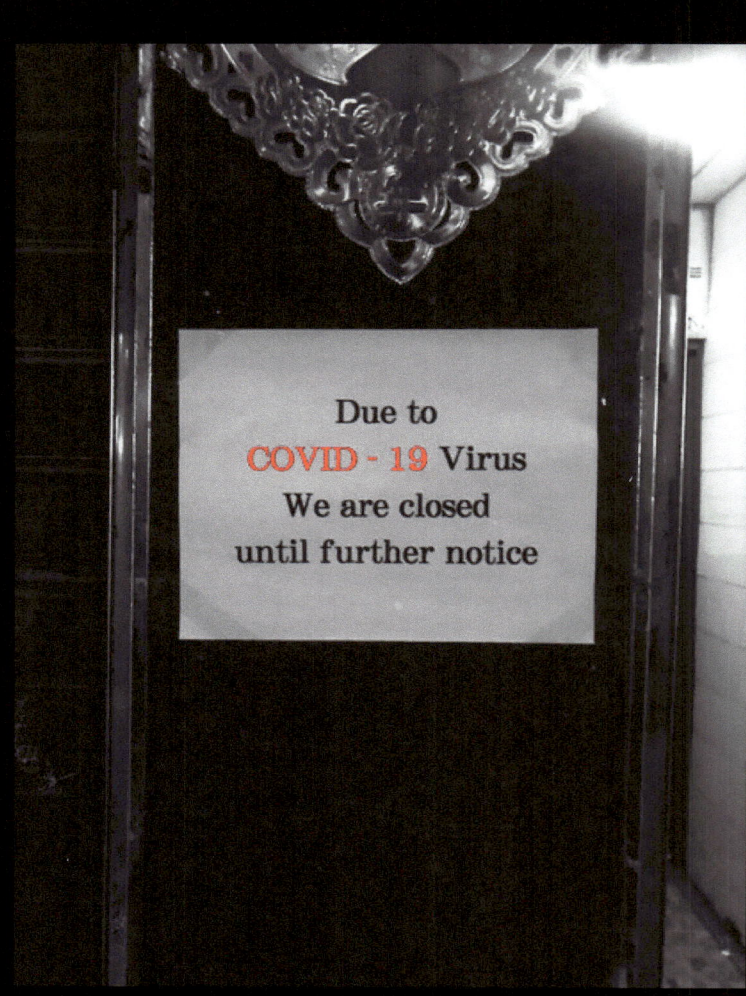

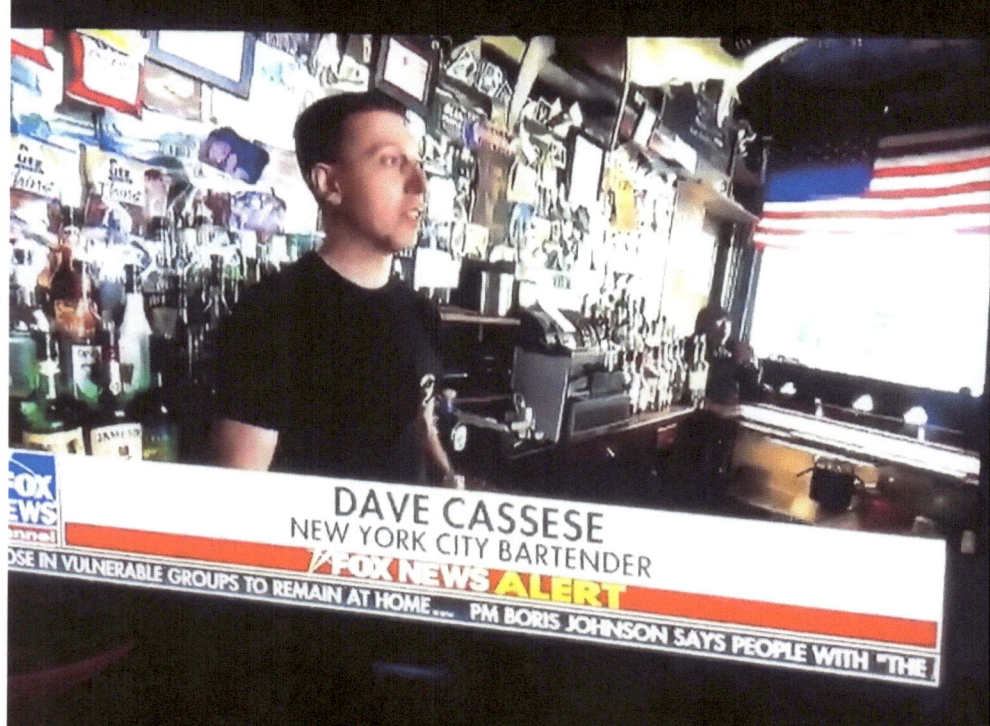

An unprecedented sight: Spring Lounge empty during the day, chairs blocking the bar. The bar was famous for being open 365 days a year, through good times and bad. But Covid shut it down. Left, one of the bar's managers, Dave Cassese, talking to the news media about the closure.

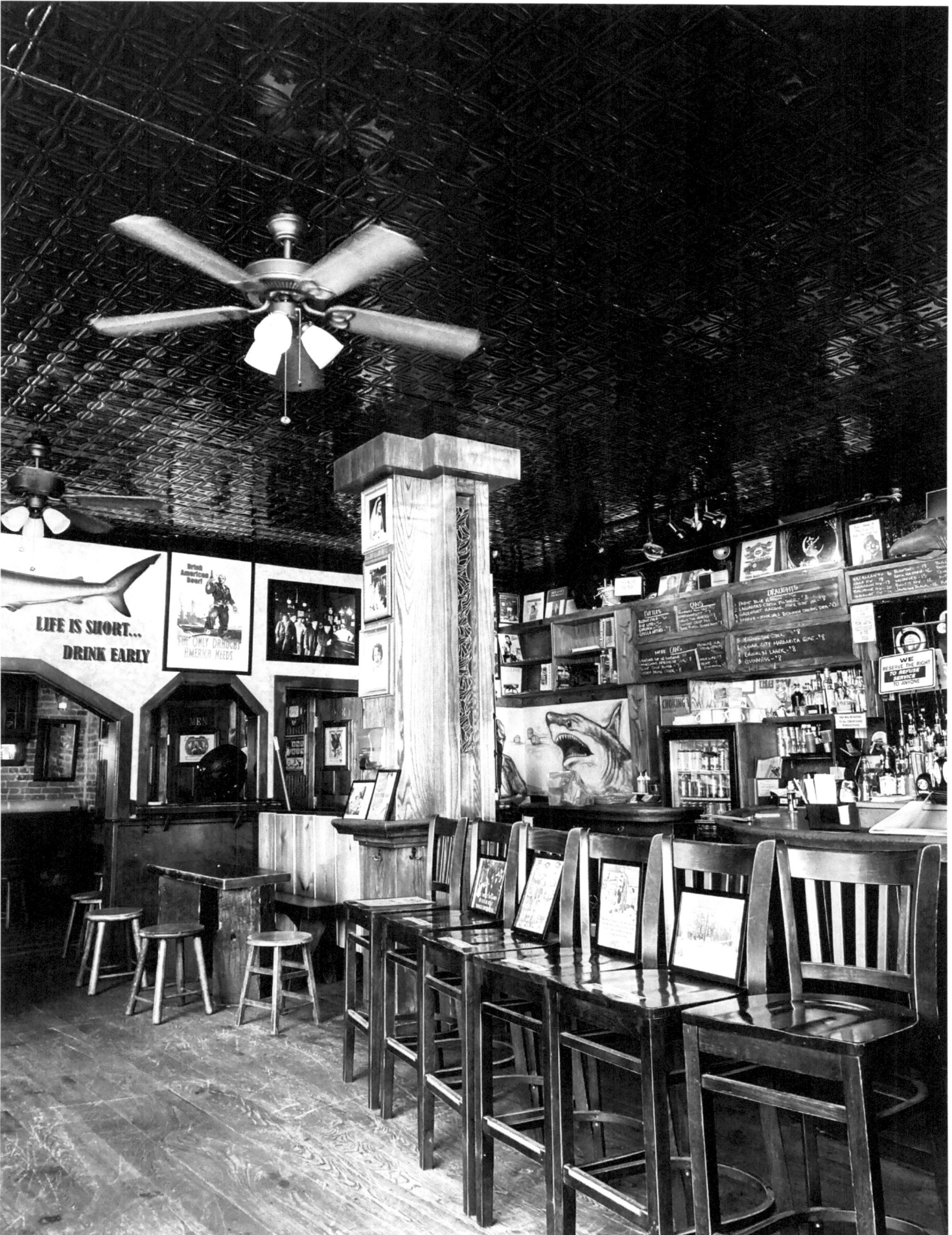

The Bar Is Open

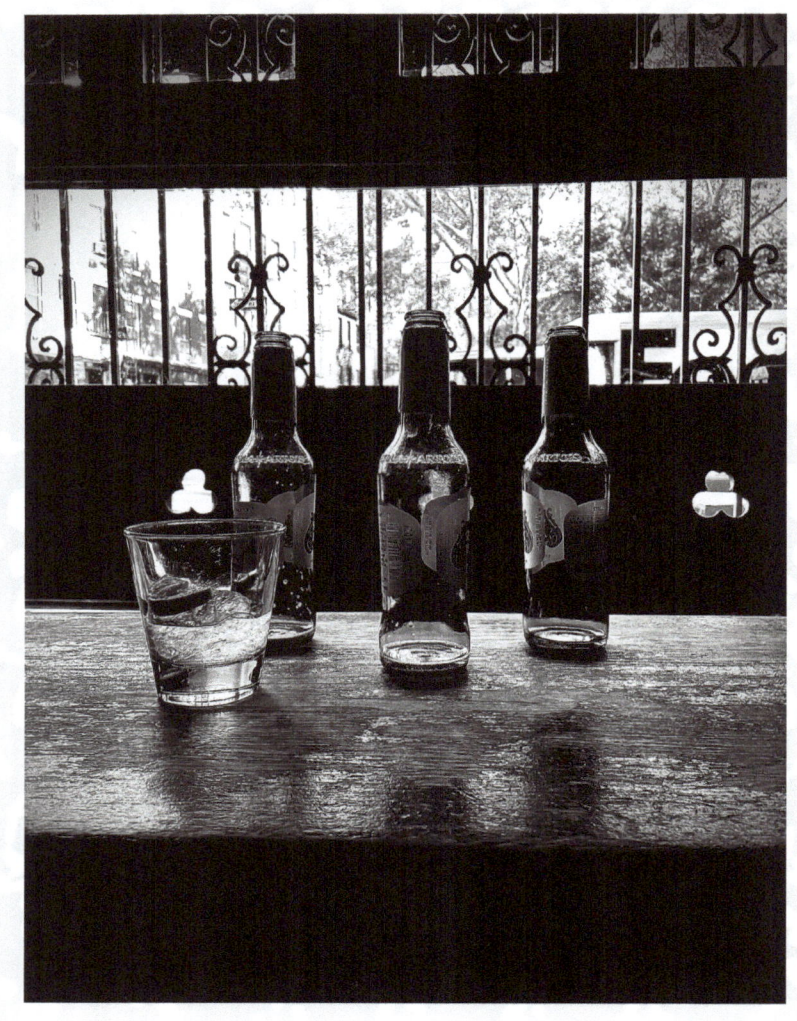

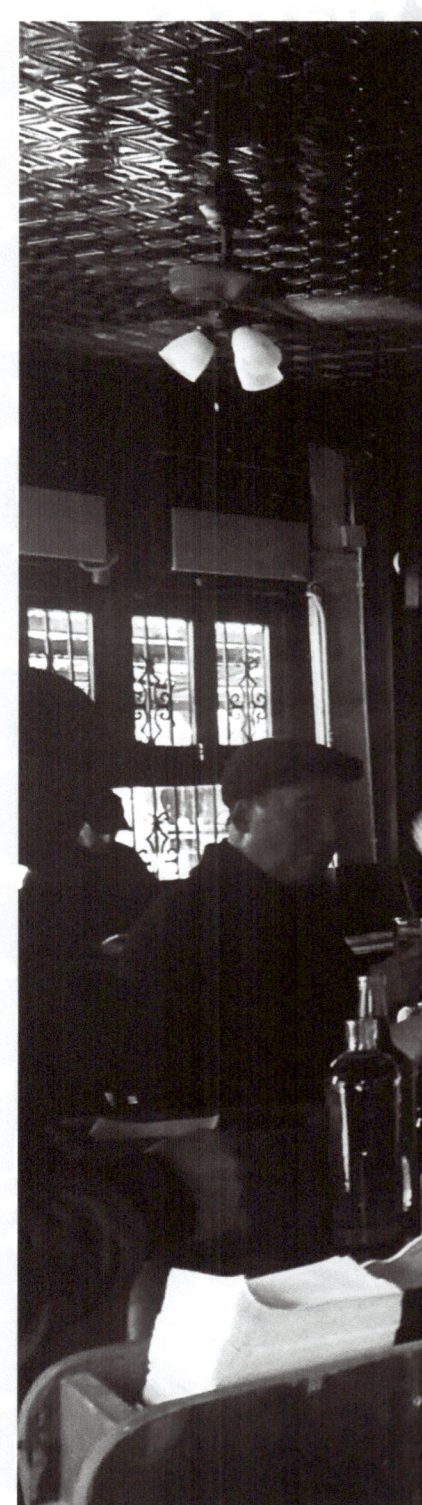

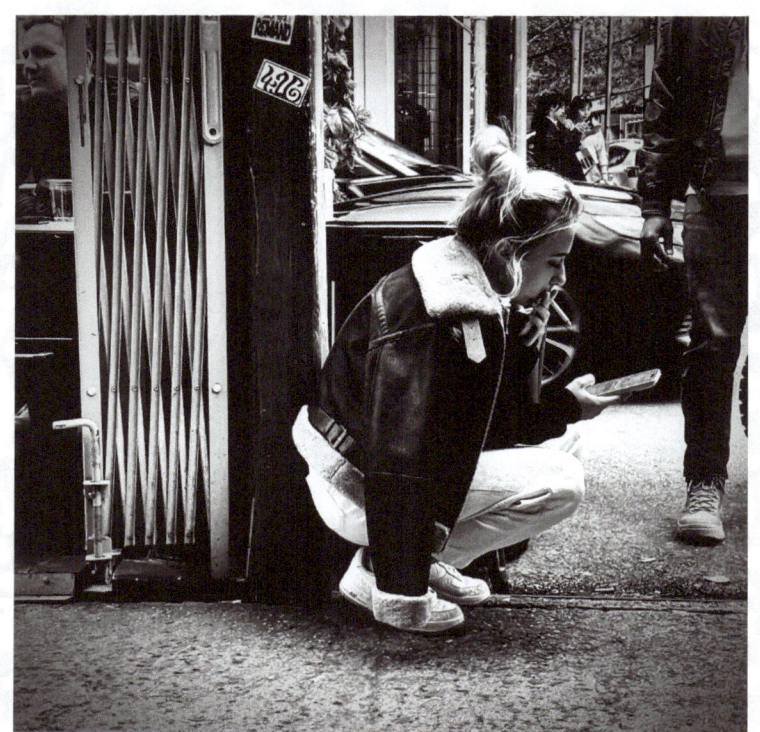

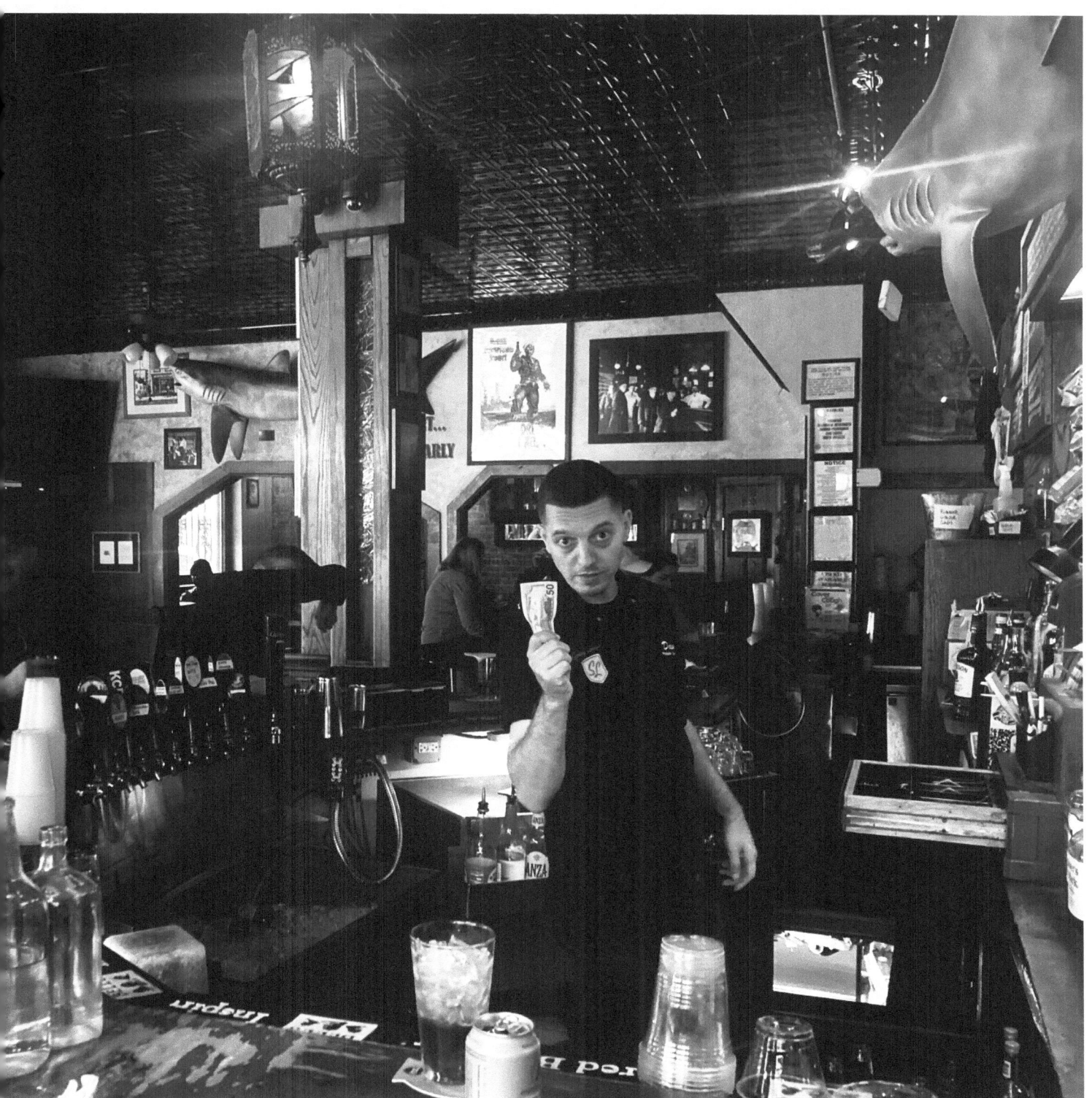

The bar's spacious interior with its signature horseshoe bar is dominated by stuffed sharks and pictures and photos of every description. A patron outside the bar consults her cellphone next to the heated outdoor seating area erected after Covid forced the closure of the bar's interior. Top left, the glass menagerie, calling to mind the famous Irish drinking song The Wild Rover.

THE BAR IS OPEN

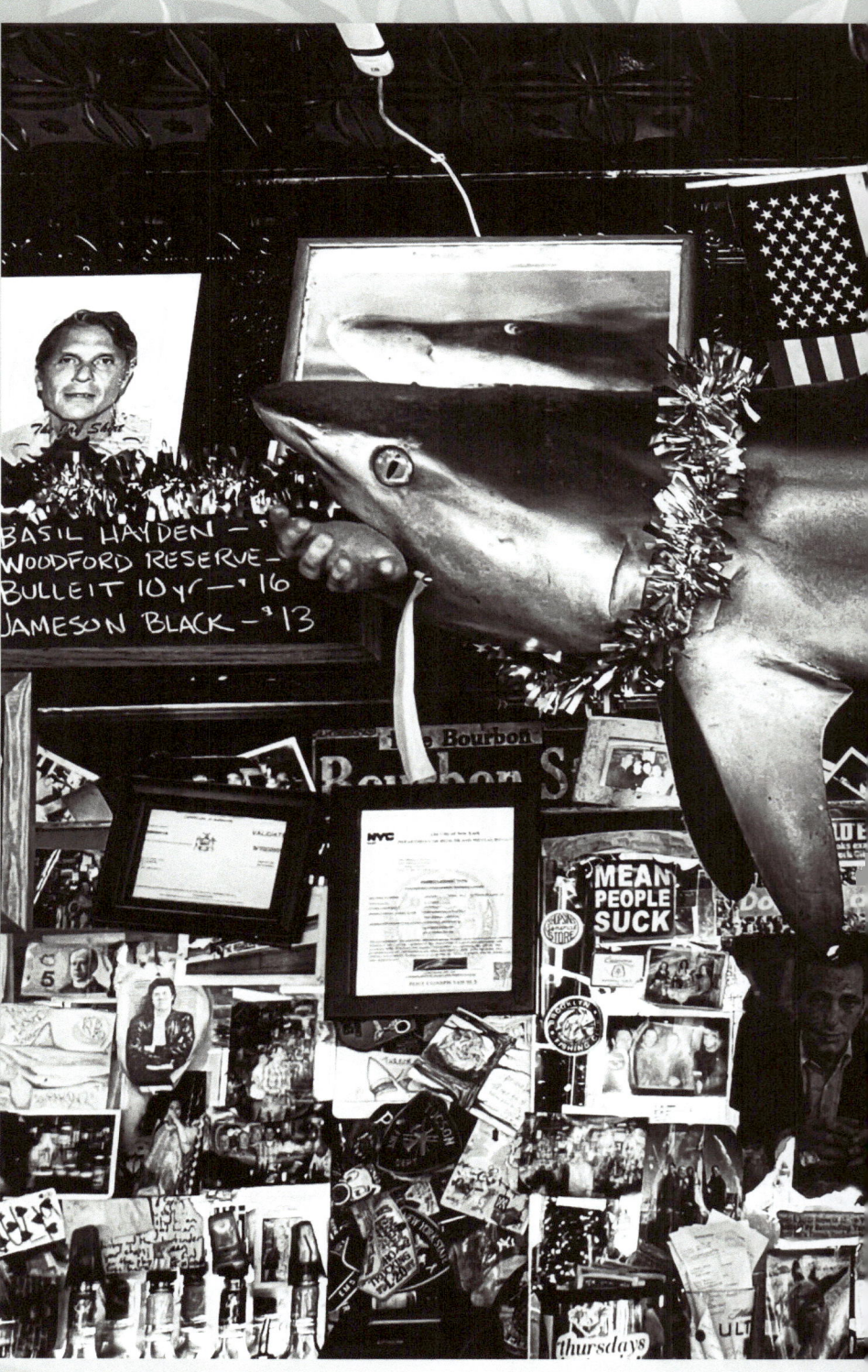

The iconic stuffed shark that seems to soar, though frozen in place, in back of the horseshoe bar. It is forever devouring a model of a severed human hand, and since Russia's invasion of Ukraine, a Ukrainian flag has dangled from the hand's fingers. The upper torso of a stuffed hammerhead shark presides over a room in the rear, and yet a third shark hangs over the archway leading to the rear room. The sharks were all caught by the bar's previous owners, Pat and Jimmy Cacerta.

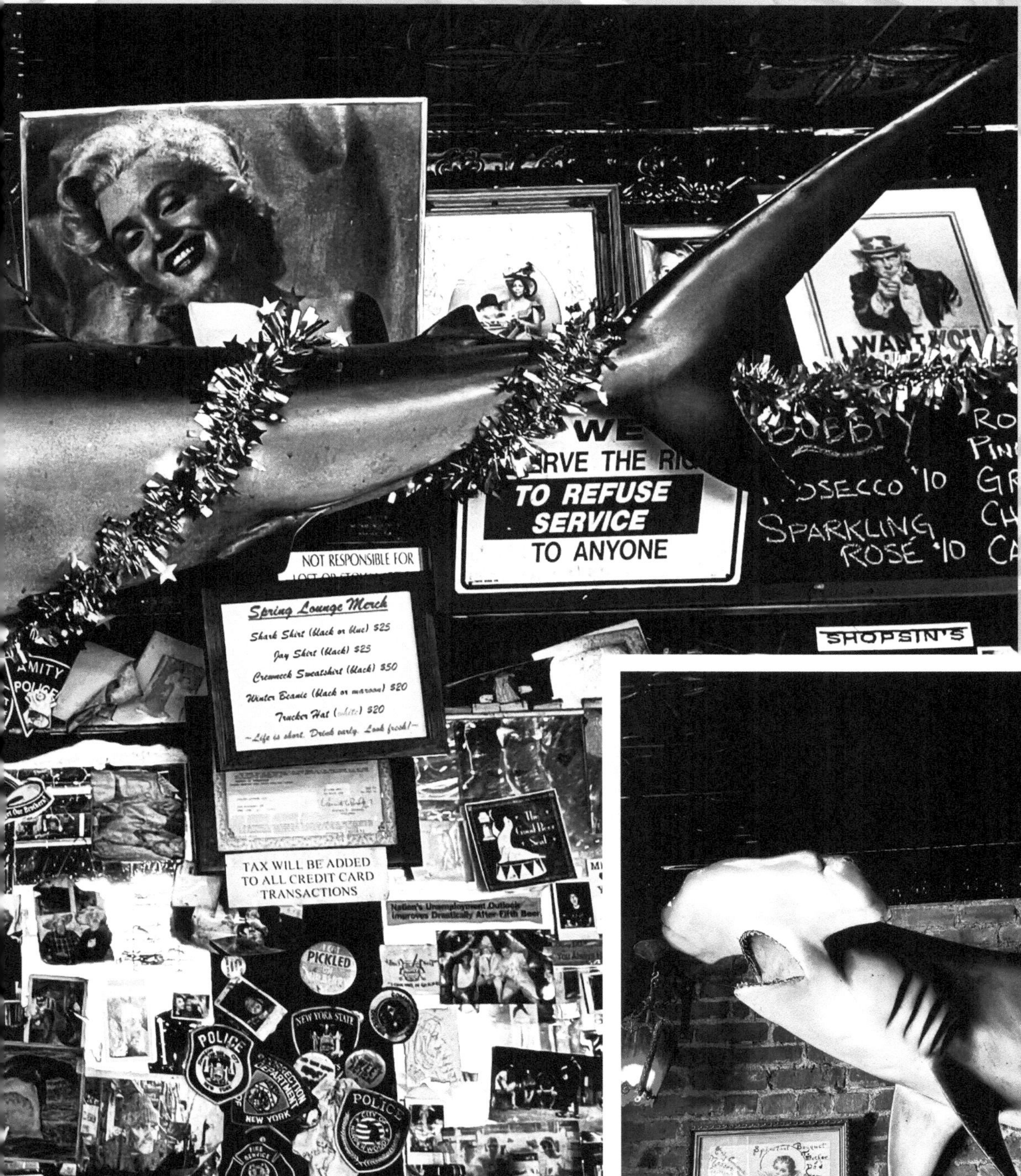

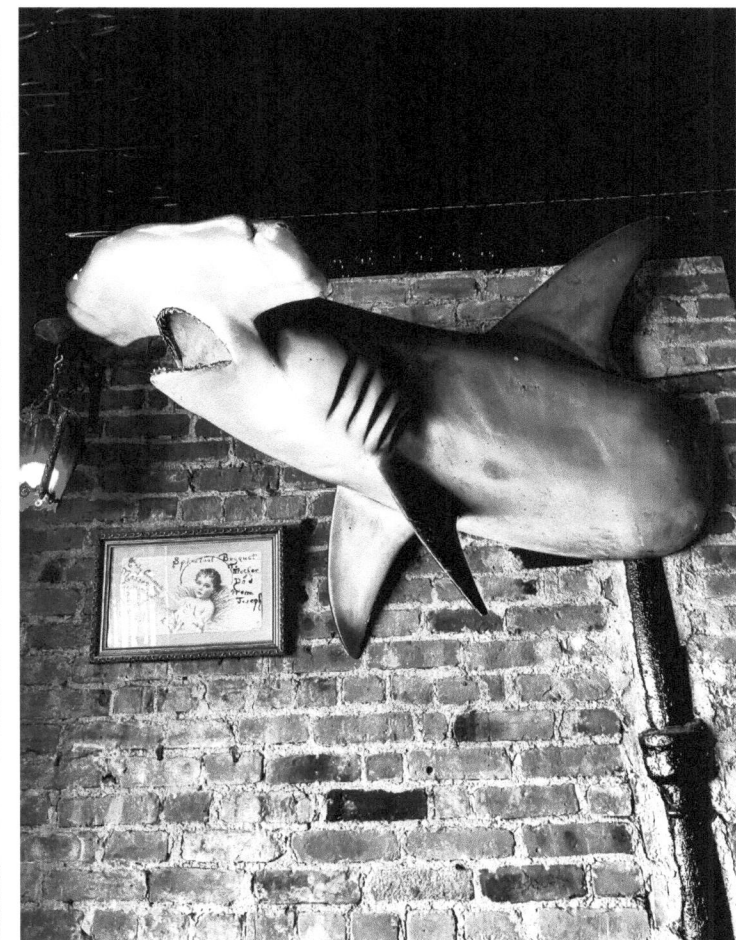

The Bar Is OPEN

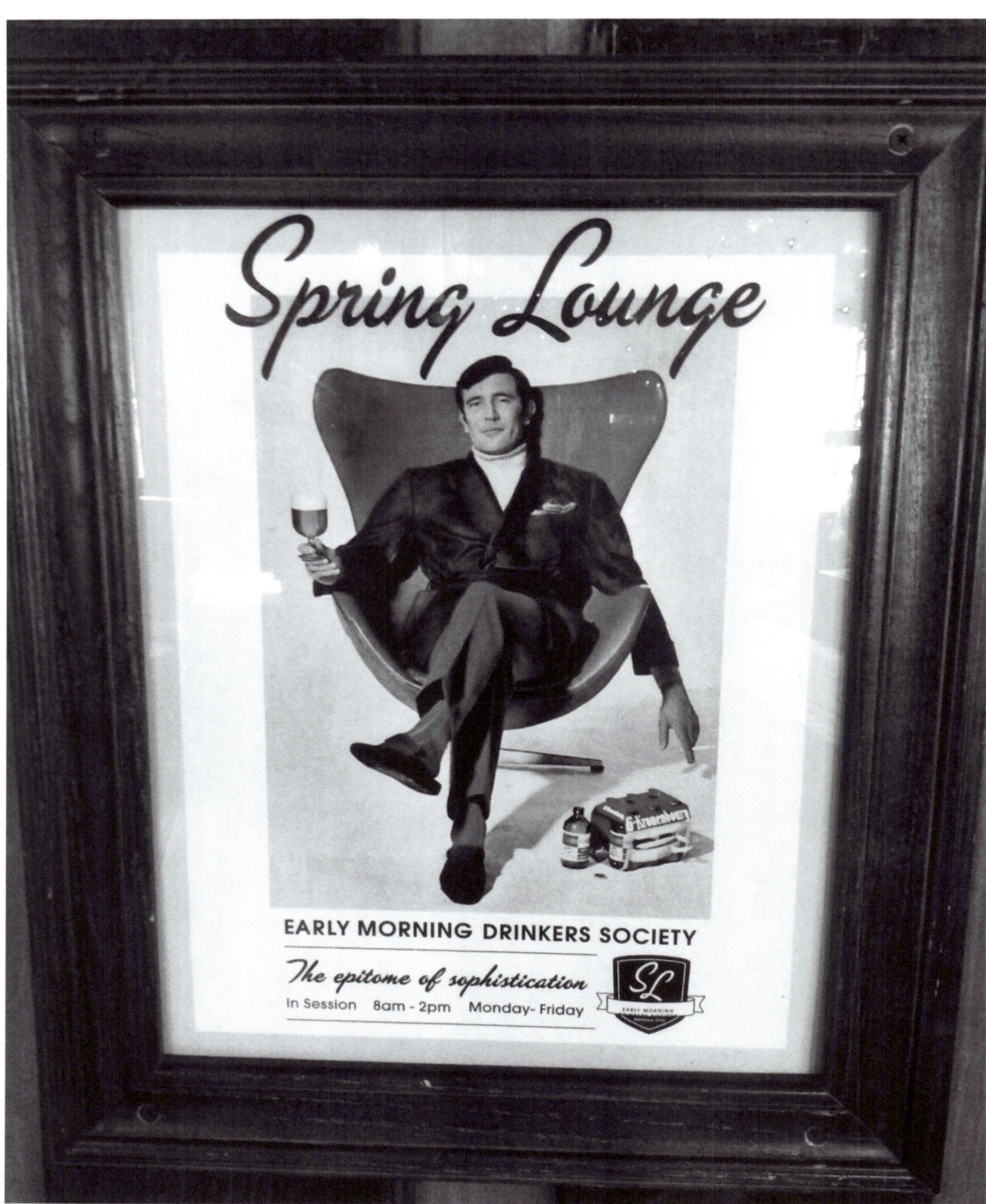

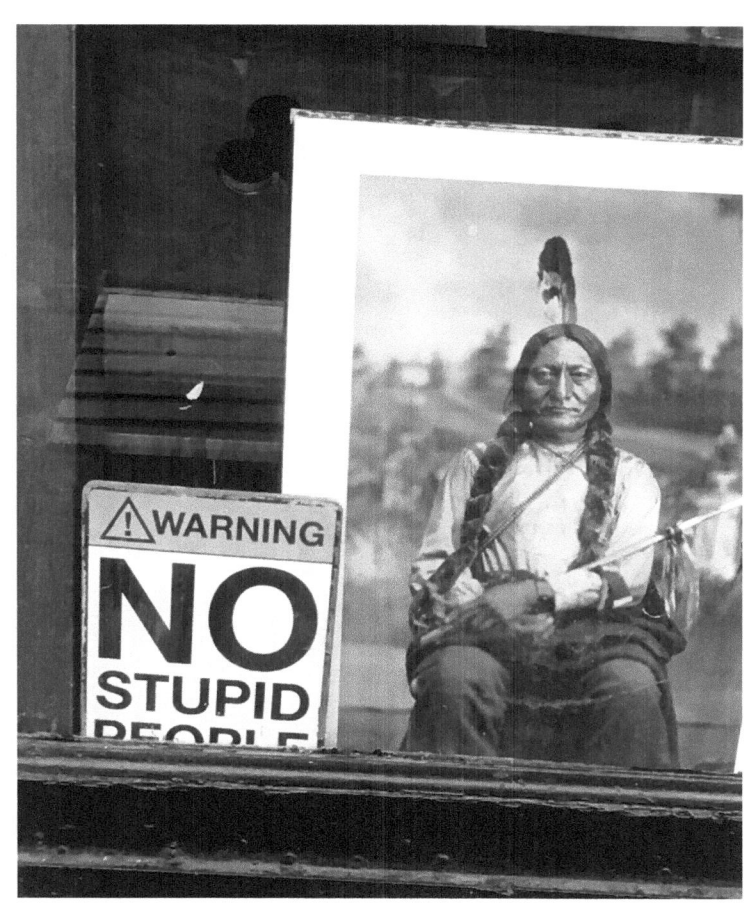

A sampling of images and signs inside and outside the bar, including a photograph of Sitting Bull. Those formally initiated into the Early Morning Drinkers Society, always with a fanfare of music, receive a T-shirt imprinted with the words and image at far left.

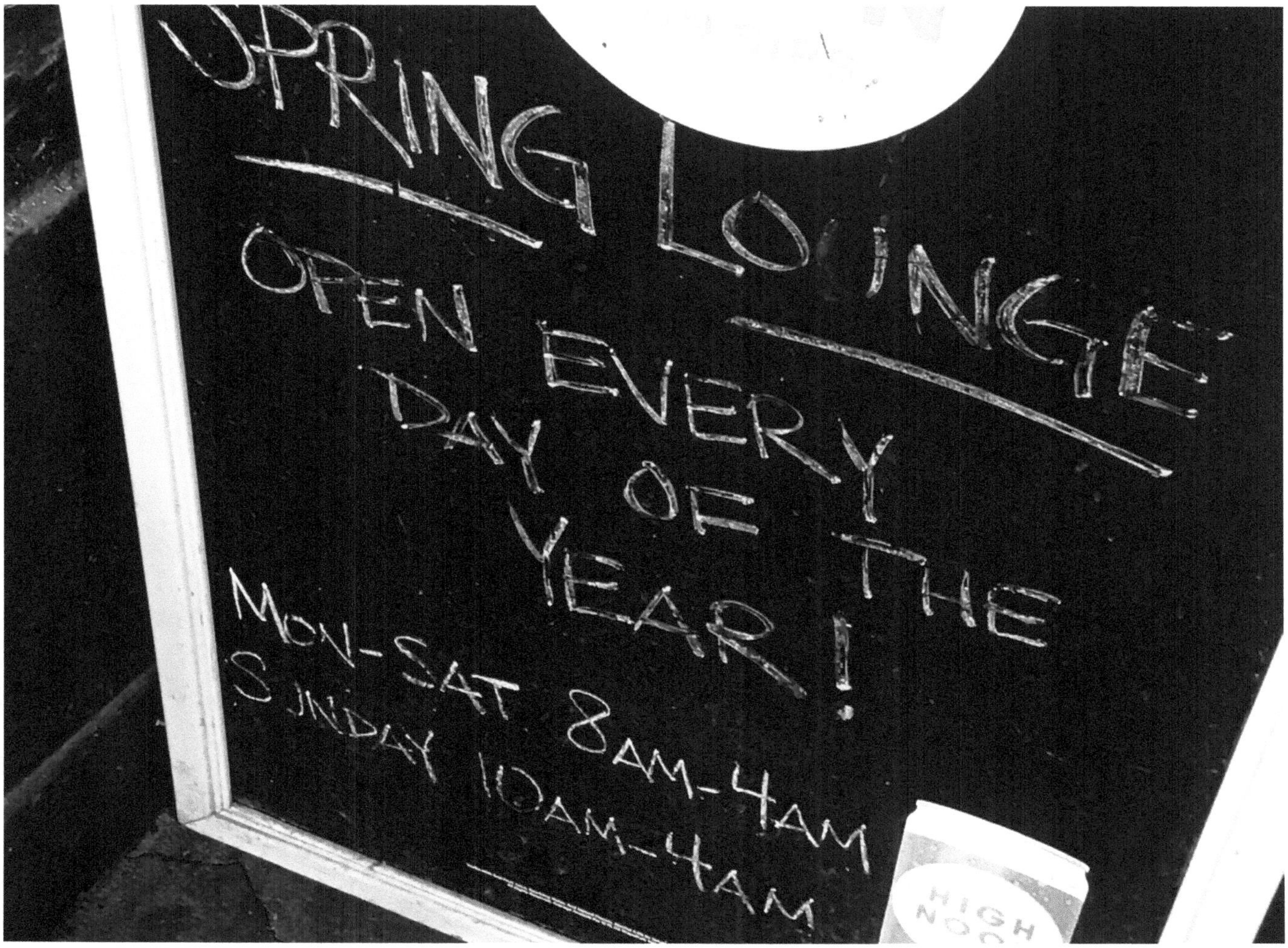

The Bar Is **OPEN**
Busy Feet

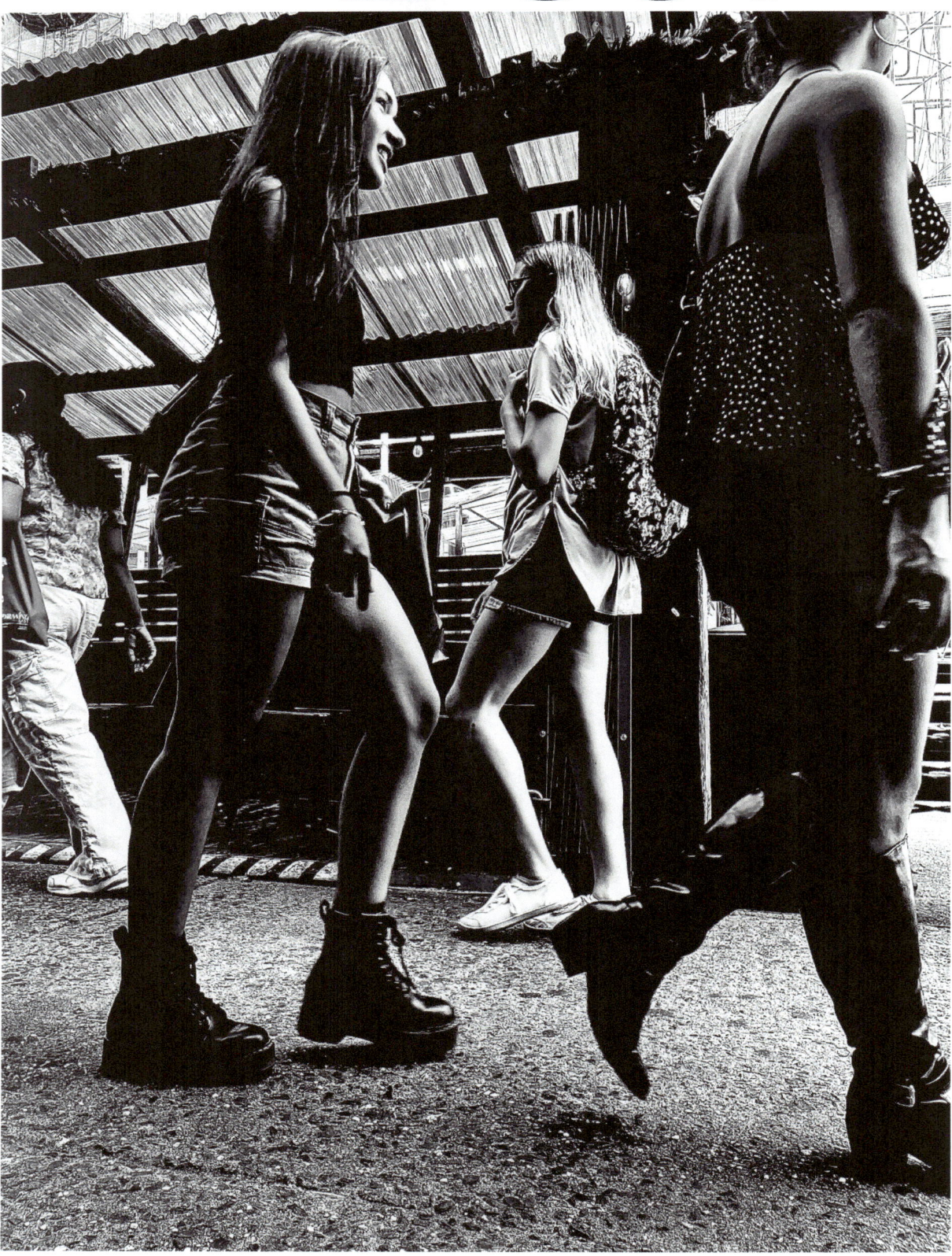

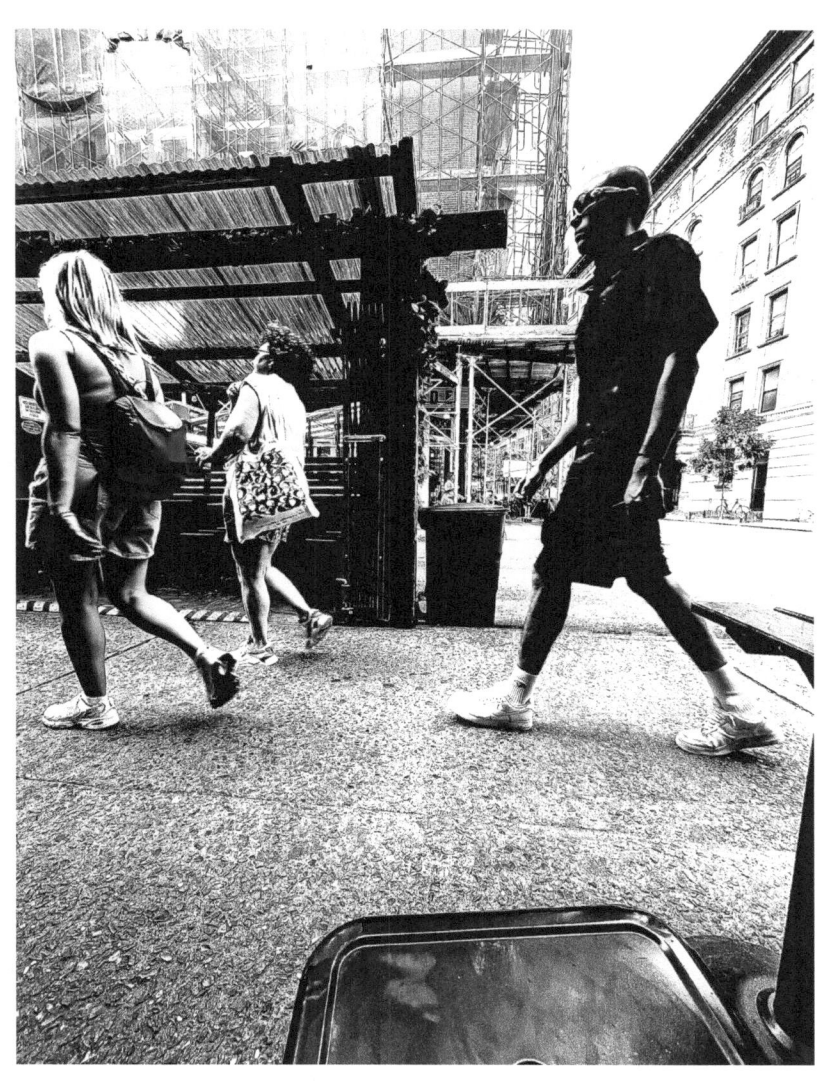

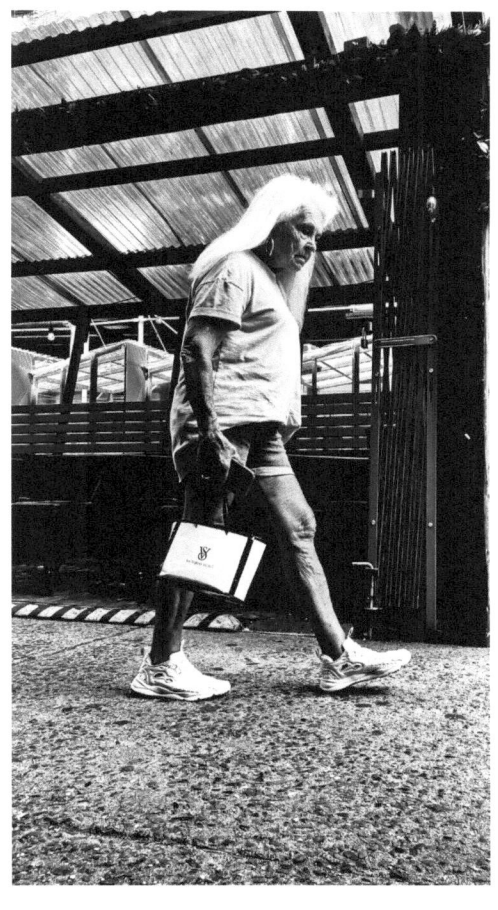

FEET
FEET
FEET

New York is a city of walkers, and pedestrian traffic, especially during the warm months, is brisk outside the bar. The bar is a magnet for many of these walkers, especially the tourists who so often wander inside for a drink and end up staying for two, three, four or more.

THE BAR IS OPEN

MOODY BLUES

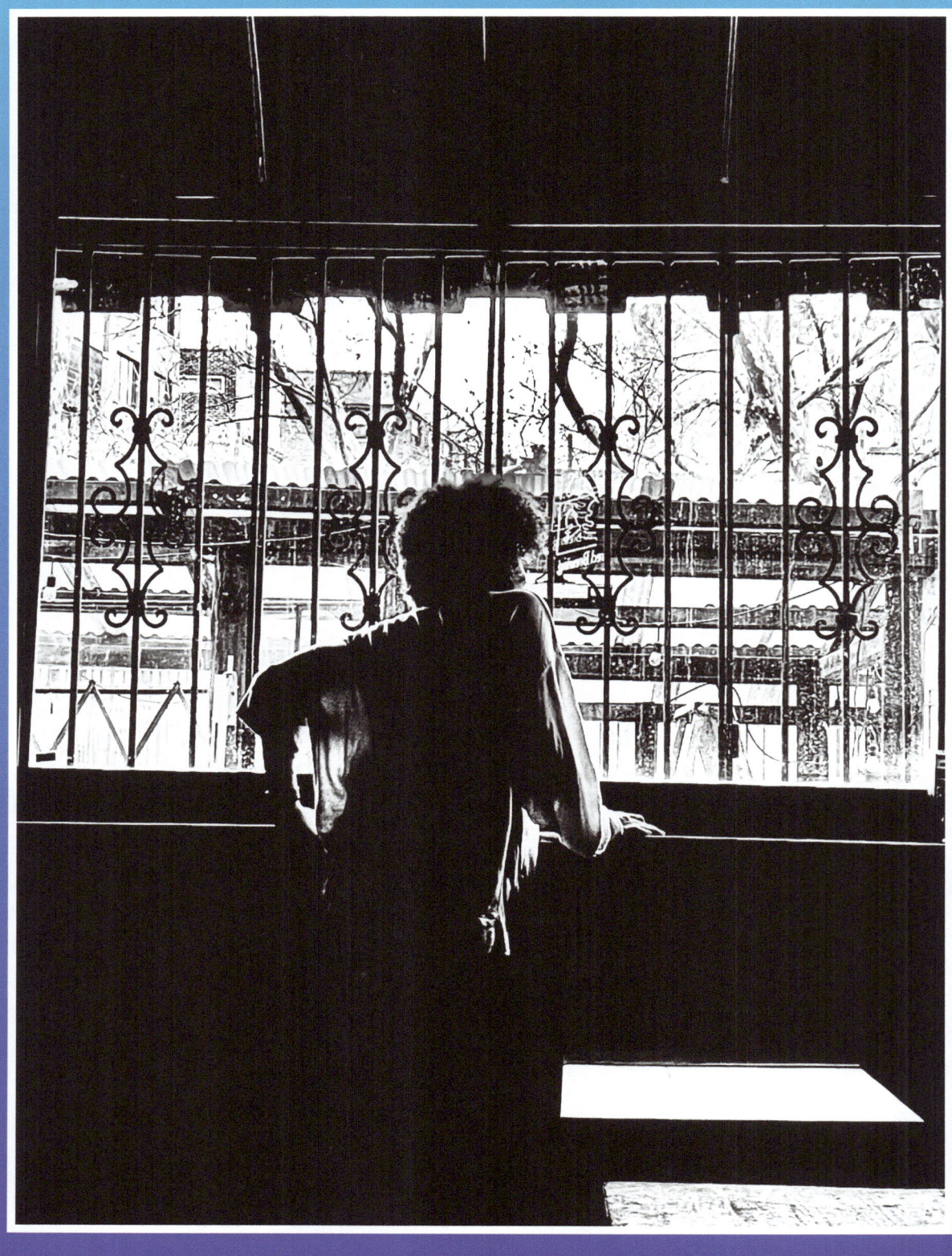

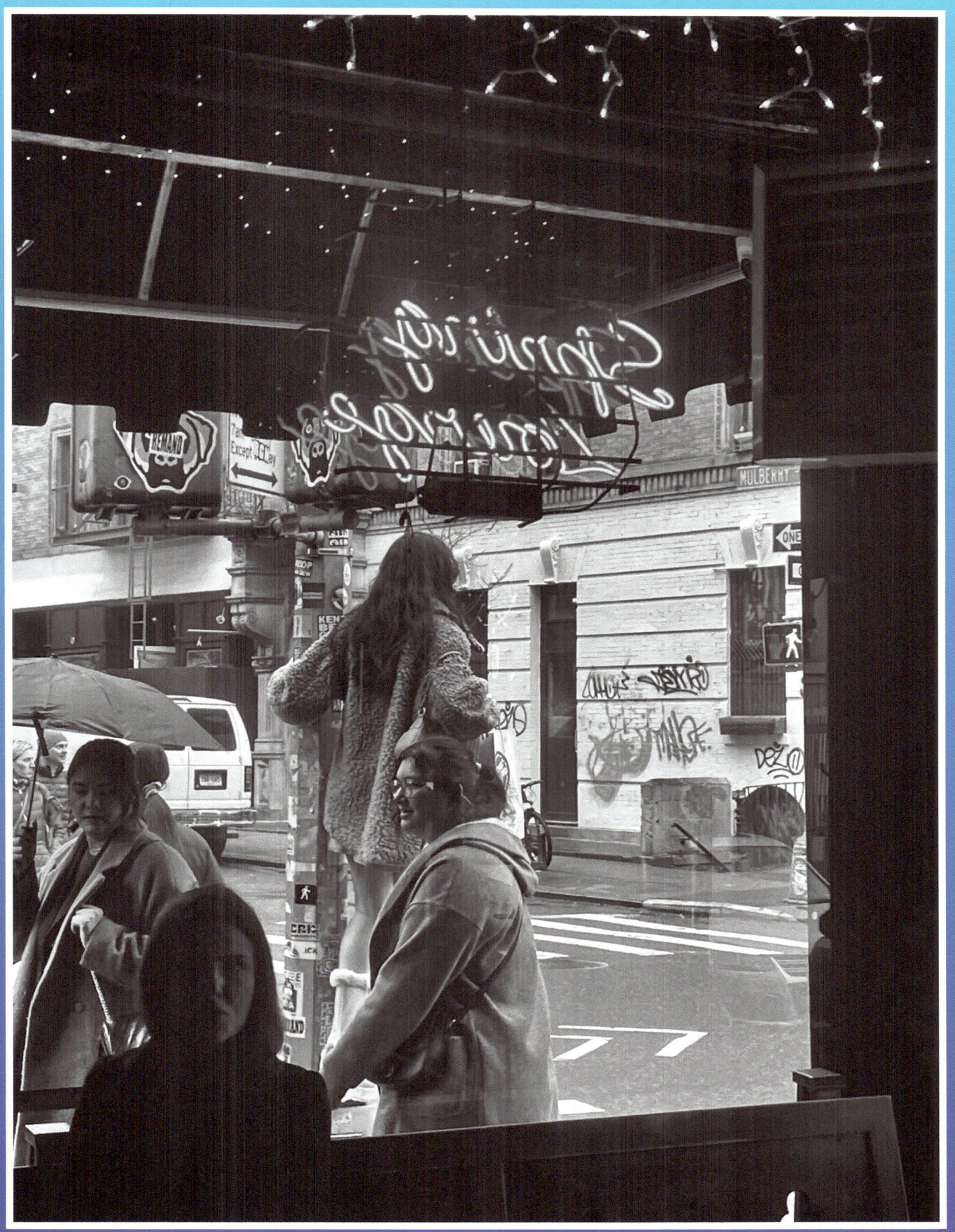

The bar, dimly lighted even on sunny days, becomes a haven when the weather turns inclement, especially during the city's long winters.

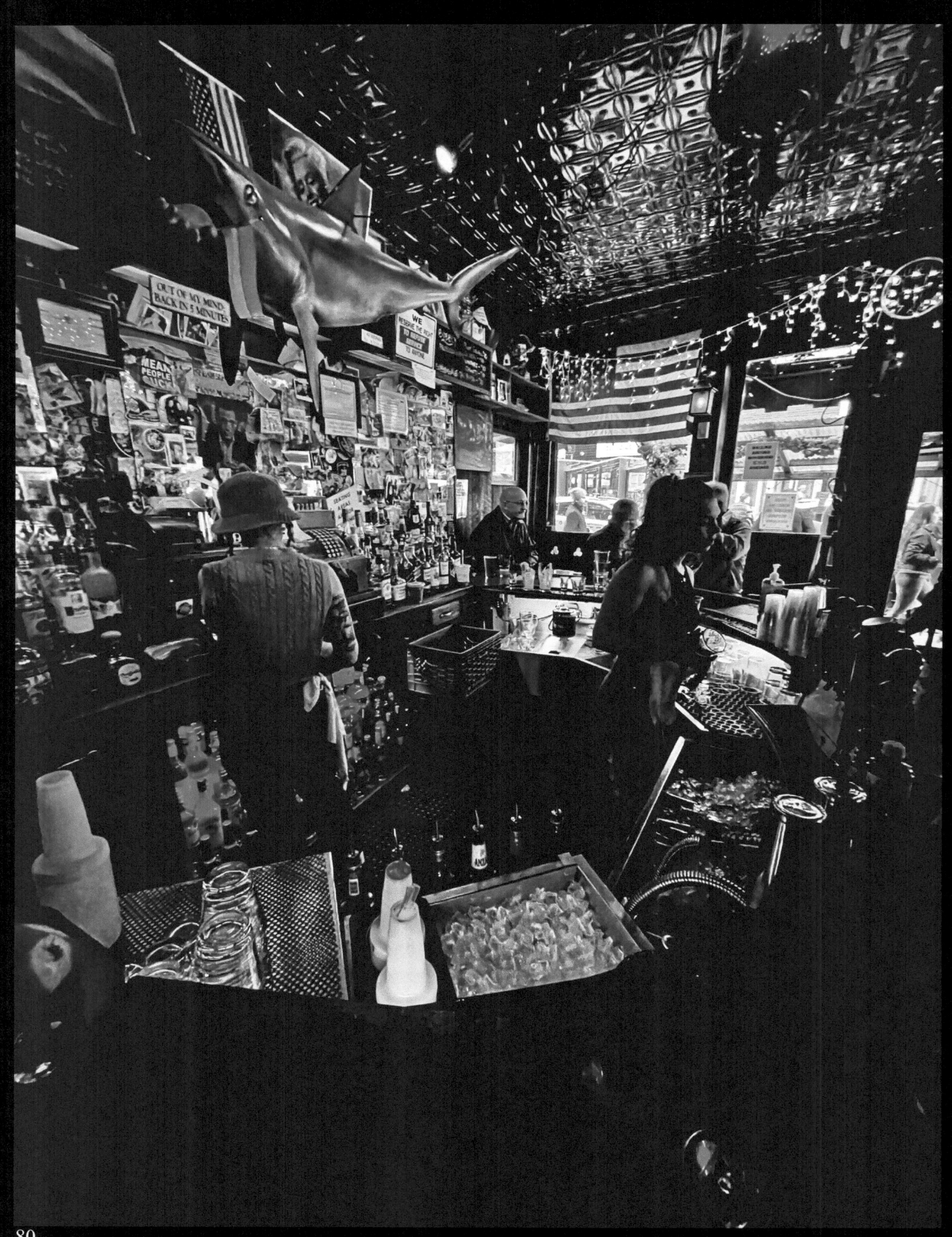

THE BAR IS OPEN

DARKNESS AT NOON

The sun never really reaches far into the bar, despite its generous fronting of large plate-glass windows. Even on clear summer days it can be cozily cave-like, and the suspended shark, the framed photos and general bric-a-brac behind the bar evoke a sense that one is spelunking among the cave paintings of prehistoric yore.

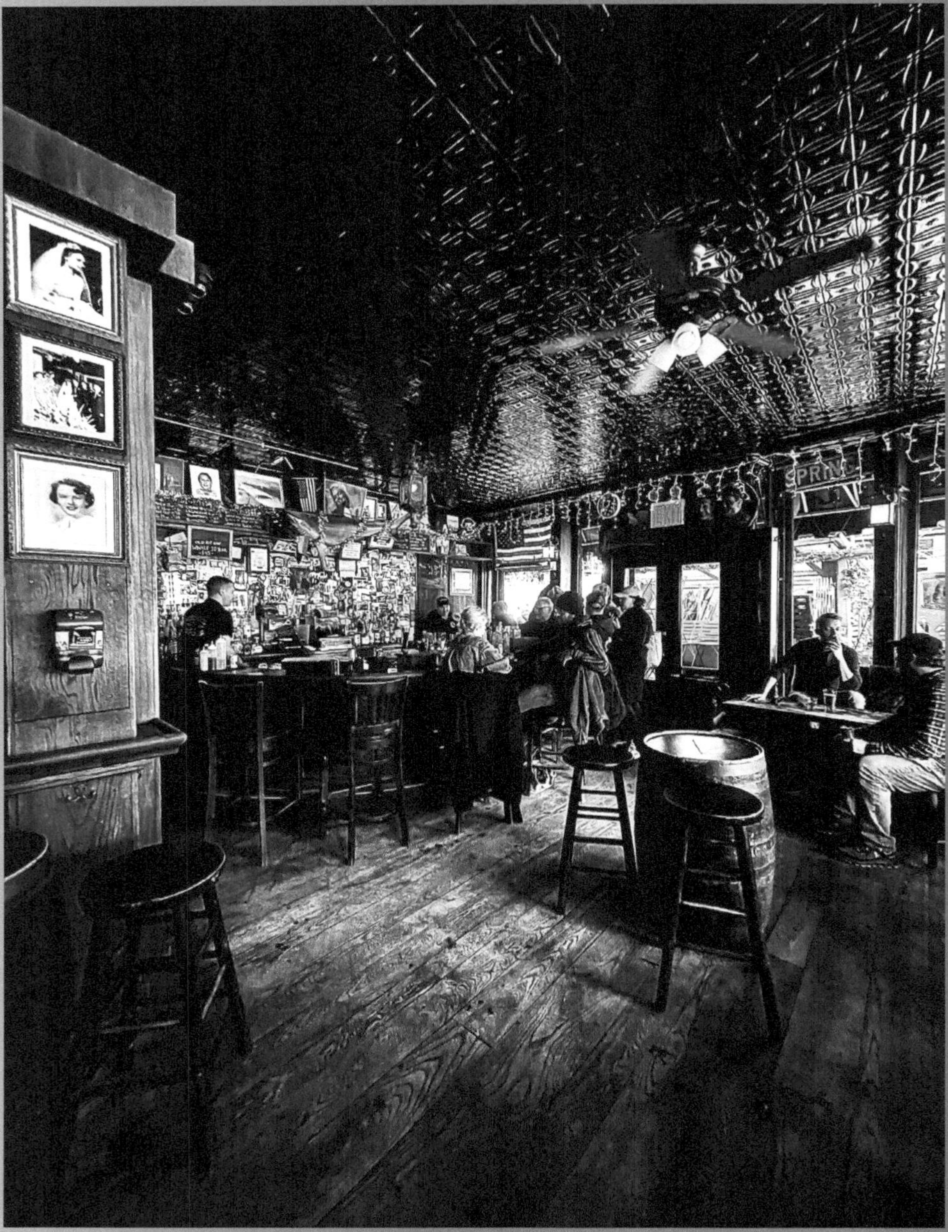

The establishment as seen from the rear, where a stuffed moose head presides over the bathrooms.

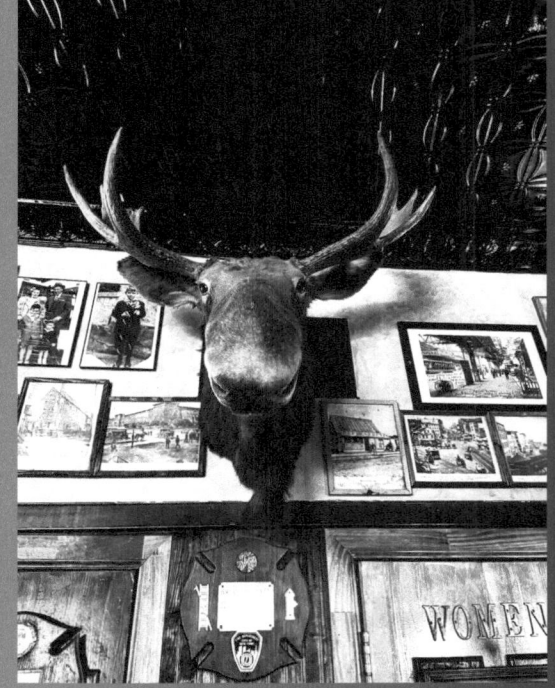

The Bar Is Open

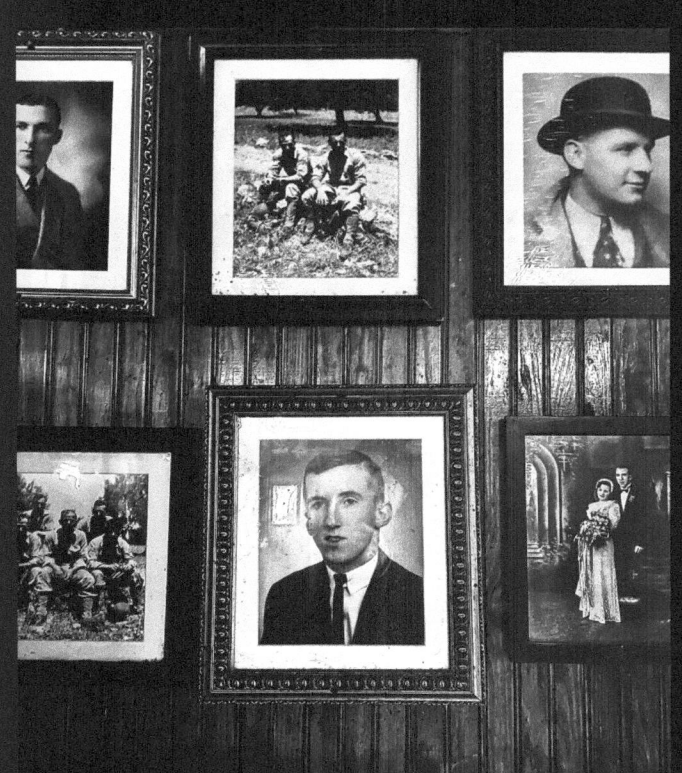

A sampling of photos, some of them enigmatically of unidentified people from decades long past. A glimpse of a corner in the rear, which by early afternoon is often packed, and the entire bar generally remains packed until closing time at 4 in the morning.

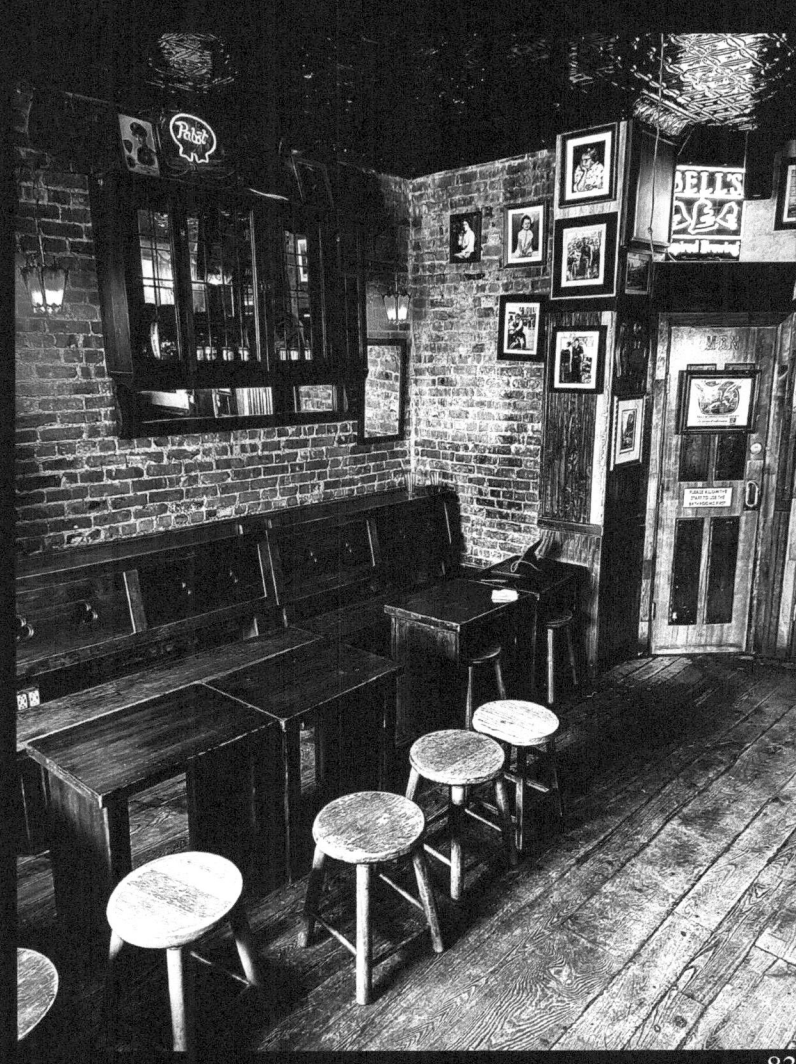

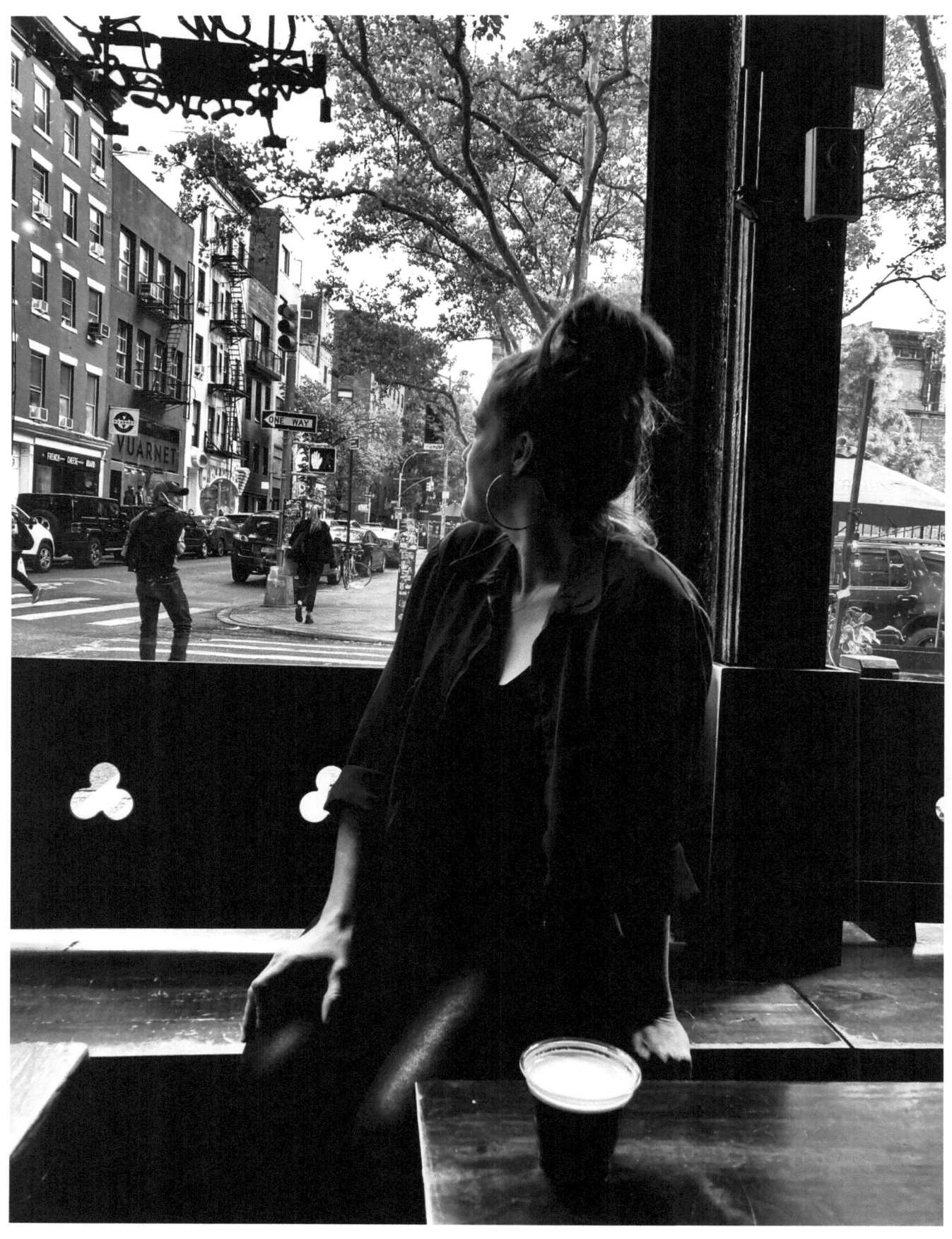

A glimpse down Spring Street, for which the bar is named, at the intersection of Mulberry Street. Laurel and Hardy are immortalized over the exit.

The Bar Is Open

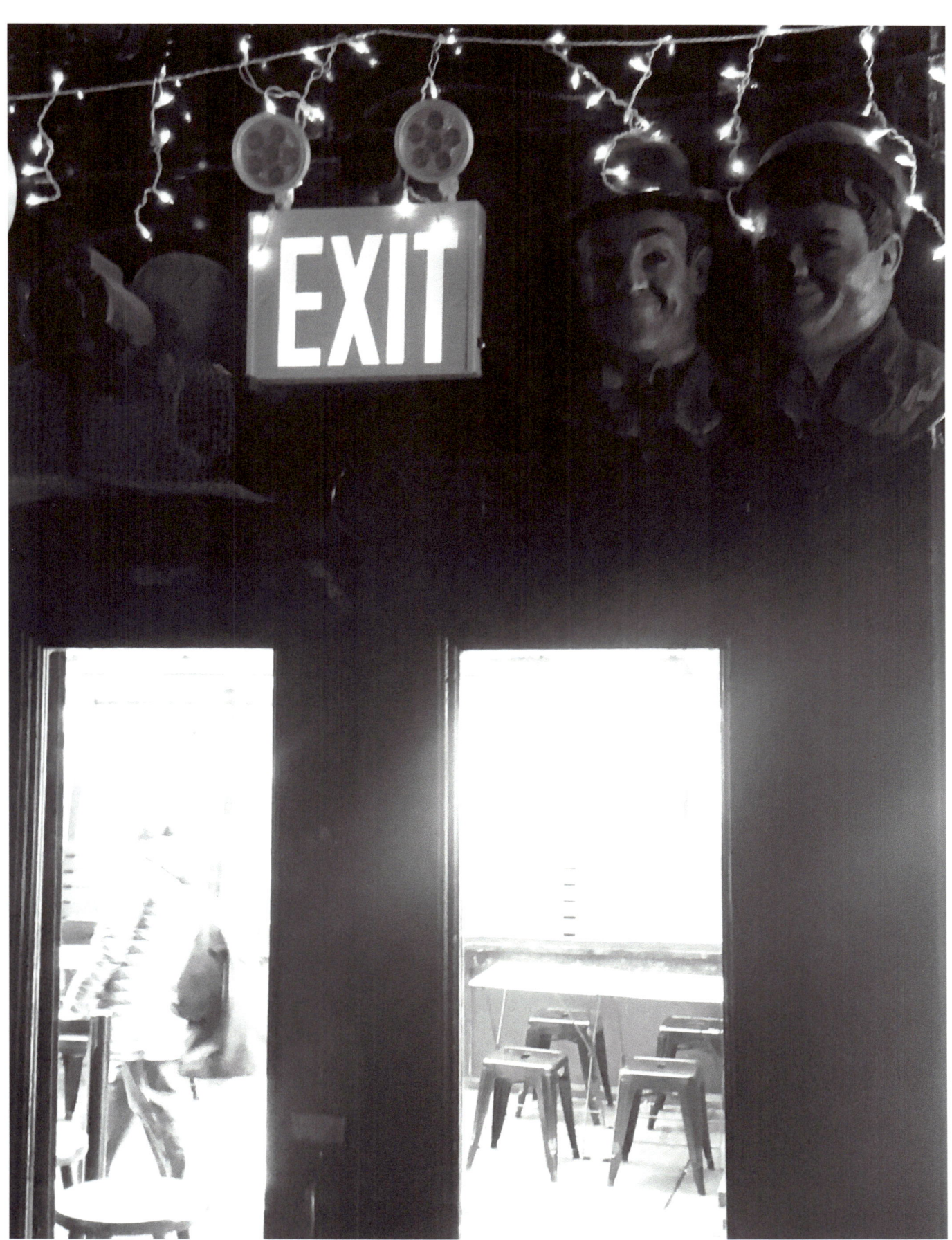

SHARK BAR

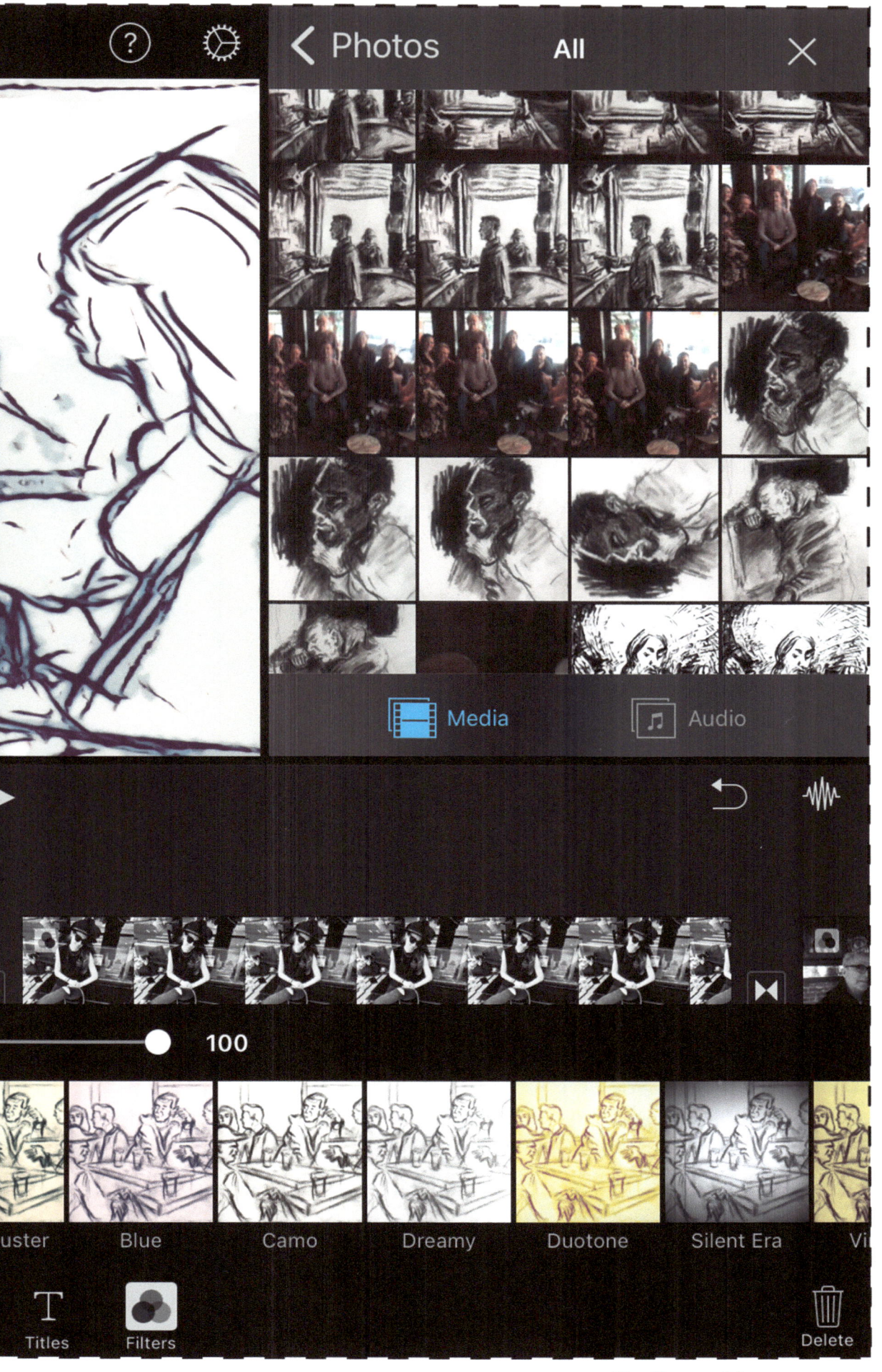

SKETCH BOOK

BY DAVID MISIALOWSKI

THE BAR IS OPEN

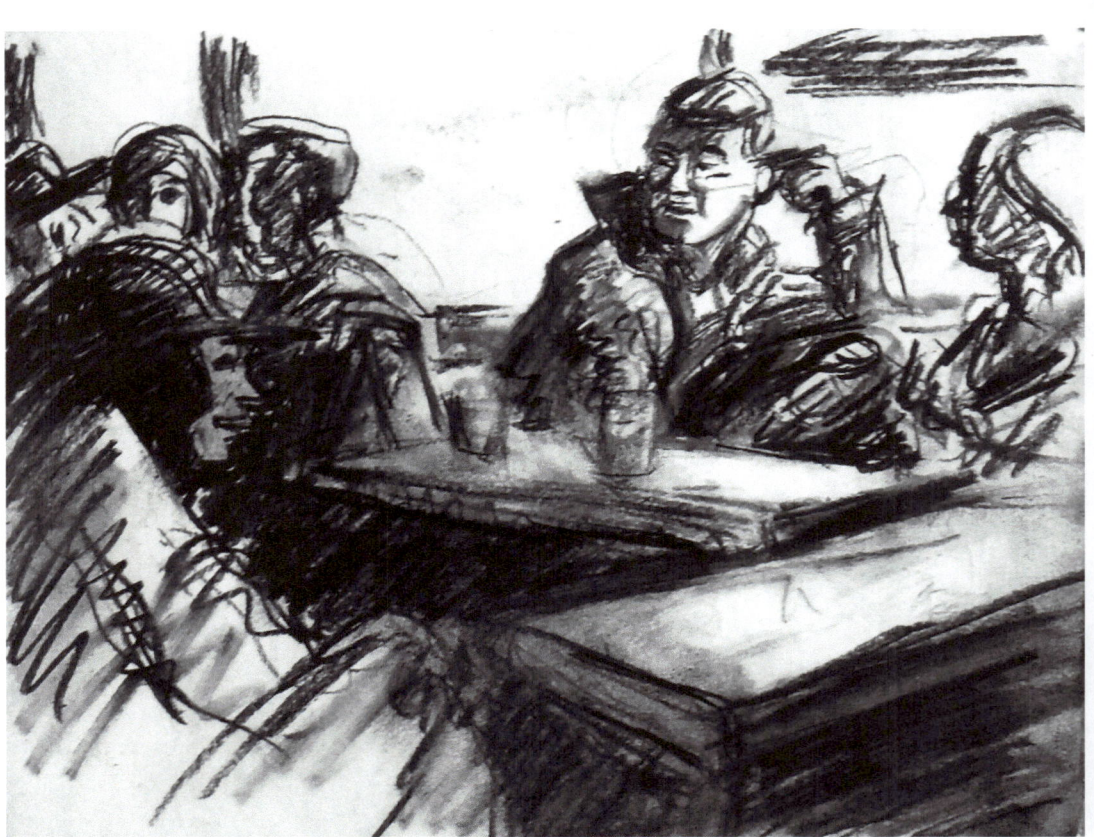

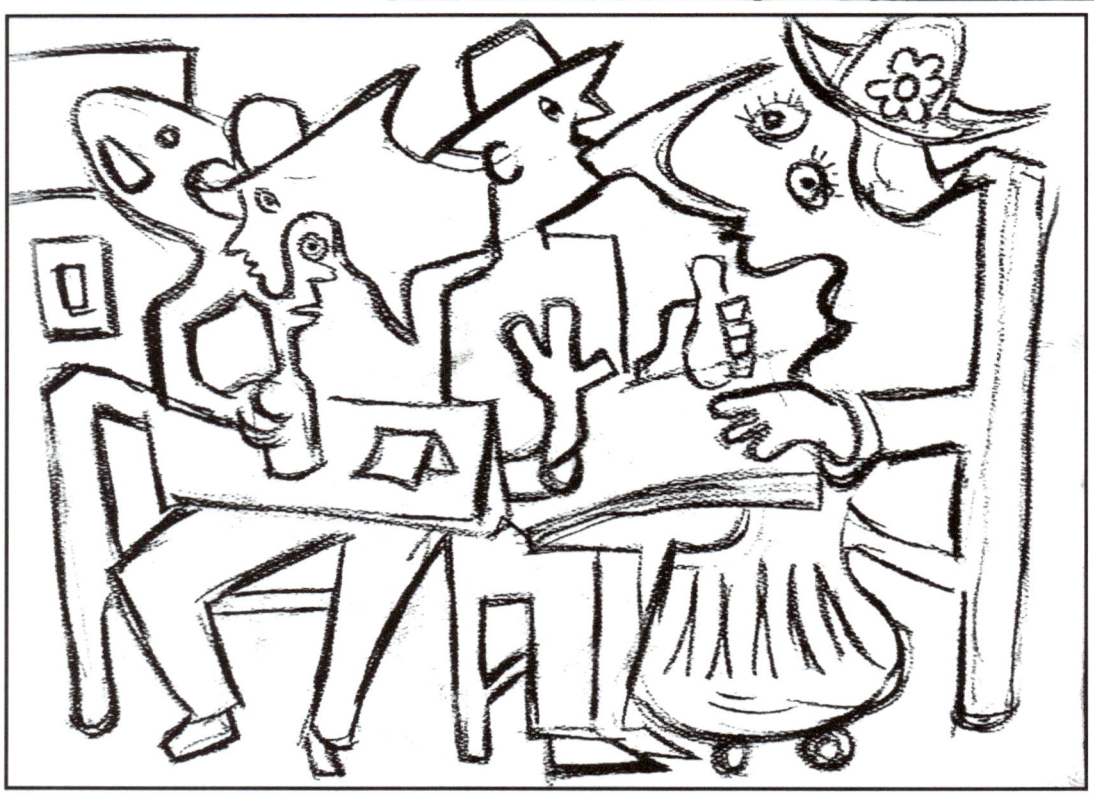

Two of my quickly executed charcoal and pencil sketches of the bar's interior and its patrons. Directly above is a drawing of day drinkers and one of the establishment's famed stuffed shark, rendered in a synthetic Cubist style inspired by Picasso's Three Musicians.

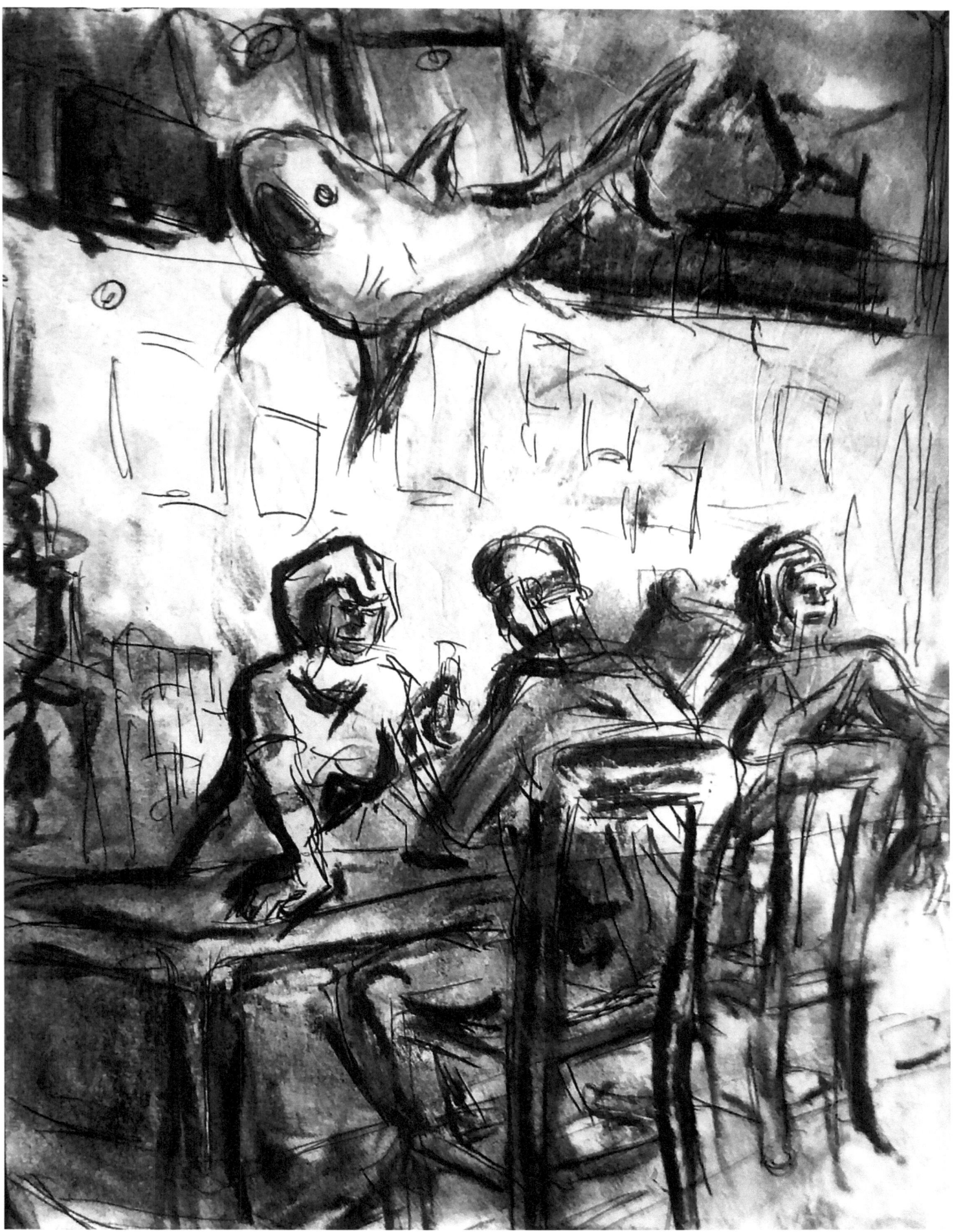

The Bar Is Open

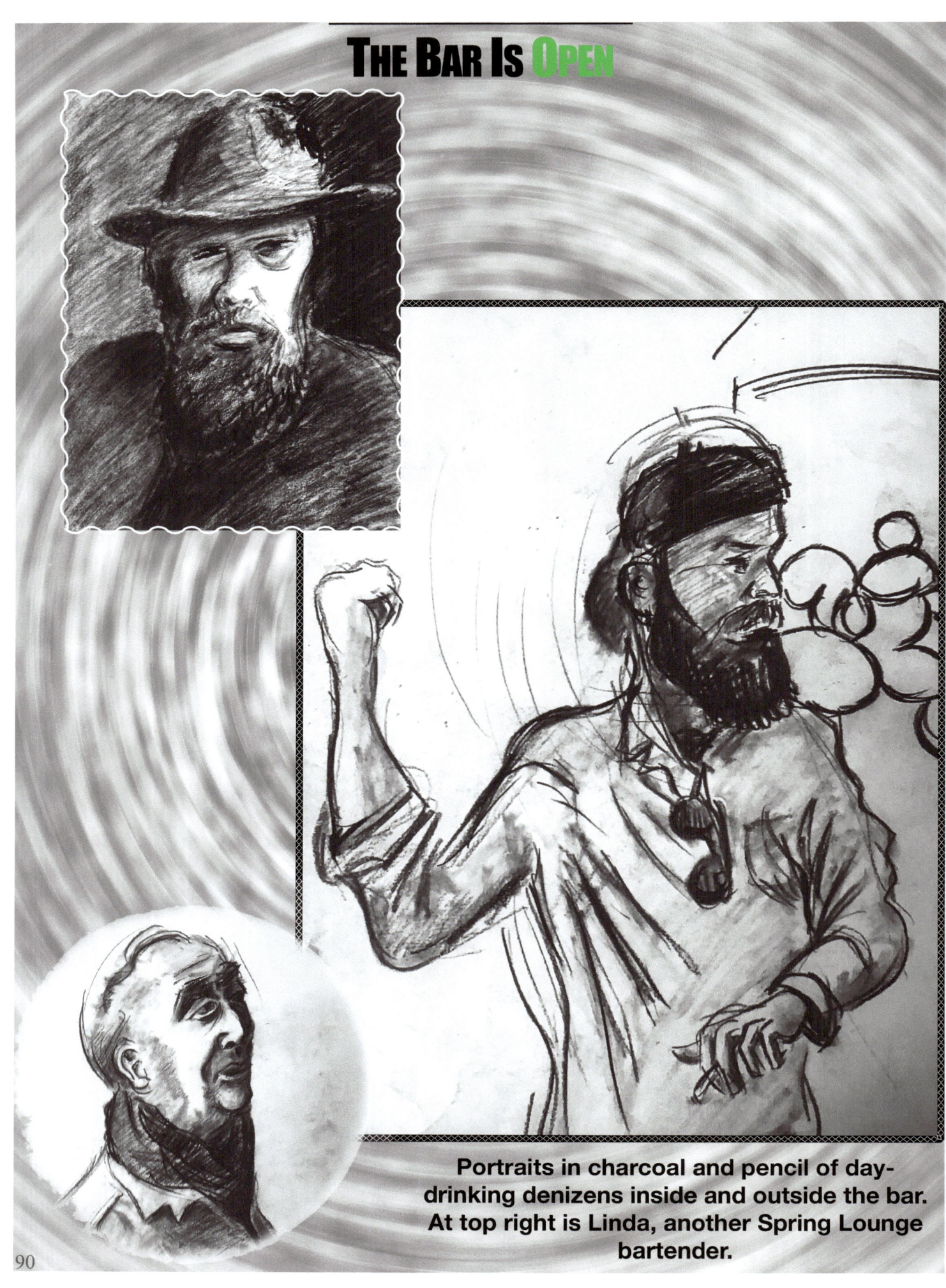

Portraits in charcoal and pencil of day-drinking denizens inside and outside the bar. At top right is Linda, another Spring Lounge bartender.

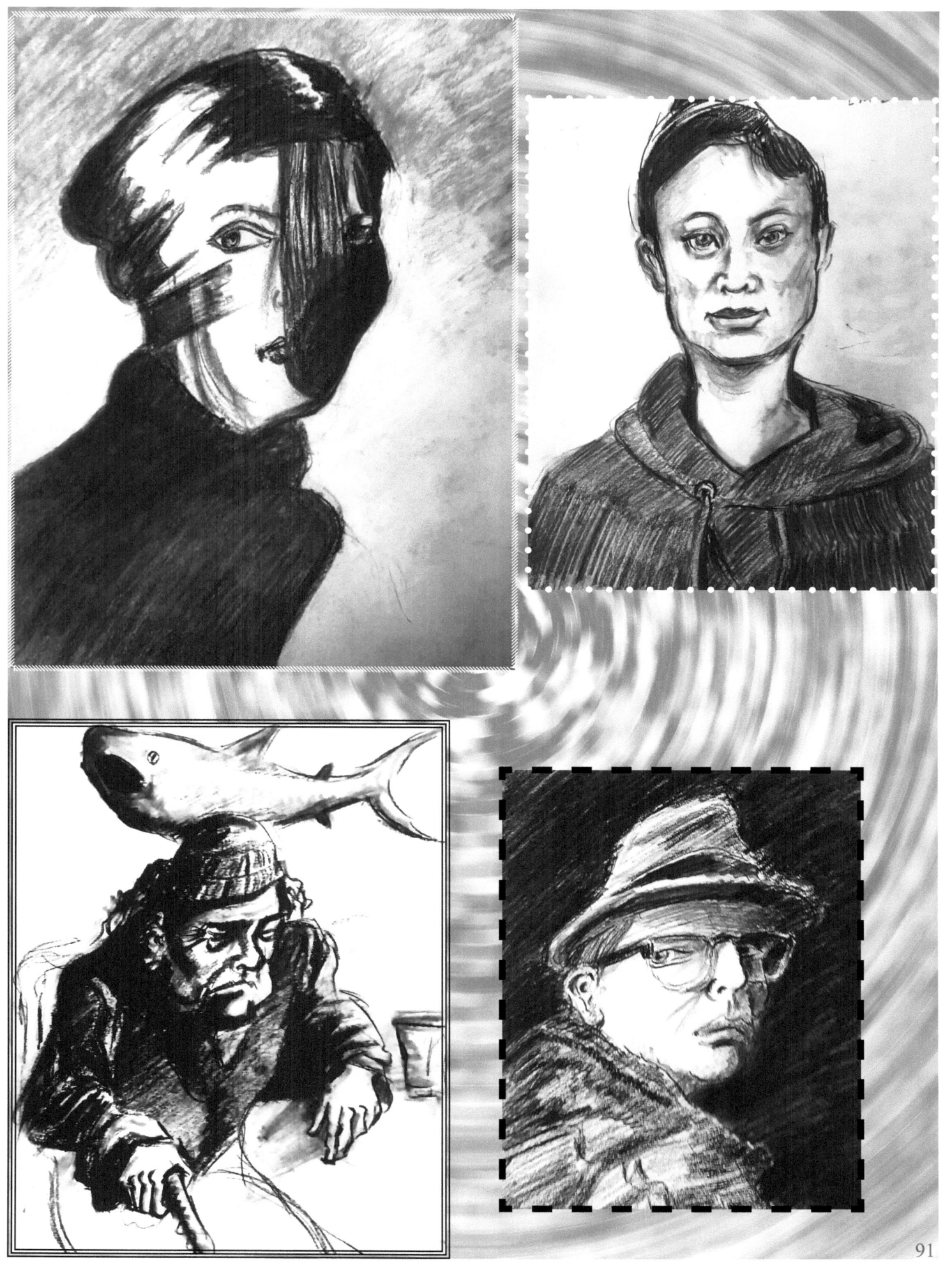

The Bar Is Open

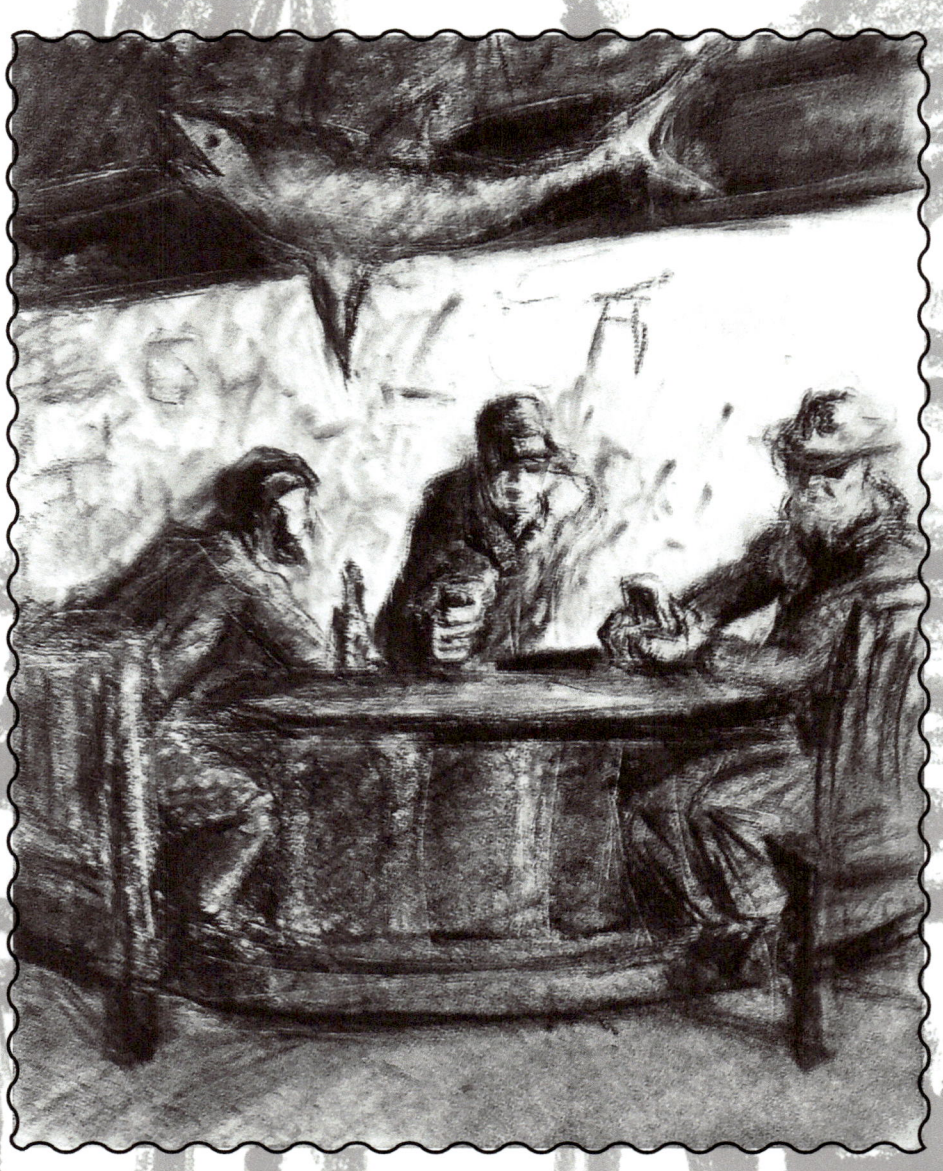

Pencil and charcoal sharks galore, including a view at right of the main shark devouring a model of a human hand. For an artist's eye, the graceful form of the shark is endlessly alluring, especially when viewed from different angles and changing perspectives.

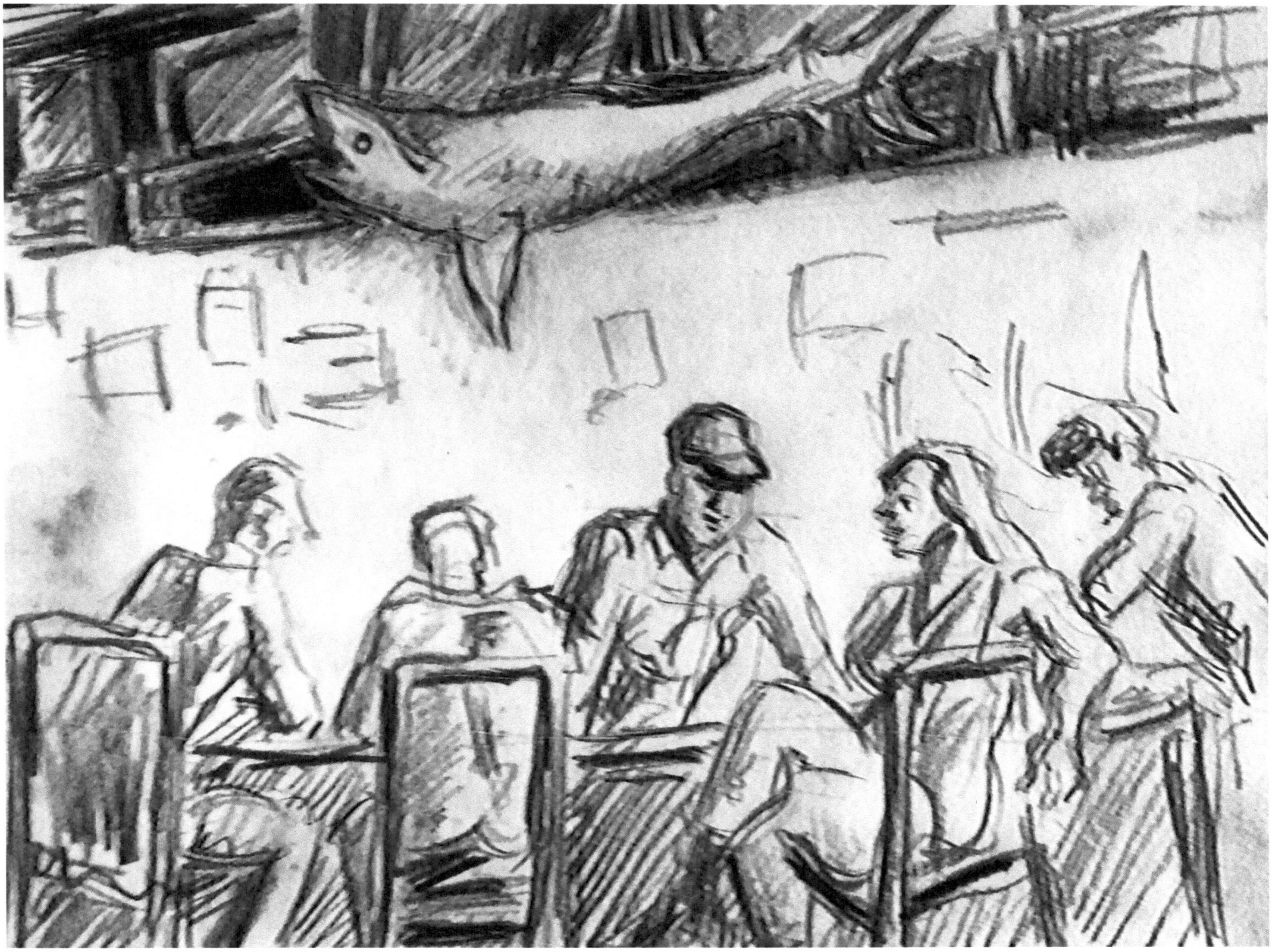

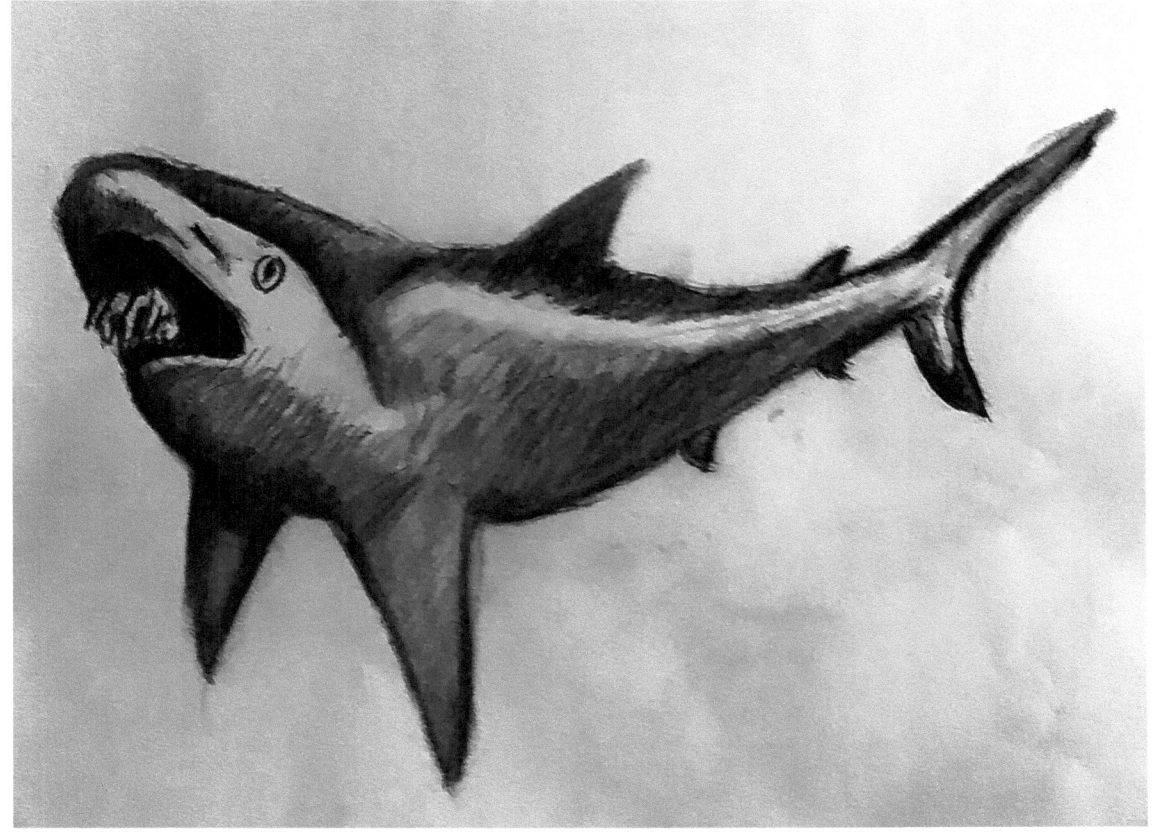

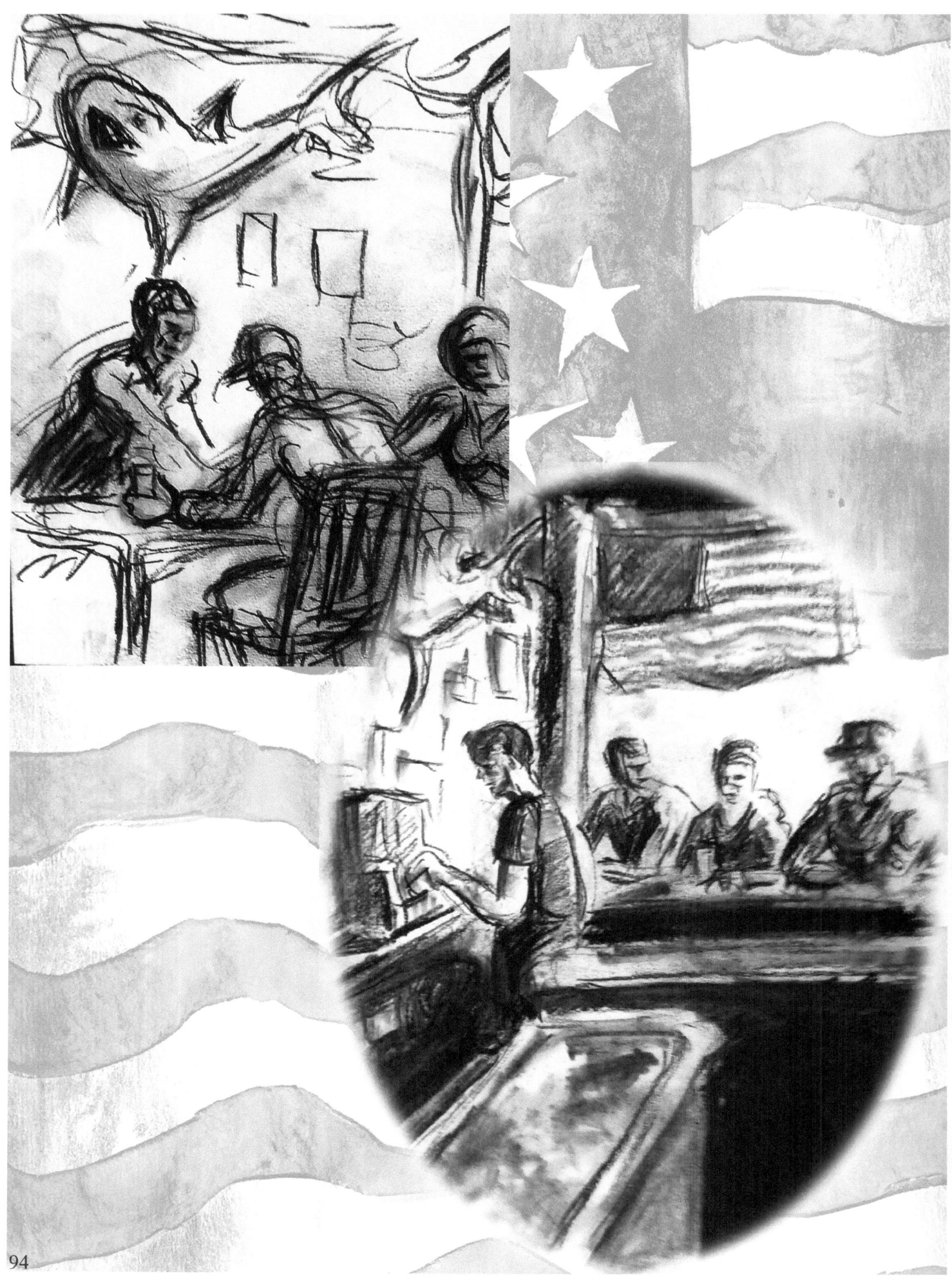

The Bar Is Open

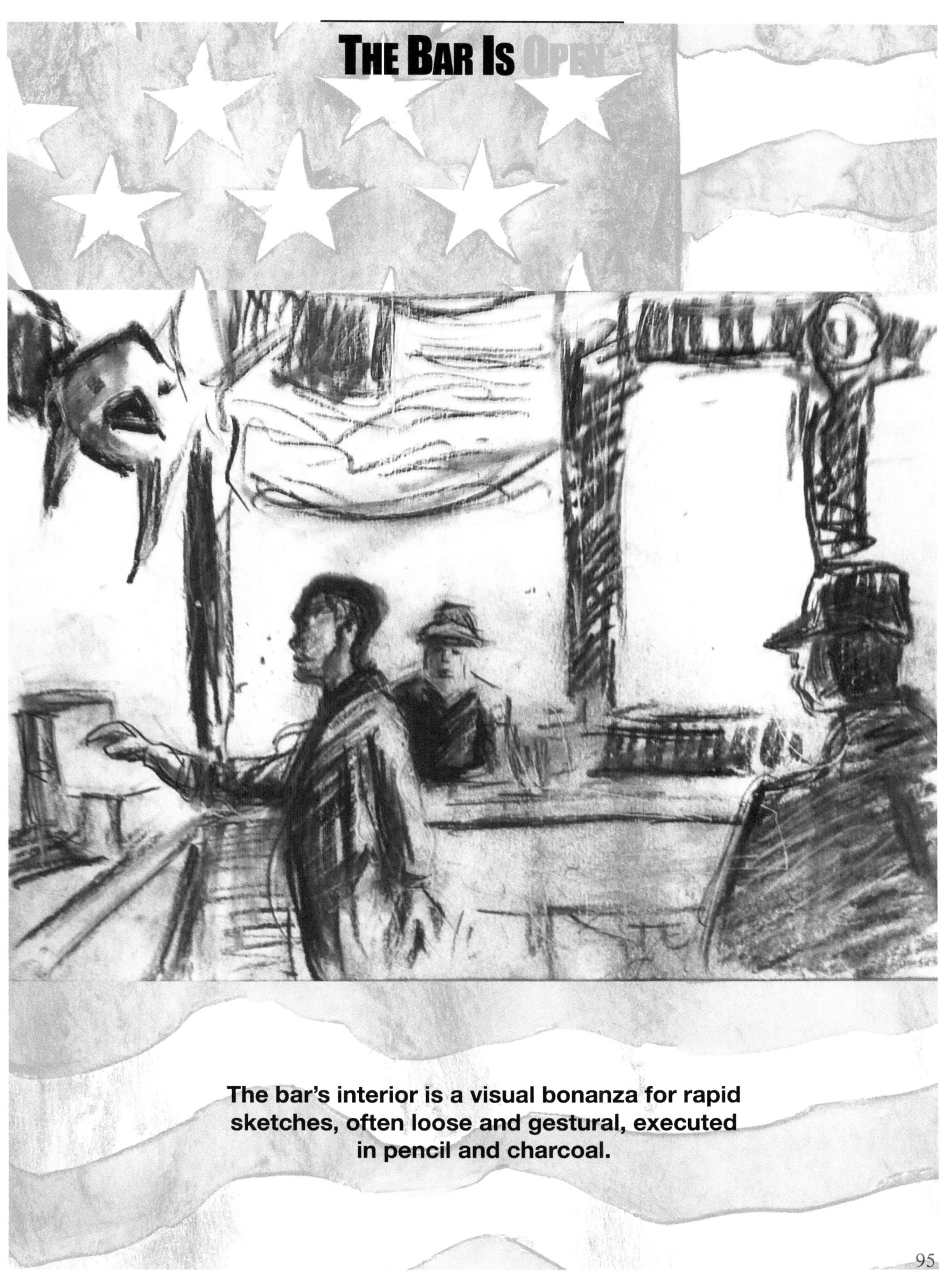

The bar's interior is a visual bonanza for rapid sketches, often loose and gestural, executed in pencil and charcoal.

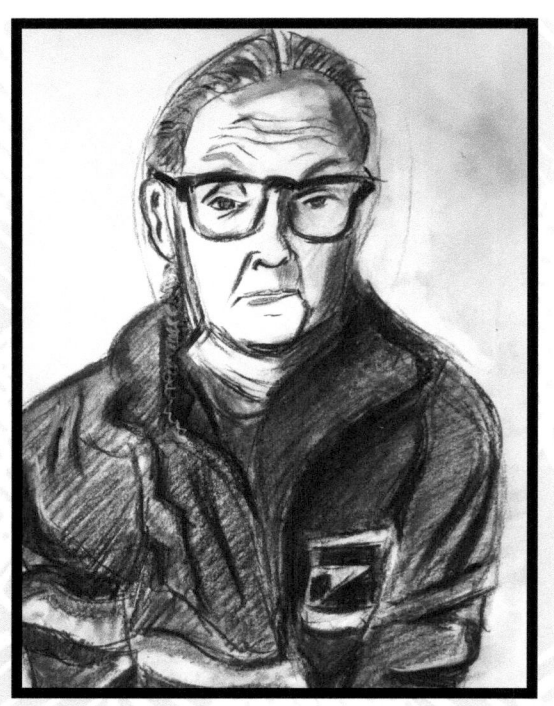

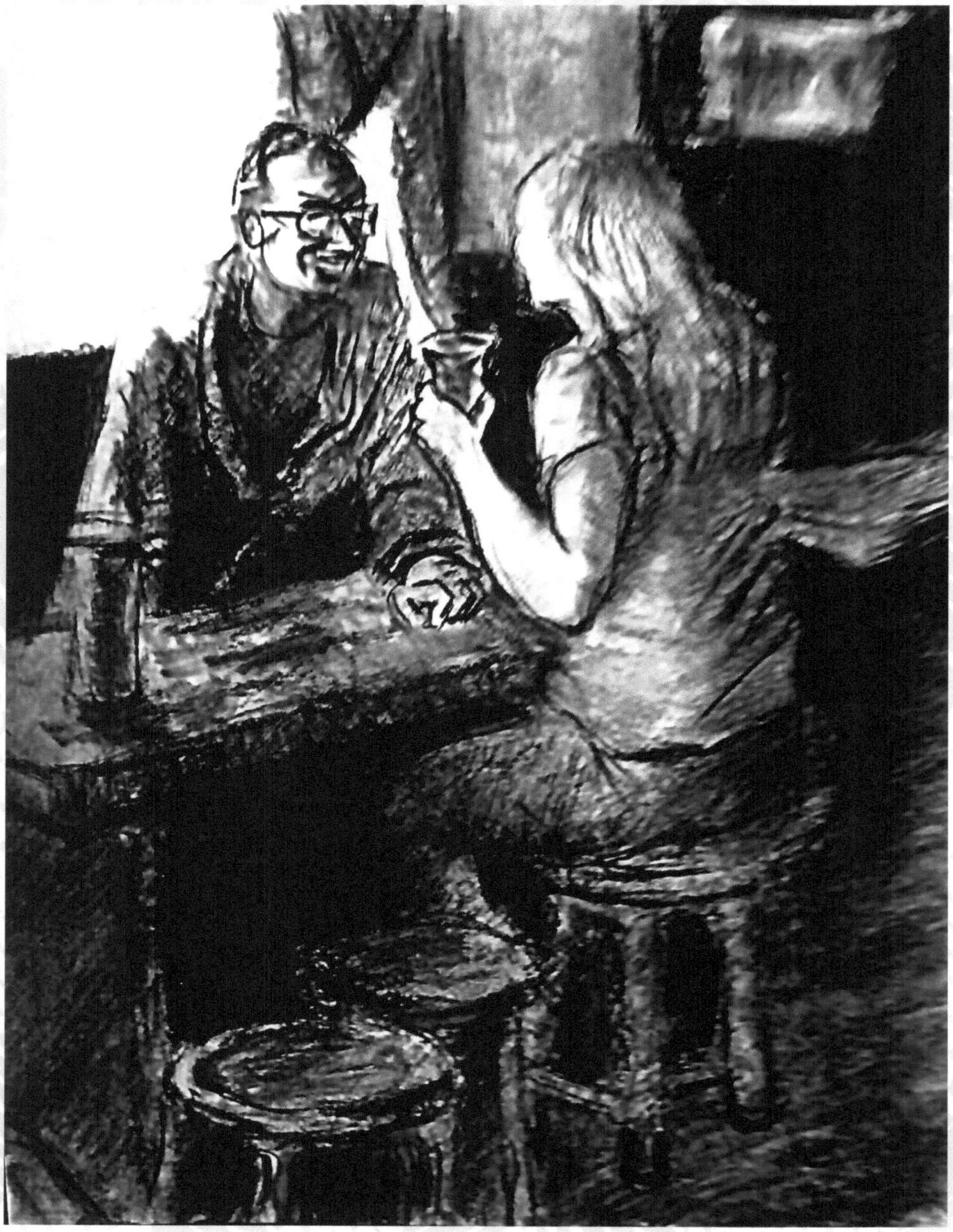

The Bar Is Open

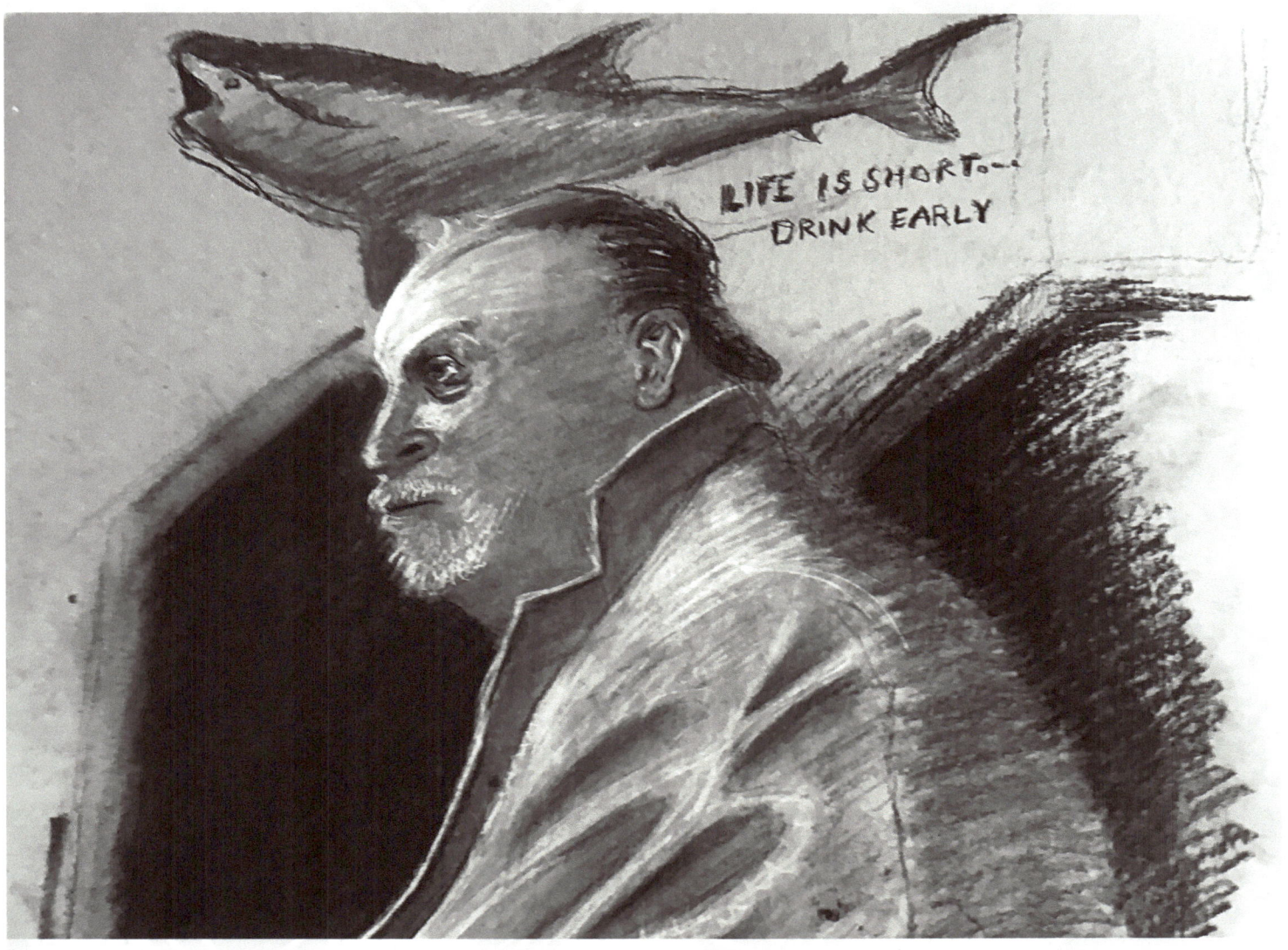

Top left, a portrait of the postal lady Annie outside the bar, after she has dropped off the mail. Left, a couple enjoy cocktails and conversation by window light. Top, doughty old Tom, a court police officer and a former prison guard, in a thoughtful pose under one of the stuffed sharks, with the bar's motto emblazoned on the wall.

THE BAR IS OPEN

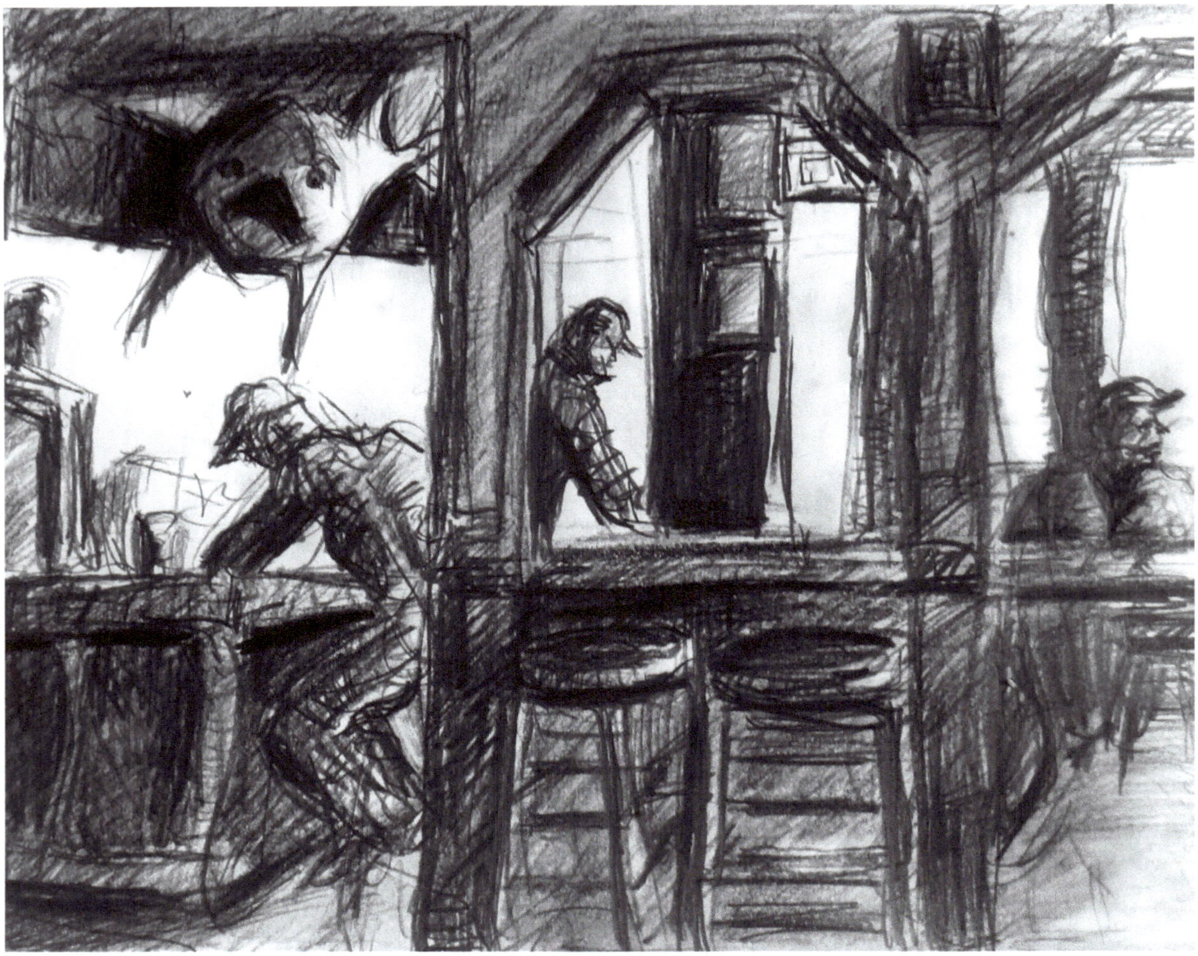

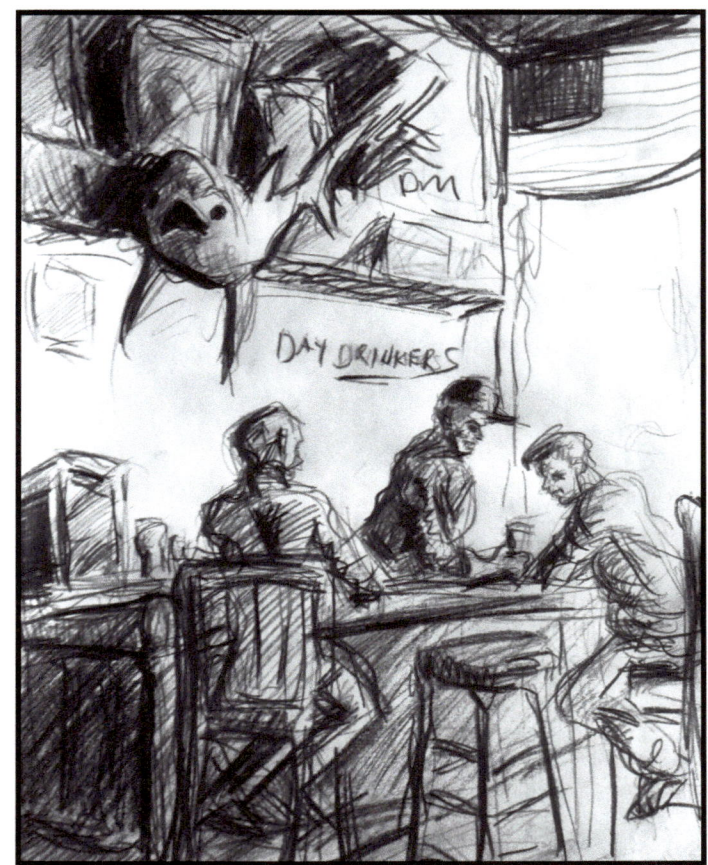

Day drinkers at the Spring Lounge, including a neo-Cubist view at top right.

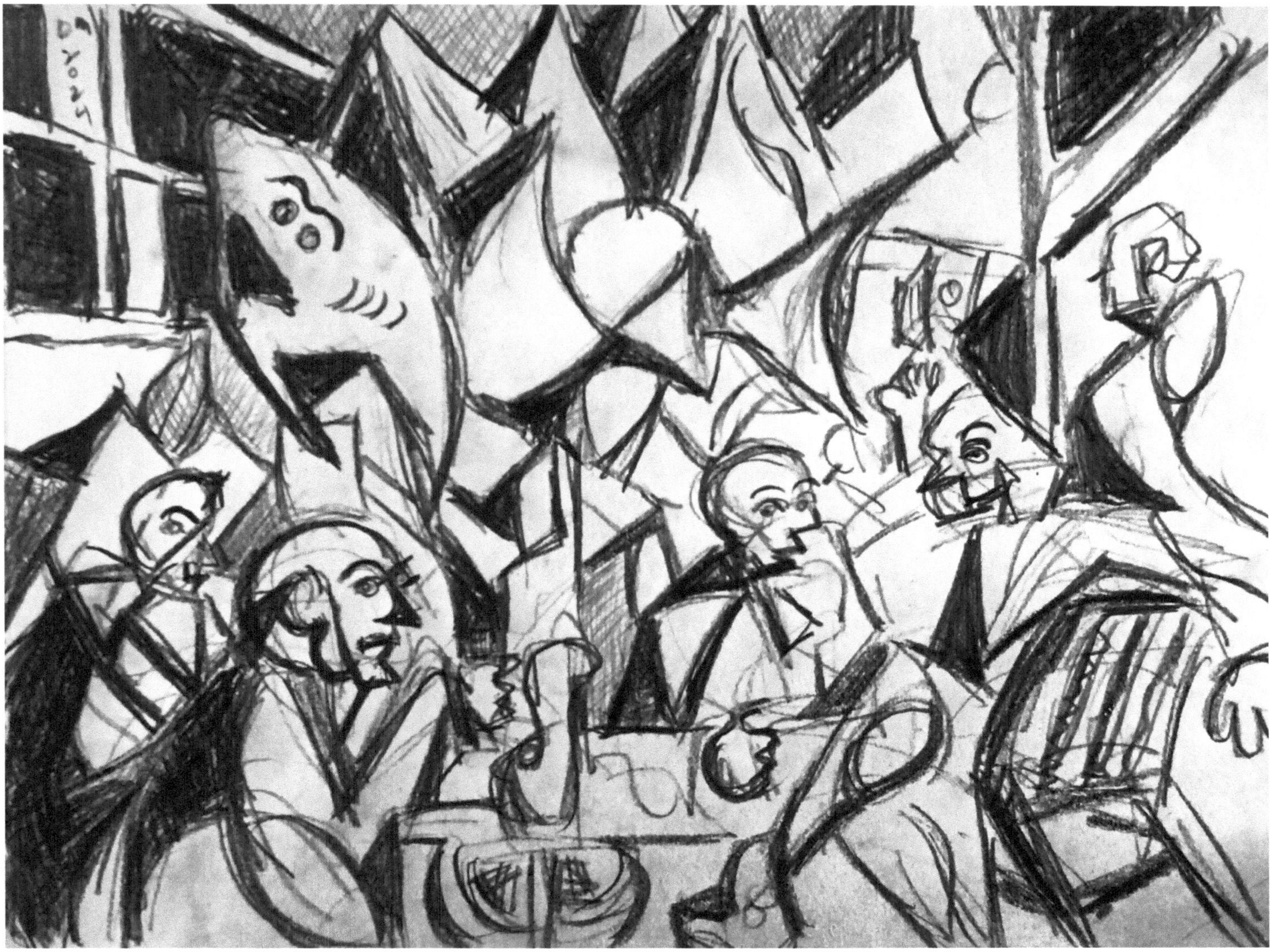

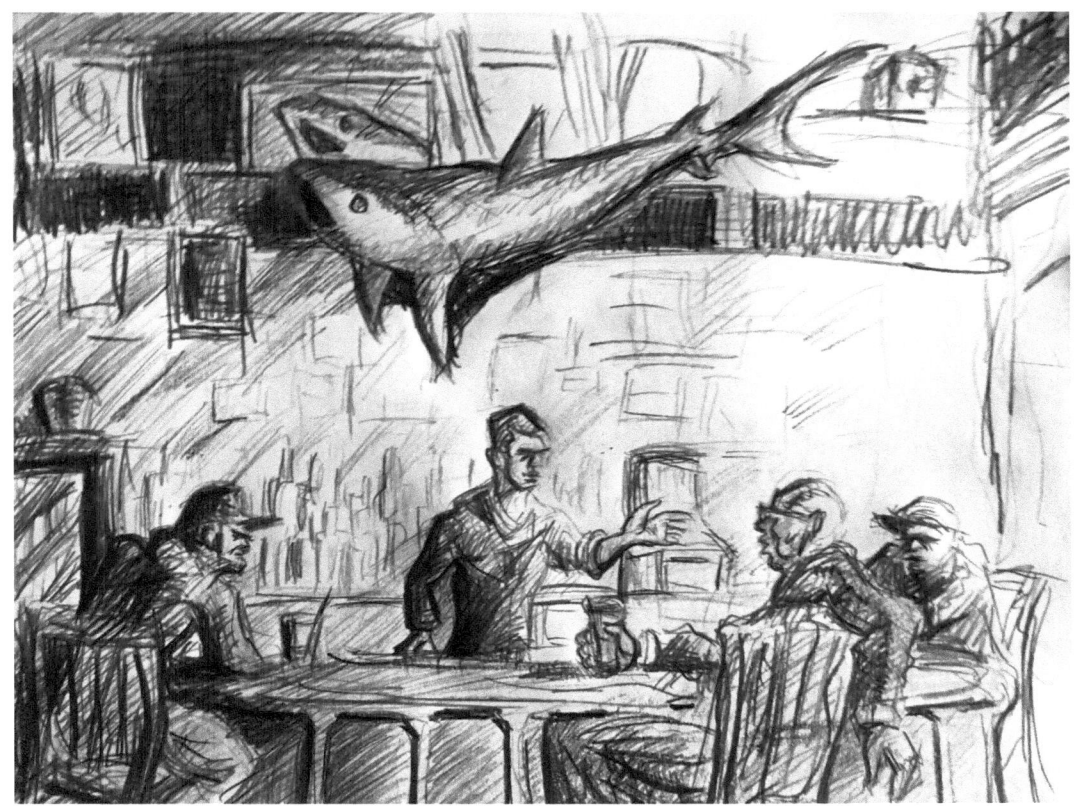

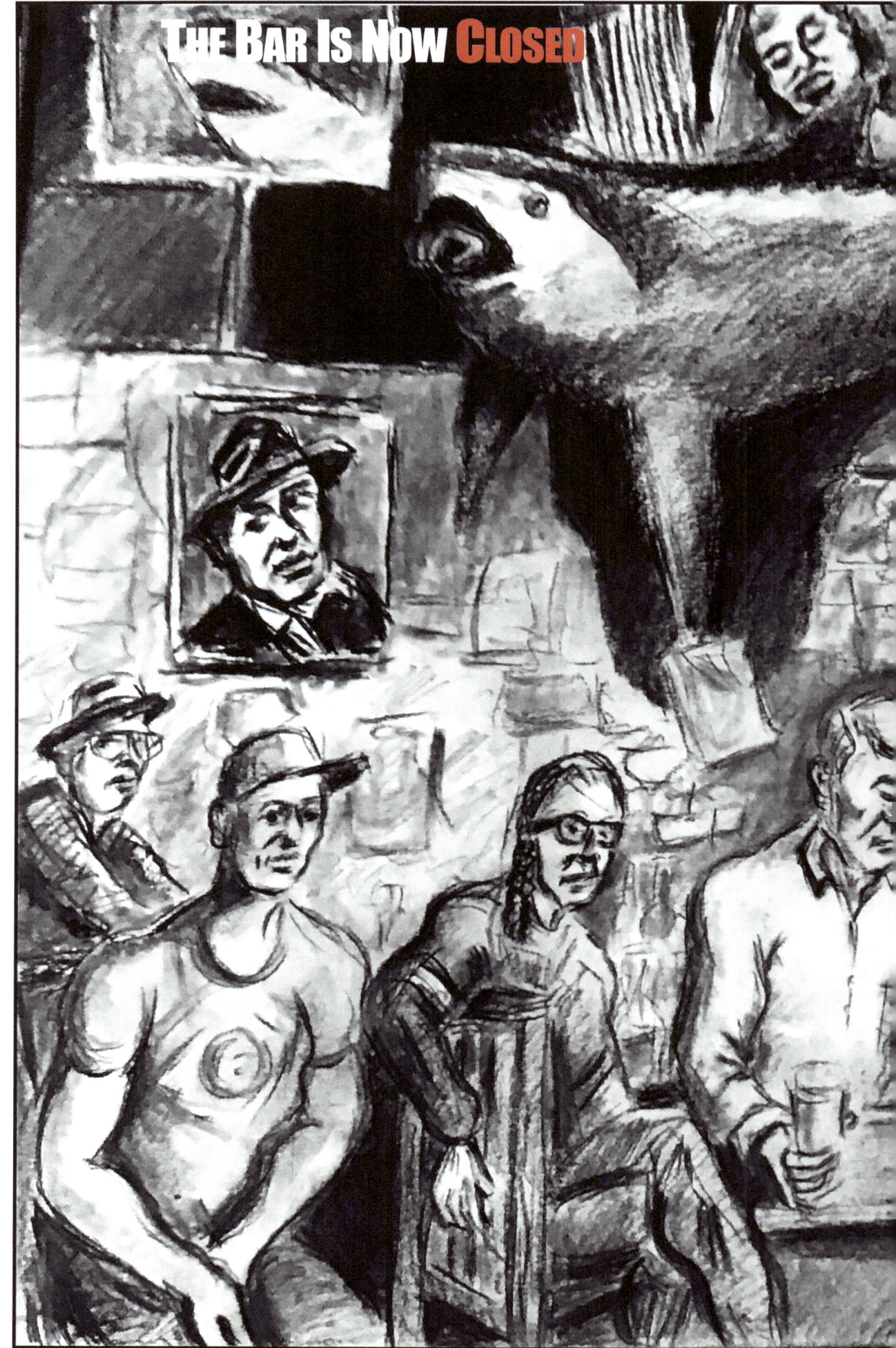

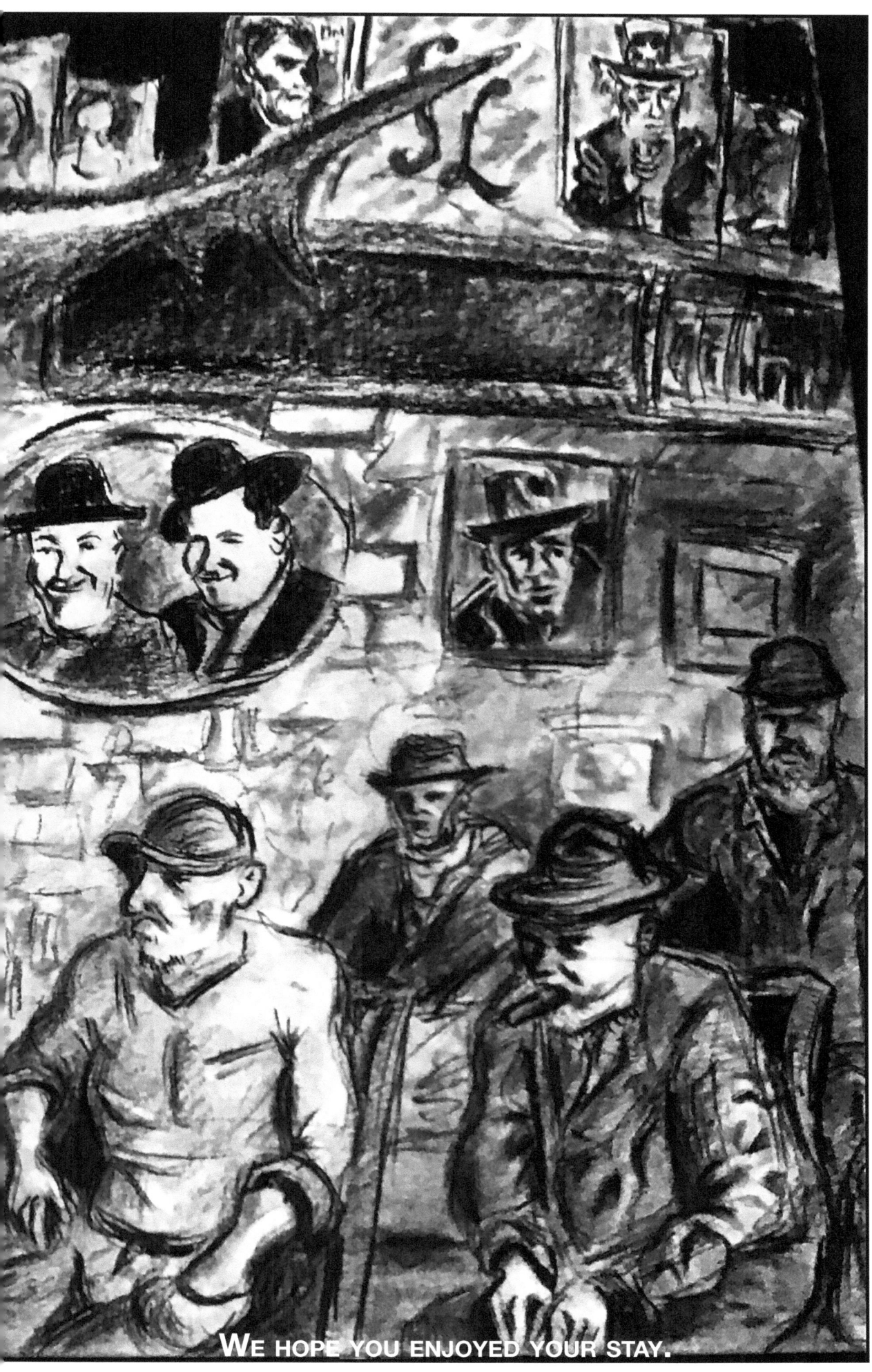

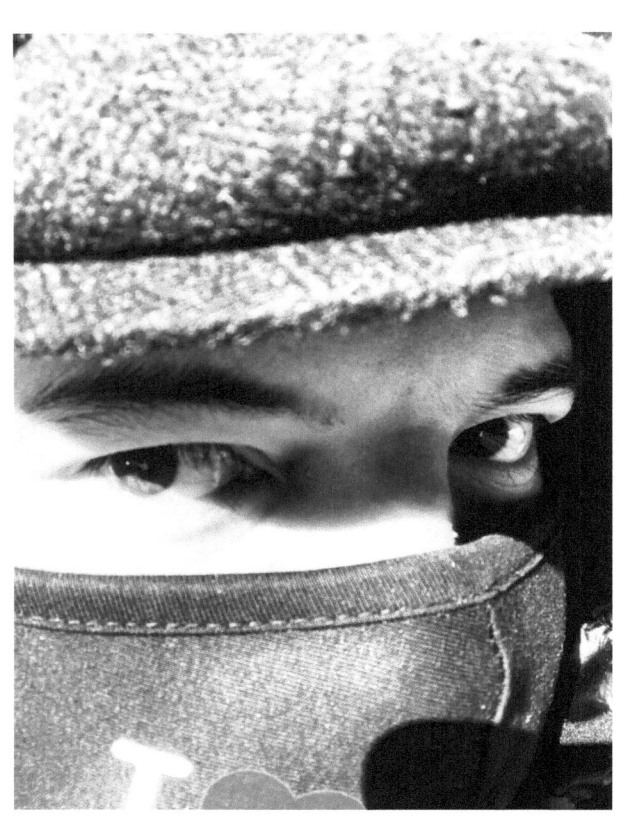

Feo

Who is that masked man? He's a New York City poet and photographer, and this is his second book of photography. His first, The Light Fantastic, was recently published, also by Pood Paw Prints.

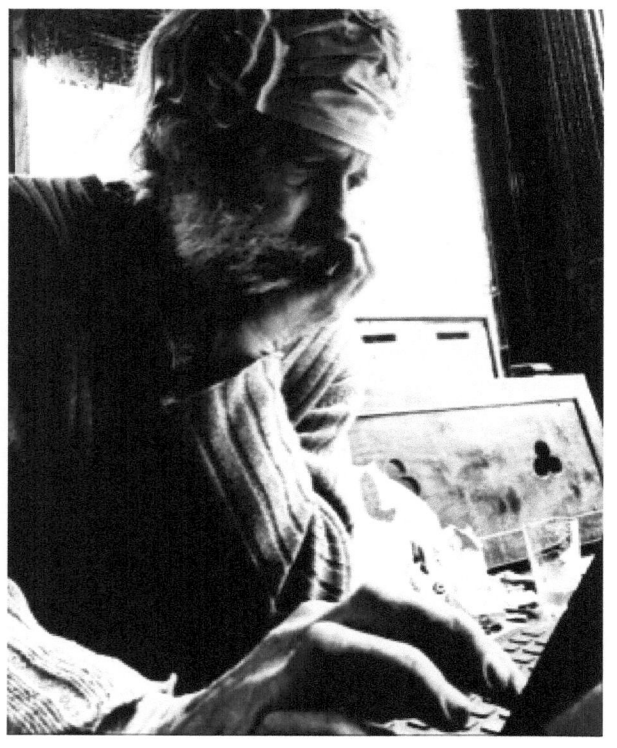

David Misialowski

Is a published New York City fiction writer, poet, and professional artist. He worked for 18 years as a staff editor on The New York Times. Since leaving The Times, he has reverted to his standard role as a curmudgeonly misanthrope.

Other Books by Pood Paw Prints:

The Pood: Michigan's Inferno
Pantheon: Heterotopia
Pantheon: Heterothanasia
Abe 2.0: Welcome to the Asylum, Mr President
Eternity Invasion
The Light Fantastic by Feo

www.poodpawprints.com
facebook.com/poodpawprints
youtube.com/@poodpawprints
instagram.com/poodpawprints

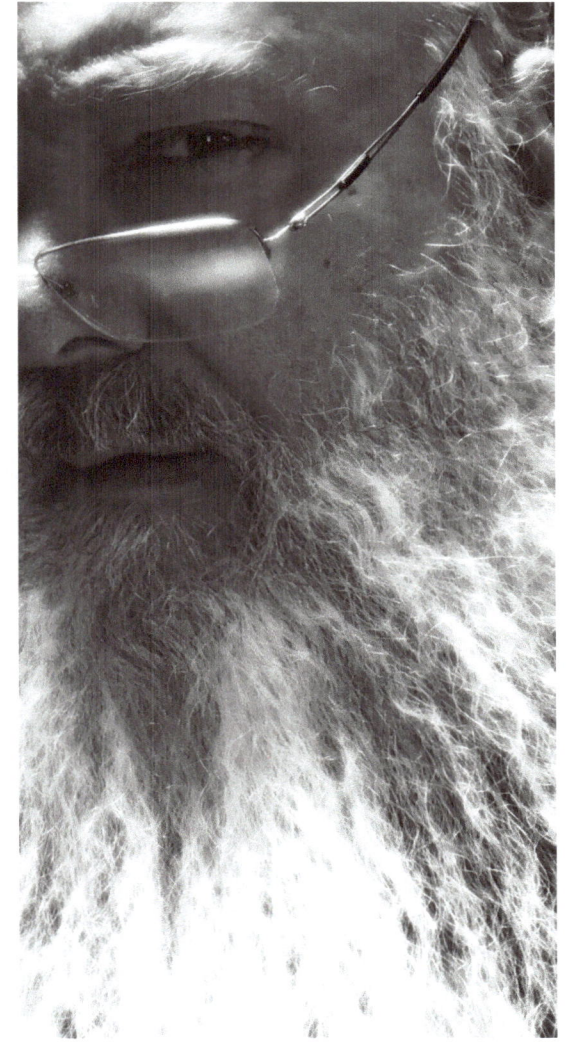

Scott Thorson

Publisher.
Published Author.
Dancing girl on Thursdays.
Knows Liberace from film.
Watching to see if you are
good or bad. He knows.
Doesn't drink early.

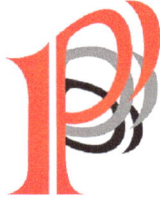